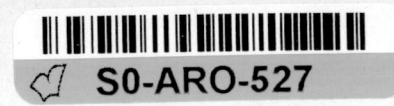

The Seeds of Freedom:

Personal Reflections on the Dawning of Democracy

By
Senator Al Graham

The Canadian Peacekeeping Press
1996

Modern international stability operations frequently involve several warring factions, an unstable or non-existent truce, and a national theartre of operations. To deal with these operations there is a *New Peacekeeping Partnership*: The **New Peacekeeping Partnership** is the tern applied to those organizations and individuals that work together to improve the effectiveness of modern peacekeeping operations. It includes the military; civil police; government and non-government agencies dealing with human rights and humanitarian assistance; diplomats; the media; and organizations sponsoring development and democratization programmes. The Pearson Peacekeeping Centre serves the *New Peacekeeping Partnership* by providing national and international participants with the opportunity to examine specific peacekeeping issues, and to update their knowledge of the latest peacekeeping practices.

Canadian Cataloguing in Publication Data

Main entry under title:

The Seeds of Freedom

ISBN 1-896551-11-4

1. Graham, Al   2. Election monitoring.   3. International police.   4. Canada -- Foreign relations. I. Title.

JF831.G73 1996   324.6'092   C96-950211-7

The Seeds of Freedom: Personal Reflections on the Dawning of Democracy

By
Senator Al Graham

The Lester B. Pearson
Canadian International Peacekeeping
Training Centre
President, Alex Morrison, MSC, CD, MA

The Pearson Peacekeeping Centre supports and enhances the Canadian contribution to international peace, security, and stability. The Centre conducts research and provides advanced training and educational programmes, and is a division of the Canadian Institute of Strategic Studies. The Canadian Peacekeeping Press is the publishing division of the Pearson Peacekeeping Centre.

The Centre (a division of the Canadian Institute of Strategic Studies), established by the Government of Canada in 1994, is funded, in part, by the Department of Foreign Affairs and International Trade and the Department of National Defence of Canada.

Le centre (une division de l'Institut canadien d'études stratégiques) à été établi par le Gouvernement du Canada en 1994. Le soutien financier de Centre provient, en partie, des ministères des Affaires étrangères et du commerce international et de la Défense nationale.

Canadian Peacekeeping Press publications include:

Pearson Roundtable Series, Report No. 1:
Peacekeeping and the Coming Anarchy (1996)

The Centre-Periphery Debate in International Security (1996)

Rapid Reaction Capabilities: Requirements and Prospects
*Les capacités de réaction rapide de l'ONU:
exigences et perspectives* (1996)

The New Peacekeeping Partnership (1995)

The Persian Excursion: The Canadian Navy in the Gulf War (1995)

Peacekeeping and International Relations (bi-monthly)

The Peacekeeping Profile

For publications information, please contact:

James Kiras, Publications Manager
The Pearson Peacekeeping Centre
Cornwallis Park, PO Box 100
Clementsport, NS B0S 1E0 CANADA
Tel: (902) 638-8611 ext. 161 Fax: (902) 638-8576
Email: jkiras@ppc.cdnpeacekeeping.ns.ca
Or visit the Pearson Peacekeeping Centre website:

http://www.cdnpeacekeeping.ns.ca

Table of Contents

Dedication vii

Acknowledgements ix

Author's Preface xi

Introduction xiii

PART ONE: A Little Help From My Friends 1
1. The Little People Together is a Giant 3
2. If You Come Back Broken, They'll See That You Mend 9
3. A Road Less Travelled 17

PART TWO: The Dawning Of Democracy 25
4. The Soul of our Foreign Policy 27
5. A New Law on Earth 34
    Democratic Consolidation 37
    Deepening Democracy 40
6. Don't Love Them and Leave Them 46
    After the Elections: South Africa 47
    After the Elections: Mexico 52
    After the Elections: Bosnia 55

PART THREE: The Seeds Of Freedom 59
7. Defining Moments 61
8. An Assault on Discouragement 66
9. Brokering Democratic Development: 70
    The UN's New Chapter 70
    The UN and Civilian Peacekeeping 76

PART FOUR: Democratic Craftmanship 79
10. To Observe or not to Observe 81
11. Don't Sit on the Sidelines 87
12. Have Some More Democracy 93
13. The Problem of Determining the Fair and the Free 98
14. Fraud or Chaos 103

PART FIVE: Sowing The Seeds Of Freedom 111
15: The Philippines: The Habit of Democracy 113
16. Paraguay: The Invention of Democracy 122
17. Namibia: A Marvellous Devotion to Democracy 128
18. Bulgaria: A Bright Light in a Dark Place 141

Appendicies

Cover Photograph: The cover picture illustrates a tense moment for US President Jimmy Carter and the author late on the night of the 1993 Presidential Elections in Paraguay. The election Commission had yet to release any results, and many citizens feared another military coup.

Dedication

Reverend John Capstick
1929-1996

For Father John Capstick, my long-time friend and mentor, who went far beyond his priestly vocation to increase the amount of dignity, justice, tolerance and freedom which all human life deserves.

PRIME MINISTER · PREMIER MINISTRE

*Senator Al Graham is a dedicated and compassionate champion of the values
that humans prize most highly. I am delighted to see that he is sharing his
considerable expertise and his memorable experiences after years of working
to nurture democracy around the world. Many of us in established
democracies tend to take our political liberties for granted, but no one could
do so after reading this fascinating account.*

Canada

Rt. Hon. Jean Chrétien

The Prime Minister with the Author

Acknowledgements

In the creation of many things, including books, the author is often assisted by many others; this work is no exception. For encouraging me even to consider putting my thoughts and recollections permanently on the record, I am indebted to numerous people.

My friend and advisor Elizabeth McIninch merits a very special note of gratitude. From its most incipient stages through to the mature form which has finally emerged, her creative suggestions, thoughtful judgement and imagination were indispensable to the completion of the text.

My long time pal Ken Boyce continually insisted that a book was a must to preserve the stories he was forced to endure after my most recent venture into another country.

On the long journey back from the 1993 elections in Paraguay to Atlanta and Washington with former President Carter, the renowned international political theorist and author James Rosenau of the George Washington University took the first look at a very tentative text, and inspired enough confidence for me to continue the effort.

A number of other individuals commented on early drafts and provided helpful suggestions for subsequent writing. They included former University College of Cape Breton Political Scientist and Community Leader, Sister Peggy Butts; distinguished author/historian John English, M.P.; Sir David Steel, for 31 years a Member of the British House of Commons and former President of Liberal International; Ken Wollack, the very astute President of the National Democratic Institute in Washington; Ron Gould of Elections Canada, one of the world's most respected authorities on International Election Observing; and Christine Stewart, Canada's knowledgeable and experienced Secretary of State for Latin America and Africa.

Mary E. Finn and Nicole C. Brunet deserve special mention for their patience, dedication and administrative assistance during the writing and publishing of the manuscript.

The Library of Parliament, in particular Mr. Don Curtin, is thanked for fine tuning the list of works cited.

For his editorial guidance and constant encouragement, I give particular recognition to the visionary Alex Morrison, President of the Lester B. Pearson Canadian International Peacekeeping Training Centre, as well as several very professional members of his staff: Dale Anderson, Peter Dawson, Christine Dodge, Pamela Forsyth, Patricia Goldman and James Kiras; their support proved invaluable in ensuring the manuscript became the book it is today.

And finally I want to thank another old friend, Donald L. Gillis, Publisher of the Casket Printing & Publishing Co. as well as his staff, for their diligence and skill in printing the book.

Author's Preface

For some time now, Canadians have been reflecting on the vital questions pertaining to the future of our vast, multicultural federation. At no time in history have I personally had a greater sense of the frustration of our people and the fragility of our nation. The world watches as Canada, one of the great symbols of peace and tolerance in the international community is increasingly assaulted from within by some individuals who consider cooperation and compromise - the glue of our federation - to be impossible.

I have written this manuscript as a means of rediscovering some of the first principles about the values of liberty and the strength of people-based institutions. As a long-time international election observer, I have been fortunate to witness the struggle for freedom at first hand and the very real courage shown by citizens of states in transition as they move into the dawn of democracy.

In the process, I have rediscovered what freedom means, and all the privileges and responsibilities which are associated with liberty. I have acquired an insight into the danger that all mature democracies face when their populations lose touch with the fundamental principles anchoring free societies. Now I want to share my experiences with my fellow citizens at a time when too many of them feel that our compassionate society north of the 49th parallel has become an unattainable and unworkable dream.

Seeds of Freedom is a tribute to the courage and determination of all those ordinary people I have seen across the world who have caught a glimpse of the possible, and who have overcome fear and intimidation in order to build a better society for themselves and their children.

It is also offered as a tribute to some of the great Canadians with whom I have been privileged to work over the decades in building what the United Nations Development Program has called the best country on earth. I mention only a few of so many. Senator Allan J. MacEachen, former long-time Cabinet Minister, my first and finest political mentor, has exemplified a deep intellectual commitment to a tolerant, equitable, and compassionate Canada. Prime Minister Lester B.

Pearson taught many of us, as we entered politics as young men and women, about statesmanship and Canada's responsibilities in the world. As Prime Minister, Pierre Elliot Trudeau's passion for a level playing field and a just society proved to be the cerebral underpinnings of the years I spent as President of the Liberal Party of Canada. As Cabinet Minister and Prime Minister, John Turner's fierce love of Canada was infectious and an example to all of us who served under his leadership.

Today, Prime Minister Jean Chretien, with his extraordinary commitment to fairness and the well-being of ordinary Canadians carries the most difficult burden since Confederation. I am deeply honoured to serve the Prime Minister as Deputy Leader of the Government in the Senate.

As well, it is a tribute to the National Democratic Institute in Washington, D.C. which opened the windows of the world to me, and under whose aegis I have monitored so many elections.

It is a tribute to the people of Cape Breton, whose sense of community and resilience and strength in adversity has given me hope and faith in a better future for all of us.

Finally, it is a tribute to my family, without whose support and love I could not have achieved the many fine moments in time I have been so privileged to enjoy.

Introduction

Over the course of the last decade, I have served as an international election observer in many countries undergoing the painful, yet joyful transition to freedom - a transition symbolized by the simple act of casting a secret ballot.

International election monitoring is a complex process which can begin months before the drama of election day and can last weeks in the aftermath of the historic events. As is commonly understood, observers are sent to transition states to determine whether an election is fair and free.

The reality is, of course, much more complex as the ensuing chapters will make clear. But for now, and taken in the broadest sense, observers act primarily to ward off the discouragement which can often sap the morale of people voting in difficult, first-time processes.

Fear and intimidation are only a few of the enemies of democratic transition. Yet, when I first began to observe elections, I was struck by the festive atmosphere which enveloped the long lineups of, in most cases, first-time voters. No matter what country, no matter what terrible poverty the people in those lineups had seen and with which they had lived, the words best descriptive of their collective mood are dignity and hope.

People all seemed to walk with their heads a little higher as they approached the polling stations. What they had in common was a belief that they could play a part in building a better society for themselves and their children.

The big challenge for fledgling democratic governments would be to keep that belief alive. Along with this would come the reshaping of entire countries with prerequisite, some might say heroic virtues of patience, sacrifice, and unending hard work. As the dawn of democracy breaks in many countries around the world, the factors and institutions critical to the consolidation of pluralist societies are still in the formative phases. At first glance, the very idea of democracy offers hope and good will to believers, if little else.

An elderly lady who waited patiently in line to cast her first, precious ballot put it to me this way during the October 1991 elections in Bulgaria: "Now that we have the election, the people will be free. We are not afraid anymore."

That comment was telling. The success of an election is an important source of the empowerment of people, a key spiritual factor which I would regard as the engine of democratic transition. Elections are but the first step in the long, often very frustrating process of democratization. But that first step is essential to the development of civilian societies around the world.

In many ways, my experiences as an international election observer have brought me back to the first principles of what the democratic experience means. I have relearned long held truths and assumptions about the rights, as well as the responsibilities of real citizens in free societies. Most importantly, I have become more sensitive to what happens when people lose their vigilance, when they begin to believe that freedom is a gift to which they have a right, but no responsibility to defend.

The great strength shown by ordinary people from all walks of life in the often very difficult circumstances surrounding first-time elections is sustained by a simple conviction. Put simply, it is that all citizens - irrespective of creed, race, colour or class - are entitled to participate in the development of peaceful societies that are respectful of the laws of which they, the people, are the authors.

Seeds of Freedom is a title which loosely translates into that largely spiritual conviction. Belief and commitment, however, must be balanced by democratic craftsmanship on many levels if elections are to succeed. *Seeds of Freedom* chronicles the interplay between these two essential ingredients of transition processes.

Election monitoring must be looked at holistically in order to understand the very practical mechanics essential to success in conditions where institutional chaos, fraud, and intimidation are formidable obstacles. This is the kind of mediating activity which has interested me over the years and which will be discussed and analyzed in the pages to come.

Election assistance is a vital component of democratic development; it is obvious that elections and the whole course of democratic development are inextricably linked.

I believe my own experiences as an international election observer enable me to contribute most effectively to an understanding of the forces at work in the early phases of democratic transitions. I have subtitled the book *Personal Reflections on the Dawning of Democracy.* This has been done in order to emphasize my belief that elections are beginning and critical factors in the global evolution of democracy - in the growth of a new law on earth[1] - largely because they embolden people to believe that the development of free, civilian societies is possible.

Seeds of Freedom is a book of and about hope. It has been written with the intention of showing that it is in the best interests of western liberal democracies to support constructively international election assistance at what is, in my opinion, a key and unprecedented moment in time.

Elections are a means of allocating power peacefully. Observers have sustained many critical elections in countries where the inhabitants are frightened and where distrust threatened to subvert the process. When elections fail, not only domestic peace, but the larger peace of the global community is also threatened. Perhaps this may best explain why the act of watching other people vote has implications for all of us.

PART ONE
A LITTLE HELP FROM MY FRIENDS

But first, let me tell you where I came from. I was raised in a resource-based economy where many people were very much at the mercy of forces they felt they could not control. I was privileged to witness activist roles of individual leaders in the close-knit communities on Cape Breton Island, Nova Scotia, who taught men and women how to become masters of their own destiny. The power of education and self-help, along with an overwhelming belief in the capacity of the little guy to effect change were all part of the ideas envelope we grew up with.

While we understood the necessity of self-help in my part of the world, we all knew intuitively about the responsibility of helping others. The vagaries and uncertainties of life in the coal industry ensured that community caring and concern was not just based on pious notions of justice; it was based on the practical realities of the society and economy in which we lived.

As my political career evolved, I was fortunate to be associated with a remarkable period of socio-economic reform in my own country. The Canadian social security net, the heart of which was a system of nation-wide comprehensive health insurance, or Medicare, was designed and instituted during the Pearson years. I was witness to the growth and development of a political culture of respect for people. We were building a compassionate infrastructure, the values of which became more and more an anchor for our national identity as the decades ensued.

I began to learn about the world beyond Canada through my initial contacts with Liberal International, an association of liberals from many countries around the world which enriched my life in many ways. My colleagues were, on the whole, pragmatic idealists on the cutting edge of reform in their own countries and throughout the international community at large. They believed, as had my early mentors in Cape Breton, that little people could become masters of their own destiny. The road of compassionate idealism may be a road less travelled, but in my life it has made all the difference.

Victor Hugo described the spiritual power of belief and conviction over a century and a half ago when he wrote that: "an invasion of armies can be resisted, but not an idea whose time has come."

The time of democracy has come. I have been privileged to watch the clock of freedom tick inexorably on as the century comes to a close. In all of this I have been a very receptive witness. Much of this was due to the support and assistance of the community in which I was raised and, of course, a lot of help from my friends.

1. The Little People Together is a Giant.

Cape Breton is a lovely, tranquil island where the land is hard, the valleys are deep, and where some of the most spectacular vistas of lake, mountain, and sea known to man unfold under wide, open horizons. The quiet beauty of the place, mixed with the rich culture and fierce pride of its inhabitants make this a place which instills incredible love and loyalty in those fortunate enough to call it home.

The economic insecurities of the largely resource based economy have led to the departure of many talented young Cape Bretoners, but, in their hearts and minds, very few ever really leave the island. This strange and magical place of legends and myths and music continues to tug at the heartstrings of all its expatriate sons and daughters.

The story of Cape Breton, most particularly of Dominion and Glace Bay, where I was born and raised, is really a story about coal. My grand-uncle, Father Charles MacDonald, was the parish priest of Immaculate Conception Parish which served the town of Dominion and the community of Bridgeport, a suburb of Glace Bay. My father died a few months before I was born and shortly after that, Father Charlie asked my mother, his niece, to serve as the housekeeper in the local Glebe House.

My mother and Father Charlie were both from the rolling hills of Antigonish Harbour, on the Nova Scotia mainland. My mother had an education diploma from Mount St. Bernard College in Antigonish and had spent the years before her marriage teaching school in Western Canada. Father Charlie was a co-founder of St. Joseph's Hospital in Glace Bay, and served on the Board of Governors of St. Francis Xavier University in Antigonish.

My two older brothers and I were fortunate enough to have the highly respected and greatly loved miners' priest as replacement father. We grew up in the Glebe House, in the heart of the coal industry. Father Charlie bought me my first bicycle. He followed our activities very closely, whether on the playing field or in the classroom. I remember him so well in attendance at my high school graduation. As I began my valedictorian's speech, Father Charlie's voice rang out loud and clear from the first row of the Savoy Theatre. "Speak louder, boy", he demanded, embarrassing me forever.

It was Bobby Kennedy who once said that each time a man stands up for an ideal, or acts to improve the lot of others, or strikes out against injustice, he sends forth a ripple of hope. Father Charlie sent forth a lot of ripples. He had great patience and never turned anyone away, no matter how poor or how desperate. He went down in the collieries to administer the last rites after tragic accidents occurred, often the result of coal falls. He would usually be accompanied by the much loved Dr. M. G. Tompkins, the "doctor of the deeps" and of our particular community. They were miners' people and we were all coal miners' kids. They taught us about caring and sharing and generated a spirit of selfless responsibility to others. When I was in my freshman year at St. Francis Xavier University, Father Charlie died, and I remember this as one of the saddest occasions of my young life.

The coal culture taught people to look after each other. Blood and bone is the price of coal, as the famous *Ballad of Springhill* makes clear. The ballad was written as a tribute to the 75 miners who died following the Springhill, Nova Scotia mine disaster which occurred at 8:05 p.m. October 23, 1958.

For generations of miners, life was spent at coal seams of up to one metre in thickness. Many were done in by lung-swelling coal dust or by the physically crippling hard work, or by the continuous possibility of a stone roof falling in on their heads.

In the older mines, the coal faces themselves could be as far as eight kilometres under the sea bed. It is said that, in the winter months, many of the blackened and sweaty men of the deeps never saw the sun.

At the turn of the century, brutal exploitation and oppression, combined with illiteracy and the total dependence on company stores and company houses became the stuff of music and literature. The extreme inequities of those times were alleviated over the decades, but the coal industry itself remained dangerous and insecure, and excessively costly in terms of the quality of life both for the miners and their families.

The wonderful voice of Cape Breton's Rita MacNeil backed up by The Men of the Deeps, a chorus of miners, has captured the spirit of the times and made audiences across Canada misty-eyed when they sing *Working Man*. Over the decades, every Cape Breton miner could have sung along with these words.

> It's a working man I am,
> And I've been down underground
> And I swear to God, if I ever see the sun -
> Or for any length of time
> I can hold it in my mind -
> I never again will go down underground.

But King Coal was their way of life, and, despite its hardships and insecurities, all the men of the deeps and their families drew strength from a resource which was in some ways even stronger than the black gold itself. Cape Breton's greatest resource is its strong community spirit and I mean that in the cultural, social, economic and spiritual sense of the word.

The culture of the coal industry is in many ways similar to that of the military. Each man has a buddy and each looks after the other in dangerous surroundings. Each would go over the top for the other, if needed.

Everyone in the community understood the extraordinary and sometimes heroic bonds developed far under the surface of the earth. I began to understand this as a young boy in the days I delivered the *Sydney Post Record* to the miners' houses. Like all of us, I knew the unwritten codes, the bonds of trust and solidarity, which made that community one of the strongest in North America.

My understanding grew when I started to work in the summers as a young university student for the old *Glace Bay Gazette*, then owned by the United Mine Workers of America. Ernie Beaton, the widely respected Public Relations Director for the Dominion Coal Company, told me that if I wanted to write about local issues I would have to learn about them first-hand. Beaton took me down in the mines for the first-time. Little did I know at the time that one day I would become senior Vice-President of the Cape Breton Development Corporation, a federal crown corporation established in 1968. This was a very fortunate turn of the wheel for me because it brought me back to my roots. But that was all to come later.

The intensely deep sense of community which Cape Breton is so famous for has been faithfully recorded by Allister MacGillivray in his *Song Of The Mira*. In this lovely ballad, we sing of the humanity and compassion which were synonymous with the river all of us loved.

> Out on the Mira the people are kind,
> They'll treat you to homebrew and help you unwind
> And if you come broken, they'll see that you mend,
> And I wish I was with them again.

The life was hard, the communities were scattered and the isolation often difficult for the people to bear. One of the ways in which the people of Cape Breton were able to deal with the vagaries of an economy based on fish, coal and steel - on the resources of forests and sea and mines - was through co-operative action. Monsignor Moses Coady of the small settlement of Margaree in Cape Breton began to write and speak prolifically on the necessity for co-operative self help early in this century.

Monsignor Coady was affectionately known as the humble giant, a man whose great stature always impressed me as I went about my duties as a student waiter in the Priest's Refectory at St. Francis Xavier University. His energy was prodigious, his spirits unflagging. His faithful secretary, Ellen Arsenault, recounted that she kept a stenographer's pad by her bed to record Coady's ideas, often summarized to her in late night telephone calls. His mind was going 100 miles an hour all the time.

Monsignor Coady had a vision of revitalizing people and their communities, and he had enormous faith in the power of individuals to become Masters of their own Destiny. He believed a person learned by doing. He always said that to give a person a fish was to provide food for a day, but to teach them how to fish, was to provide self-sufficiency for a lifetime.

This was a message of liberation and empowerment and the co-operative movement which developed from his teachings gave hope to uneducated men and women. By his word and his example, the seeds of freedom were sown in much of Atlantic Canada. This was freedom from the loss of will and the degradation of spirit which so often resulted from the hardships and isolation endured by miners and steelworkers, and those who fished the sea.

The humble giant knew that real democracy would only develop if people could manage their own affairs and work overtime in their own interests. His teachings gave them a glimpse of the possible. It was then up to them to create a new society in which all men and women would be free.

St. Francis Xavier University became the centre of the spirit of organized self-help which gained world-wide renown as the Antigonish Movement. Coady became the Director of the Extension Department which brought the concept of mutual self-help through co-operatives and credit unions to generations of students. His work was internationalized when the University established the Coady Institute to bring the founder's concepts to students from developing countries.

I tried to capture some of the spirit of the Antigonish Movement in a speech to the Closing Exercises of the Coady International Institute in December, 1972.

> You are expected now to go home to your countries to encourage and instruct people on how they might best participate in the economic life of your communities...you are asked to develop in your countries and in your communities a society that respects the humanity of man... you are asked to impress upon your fellow countrymen that...through a process of continuous education you will in fact become masters of your own houses... a society where human life is respected, where economic insecurity is eliminated, where all institutions exist to serve man.

Father Jimmy Tompkins was Coady's cousin and an equally powerful force behind the adult education movement in eastern Nova Scotia. In 1935 he invited his parishioners at Reserve Mines (much later, my brother, Father John, would follow as Parish Priest at St. Joseph's) to come and borrow books from his front porch, thus opening the first public library in Cape Breton.

Tompkins' simple gesture underscored the importance of community libraries in the evolution of real democracy. He felt they should belong to people. He once said: "I want regional libraries because I want the people to know a fool when they see one." Father Tompkins knew that if you give people ideas they will put them to work. The porch-front library provided a glimpse of the potential to change the lives of ordinary people forever.

Education meant the possibility of social change because it allowed people to influence the otherwise overpowering forces which controlled their lives. In other words, as Father Jimmy once put it so well, "...the little people together is a giant. You've only got to give them ideas and then they'll blow the roof off."

On March 21, 1996, my friend and colleague, Senator Allan J. MacEachen addressed the Senate of Canada on the current state of the coal mining industry in Cape Breton. He spoke movingly of the foundation of the Antigonish Movement and the powerlessness of the little people which had so deeply concerned Father Tompkins and Monsignor Coady. Senator MacEachen drew from his personal store of memories of the industry; his father had been a miner who spent 46 years underground in Inverness, Cape Breton, Nova Scotia. He spoke of the insecurity of the industry, pointing out that the work schedule had been governed by a whistle and that whistle in turn was the force which governed the lives of all the miners' families. One whistle meant work; two whistles: no work. The whistle also could signal tragedy because when it blew in a certain pattern, people would rush to the colliery to find out which of their loved ones had been killed or injured.

The uncertainty depicted in the two-whistle signal was Senator MacEachen's way of explaining the purpose of the Antigonish Movement. He summarized it this way: "The whistle was the voice of the unseen forces that controlled the lives of the coal miners in those coal mining communities. The purpose of the Antigonish movement was to get a grip on these unseen forces."

For all of us at St. F.X. in the early post-war years, whether it was as a Professor of Economics, as Senator MacEachen was, or as struggling student, as I was - none could fail to be caught up in the atmosphere of hope which was a direct by-product of the Antigonish Movement. The belief in the power of the individual to effect change found fertile ground in the largely working class campus of the day. We all understood intuitively the need for self-help, and, indeed, the necessity of helping each other.

Just as the buddy system was so important in the miners' families from which so many students came, so did that spirit spill over into the student body at the university. The faculty reinforced the transfer of the unwritten codes of the coal culture in this very special institution of learning.

That same special mix of ideas and activism carried over to the University College of Cape Breton, founded in 1974. My long-time friend, Father Donald F. Campbell, was the University's first President and the driving force behind its establishment. Father Greg MacLeod is a teacher of philosophy, the Director of the Tompkins Centre at UCCB, and Chairman of BCA Holdings, a group of not-for-profit community development corporations in Atlantic Canada. He personifies the spirit of self-help and community cooperation so much a part of the Cape Breton psyche.

He builds on the same tradition of self-help and co-operative education which will be the salvation of many of our small, yet vital communities on Cape Breton Island. The Antigonish movement lives on in Father Greg. The objective is the same. People must learn to manage the unseen forces which govern their lives; forces epitomized by the sound of the whistle which determined how much would be in the pay envelopes at the end of the week.

Over the last decade, I have watched little people struggle for democracy, an ideal which promised a better life for themselves and their families. Like my own people in Cape Breton, they were beset by powerful forces which could only be controlled if they became masters in their own house.

Our delegations watched them vote in many countries and in doing so we helped accelerate the growth of democracy. There are those who feel that democracy is a process which must unfold according to the dictates of history. I beg to differ. "The little people is a giant. You've only got to give them ideas and they'll blow the roof off." That, and a little help from their friends.

2. If You Come Broken, They'll See that you Mend

When I was growing up in Cape Breton, I had two ambitions in the field of athletics: to play baseball for the Dominion Junior Hawks and hockey for the St. Francis Xavier University Varsity. I did both: as utility outfielder for the Hawks, and as third man on the third line for the X-Men.[2]

In Dominion, a town of 3,000 people, baseball was ingrained in every resident. It was truly a big part of life. The Senior Hawks played in the old colliery league at varying times against the Glace Bay Miners, Reserve Miner Boys, New Waterford Dodgers, Whitney Pier Pirates, Sydney Steel City, and the Sydney Mines Ramblers. The players were a mixture of local and imported talent recruited from among top university students in the United States.

One summer, in the first game of the provincial junior championship final, Hawks coach John Campbell started me in left field. The first visiting batter hit a "Texas Leaguer" half way between short stop Geno Scattalon and the outfield. Never fleet-footed, I chased the ball and got it on first bounce. "Take Graham out", yelled the crowd, thinking I should have easily caught it on the fly. And he did just that.

Many years later, after I had gone to the Senate of Canada, my friend John Campbell suddenly died the day before Christmas. I attended his funeral in Dominion on Boxing Day. One of the old timers was heard to observe: "Wasn't Al a great sport to come, after what John did to him?" When it came to baseball, Cape Bretoners had a long memory.

They had a long memory for self-help, and they also had a long memory for helping each other. We knew that, in the beautiful words of the *Song of the Mira*, "if you came back broken, they would see that you mend."

The deep sense of community was our greatest natural resource. I grew in my personal understanding of it after I graduated from St. Francis Xavier University and began to provide for my young family. At one time, I recall having eight jobs at the same time - all of which brought me into direct contact with virtually every aspect of community life in Antigonish County.

I was the News Editor and sports writer for the *Antigonish Casket*, the local weekly newspaper. Then I tried my hand at play-by-play broadcasting. This was more of a joy than a bread provider, although every little bit helped in an expanding family. I broadcast the first Canadian football game I ever saw in my life - an exhibition game between St. F.X. and the MacMaster University Marauders which starred the legendary Russ Jackson at quarterback.

I discovered I had a pretty free license to say whatever I wanted, because the listening audience couldn't themselves see the playing field. My old friend from Dominion, Geno Scattalon, was at the time playing for St. F.X's first Canadian football squad, and the radio accounts of their favourite son were eagerly followed by the folks back home. I didn't want to disappoint them.

One Saturday afternoon late in the season I decided that if the coach wasn't going to put him in, then I would. So with about four minutes left, I pulled one of the regulars and inserted Geno in my broadcast lineup. For those listening, in a very short space of time, he caught two passes and ran for 30 yards. I couldn't let him score because my little scam would be exposed Monday morning when his name would not appear in the newspaper accounts.[3]

In spite of some of my wilder undertakings, I subsequently became the sportscaster at the Antigonish radio station *CJFX*, following in the footsteps of my friend and fellow Xaverian, Danny Gallivan, who was the guest commentator on my first hockey broadcast in the old Halifax Forum. Danny's legendary voice would become synonymous with the poetry in motion which was the Montreal Canadiens.

At the same time, I did whatever freelance work I could with the CBC. I started off as a stringer for the Canadian Press and the Halifax Chronicle-Herald, covering events throughout eastern Nova Scotia.

But I spent most of my time in education, serving as the Principal of a two-room school in Lower South River, Antigonish County, and teaching grades six to 11. The St. F.X. Practical Teacher Training programme for Graduate Students used my school for its teacher training. That counted as an additional job for me, as did the organization of the annual Antigonish Highland Games.

I had a rich and active community life and usually managed to combine my love of sports and education. When I did a play-by-play broadcast in Halifax or Sydney, the kids at the school would draw lots and I would load up the car and take them along. In Halifax, we would go to the Provincial Legislature for example, and tour the downtown core of the provincial capital. In Sydney, we always drove around the Steel Plant and the rail yards. I took them to the sites of the old coal mines in Cape Breton.

We worked together and we played together. When the school ran into debt, we had a community picnic to help pay it off. When they needed a rink, they built one outdoors on a bog by the school. The students, with help from their parents, cut the trees, sawed the lumber at the local mill, and built the rink. Occasionally, we saved up our recesses so we could play hockey longer.

One of Canada's all time great runners, Bruce Kidd, once said that the rink is a symbol of this country's vast stretches of water and wilderness, its extremes of climate; the player is a symbol of our struggle to civilize such a land. He spoke of an important truth when he called hockey "the great Canadian metaphor."

All my life I have loved this game and to this day I continue to play it and watch it and talk about it. The respected Ottawa Citizen columnist, Roy MacGregor, in his wonderful book, *The Home Team - Fathers, Sons, and Hockey,* makes reference to my speech in the Canadian Senate in May, 1994 when I participated in the debate on Bill C-212, an Act to Recognize Hockey and Lacrosse as the two national sports in Canada. He quoted me as follows:

> The sound of the first slapshot, the first puck hitting the boards, was and is the first shock of psychic electricity that unites hearts and minds in this country. All that irrespective of regions, time zones or ethnic backgrounds, because if there ever was a visible, passionate and inspirational spirit of our magnificent multiculturalism, it was, and is, hockey.

MacGregor then wrote of the central place the rink - the great Canadian metaphor - had in the lives of two large Cape Breton families. He wrote of a family ritual that takes place each Boxing Day in Sydney, Nova Scotia, when the annual Graham-Joseph hockey game is held, with the skill level running from a puffing Canadian Senator to Fabian Joseph, captain of the silver medal-winning 1994 Olympic hockey team. That passion for the game has been repeated across the generations, as MacGregor pointed out. He recounted my references in the 1994 speech to twin grandchildren who play in Ottawa, Anna and George Barrett, each in the same minor program. He recalled that I spoke as hockey player, father and grandfather - bragging and proud of it.

With five daughters and nine sons, the Josephs typify the hard work and loyalty which makes them one of the truly great families of Cape Breton. In the days and weeks leading up to the eagerly awaited Boxing Day contest, the anticipation and the friendly banter accelerated, everything from the jokes, the boasts and the bets, to rumours about what relative or "newly engaged ringer" would be allowed to dress for the game. I would get frequent, carefully worded questions from my own boys about the current state of my physical condition, a gentle reminder that I had better be in shape for the annual event.

Another matter of considerable speculation was whether Fabian Joseph would make it home for Christmas from wherever he happened to be playing - Olympic or professional. Fabian's presence would, of course, considerably enhance the already formidable array of hockey talent on the Joseph bench.

In one particular year, as I was going into our home parish church of St. Joseph's on the Sunday morning before Christmas, I spotted Mrs. Joseph - the mother, Mabel, seated on the outside of the third pew from the back. I leaned down and whispered: "Mabel, is Fabe going to make it home for the big game?" She looked up, paused, and with a mischievious twinkle in her eye, answered slowly, and very emphatically: "we're not saying."

The spirit of the Graham-Joseph games has all been part of the continuing legacy of community which Atlantic Canada has been famous for. As I have said, we built the rinks together in the early years. When I became President of the local Teachers Union and the Antigonish County Home and School Association, we all worked hard together towards helping to establish the first Regional High School for the area.

In 1958, I was encouraged to run for the federal Liberal nomination in the constituency of Antigonish - Guysborough. We all knew this election would be tough. In June, 1957, the Progressive Conservatives under Saskatchewan prairie populist John Diefenbaker had defeated Louis St. Laurent's Liberals. That event had been cataclysmic as the Liberals had held office for 22 years. But the Chief, as Diefenbaker was known, wanted a majority and he was to get his wish nine months later in a huge sweep at the polls. In fact, it was an amazing rout. I think I knew at the time that the new Liberal leader, Lester B. Pearson or "Mike" as he was affectionately known, could do very little to stop the tide against what the voters perceived to be a tired, arrogant party too long in power. But even with my private doubts, I was unprepared for the enormity of the loss.

Mr. Pearson came to speak at a rally in support of my campaign just prior to the election. The atmosphere in the big St. Ninian's Parish Centre in Antigonish was electrifying. The place was packed in anticipation of the famous Nobel Peace Prize Winner's speech. Mr. Pearson had the ruddy Irish good looks and easy charm of the golden boy of the international world. He was a real Canadian hero. His quick wit and self-deprecating style and great personal warmth belied the brilliant, rational mind which was so essential to the creation of the United Nations and NATO. His wonderful smile which so charmed the crowd in the parish hall that night, masked a genteel cosmopolitanism derived from decades in the corridors of international diplomacy. His jovial style concealed the moral commitment of the small town Ontario Methodist minister's son.

They all came out to hear him. Allan MacEachen was there, himself a candidate in the disastrous 1958 election. Former Premier Henry Hicks, then Leader of the Liberal Party of Nova Scotia was there. So were all the Members of the Legislative Assembly for the local area. Moses Coady sat in the back of the hall wearing dark glasses. This was a big night in Antigonish.

I was introduced by Rod J. Chisholm, a local lawyer who had been my valued campaign manager and one of my earlier opponents for the nomination. He introduced me as the next Member of Parliament for Antigonish-Guysborough and invited me to "give us his address". When I stood up to speak, I agreed with him wholeheartedly and pointed out that in lieu of the tremendous reception I had received throughout "the length and breadth of this great and historic constituency", my new address would, indeed, be Parliament Hill, Ottawa. I looked down at Moses Coady and saw the big man sigh visibly. I could hear Henry Hicks behind me announce to all and sundry: "get him off that kick - he sounds too cocky". Alex Cameron, the much-loved MLA for Guysborough, was assigned to speak with me after. He said simply, "Al, perhaps you shouldn't be too confident. Perhaps you could be more modest." Maybe I deserved to lose. I consoled myself that few liberal candidates across the country had survived the Diefenbaker sweep.

St. F.X. University was located in my constituency. At least twenty-five identifiable Liberal supporters from Allan MacEachen's neighbouring riding were in residence. According to the electoral law, they were eligible to vote at home or at the University. It was felt that I needed the votes more than Allan. He generously agreed that they should stay in Antigonish and vote for me. I lost by 931 votes and MacEachen by 16. Miraculously, our friendship survived.

Richard Cashin, later an M.P. and, latterly, President of the Newfoundland Fisherman's Union, managed my campaign at the University. Brian Mulroney, then a student at St. F.X., later to be Prime Minister, ran the Tory campaign. To this day, Cashin boasts that he defeated Mulroney - on campus.

A couple of days after the election I was in Halifax and visited my friend Senator Finlay MacDonald at his CJCH broadcasting headquarters. Later, we were to be Senate colleagues. At that time he was also a prominent member of the Progressive Conservative Party, and I was told, had dumped a significant amount of "aid" for the Conservative campaign in my riding the day before the election. He greeted me enthusiastically - long strides, both arms outstretched - wide, wide grin. "Well, well, welcome to the youngest political has-been in Canadian history."

On the national front, Mr. Pearson set out immediately on the long road back. His principal contribution to the Liberal Party up to that time had been his positive, open internationalism. But there was another, equally important and less understood dimension to the new leader's intellectual armour. His years of diplomatic service in Europe during the dark years of the 1930s had given him a front row seat in the unfolding horror of fascism. Pearson's fear of the irrational was without doubt very much a by-product of this experience. It was the driving force behind his commitment to progress and the rational elements in life.

It probably should have been no surprise to Canadians that Pearson would have no fear of breaking with the past in efforts to transform dramatically the face of the nation. He was after all, an energetic and committed multilateral institution builder on the world stage.

Later, when he became Prime Minister, he was to preside over a remarkable period of social-economic legislation which reshaped the nation. He embraced the vision of a bilingual, bicultural Canada which was long overdue in our country. He was determined to march boldly into the future with a distinctive Canadian flag, precipitating a fierce Parliamentary debate in which the opposition railed against what they claimed to be a monumental break with the past.

But that was yet to come. During the years in opposition, Mr. Pearson sought out the best brains in the country. One of the people to whom he turned was Tom Kent, formerly of the editorial boards of both the *Manchester Guardian* and the *Economist*, and latterly of the *Winnipeg Free Press*. Kent was renowned for his insistence on wide-ranging social reform in Canada. Maurice Lamontagne, a highly respected Laval-educated economist, then teaching at the University of Ottawa, was, along with Kent, an important part of the new thinking which caused Liberals to veer sharply to the left. Allan MacEachen was an influential and integral part of the team which reformed the party platform and brought a new focus on egalitarianism and the concerns of the ordinary citizen to the centre of power.

When, in 1961, I was asked to serve on Mr. Pearson's Advisory Committee in Nova Scotia, the Diefenbaker government was in the final stages of the internal turmoil which would consume and destroy it. Dief was a sensational and electrifying speaker and a formidable debater in the House. He was as responsible for the triumphs of his party as perhaps he was for its demise in 1963.[4]

At the time, I became President of my riding association, and my new political associations brought me in touch with a whole roster of young Liberals of energy and intelligence, all of whom were committed to the revitalization of the party, and many of whom would achieve great prominence in government. All of us revered and idolized Mr. Pearson. All of us participated in what Richard Gwyn, a well known Canadian author and journalist, once so well described as "the politics of joy."

Those were the cerebral days of Camelot in Washington. The idealistic oratory of the Kennedy White House found receptive audiences in Canada, as it did in all the countries of the Free World. The New Frontier and the promised land seemed just around the corner. In November, 1963, Camelot died along with the assassinated young President whose charisma, charm, energy and spirit had meant so much hope to so many.

Canadians became more introspective as foreign investment figures became increasingly well-known in the country, and concerns about Canadian sovereignty began to take a focal point on the nation's agenda. As the skies over Vietnam grew dark with squadrons of American bombers, our relations with the United States became increasingly complicated and a source of much controversy at home.

I did not run in the 1962 election which the Liberals won, because I felt I simply couldn't afford it financially. But I helped recruit Dr. John B. Stewart, then a brilliant St. F.X. Political Science Professor (now a Senator) who ran a highly successful campaign and won a narrow victory. Allan MacEachen, then Minister of Labour in the Pearson Government, needed someone on his staff to help with his ministerial responsibilities in Nova Scotia. He invited me to take on the job and I accepted.

The Laird of Lake Ainslie, as MacEachen was affectionately known, combined a passion for the underdog with a logical, focused mastery of government and parliamentary procedure. As he was House leader and President of the Privy Council, he had contact with the Prime Minister in daily meetings. To me, Mr. Pearson was unfailingly courteous, kind, and personable. His commitment to the spirit of egalitarianism and social reform was palpable.

The full range of reformist initiatives and the legislation which anchored the welfare state has probably been best described in the voluminous notes and writings of one of the principal architects of the system, Tom Kent. I believe the finest hours were spent in hammering out the system of medicare which we Canadians are so fortunate to have. Allan MacEachen led the struggle for the comprehensive, universal access to health care very soon after his appointment as Minister of Health and Welfare in 1966.

I had a front-row seat as he crossed the country explaining the principles of the programme with eloquence, patience, passion and conviction. The vigorous opposition against which he struggled would have made many lesser people weaken. I was with him when he started the tour in Vancouver. And I remember so well the very cool reception he received when he outlined the plan to the Medical Society in Halifax.

The struggle for medicare, fought three decades ago, was a struggle for our citizenship. It was a struggle for our identity as Canadians. In many ways, it has turned out to be the biggest spike of the Canadian national dream. At the time of its enactment, MacEachen, more than anyone else, had the hammer in his hand. Perhaps that is why I now appreciate more than ever the significance of the Pearson years. We were building a new Canada with a human face. We were preparing the infrastructure for a compassionate society, the values of which are the anchor of our national identity in 1996.

It was in this way that the boy from Dominion and Bridgeport learned about the privileges of being a Canadian. I began to understand how much we could lose if we ever gave up on the duties and responsibilities that citizenship in this wonderful country entails.

After leaving Ottawa and managing a new broadcasting company in London, Ontario, I returned to Cape Breton in the fall of 1967 with new perspective and a huge new challenge on my plate. I became the second employee of the Cape Breton Development Corporation, commonly known as DEVCO and was partly responsible for the vast amount of preparatory work that had to be done in anticipation of the official coming into force of the Crown corporation on April 1, 1968.

Cape Breton was already in serious economic distress when the Dominion Steel and Coal Corporation - the Island's largest employer by far at the time - announced its intention to shut down the coal mines in the mid-1960s. The economic and social disruption of the shutdown would have been so devastating to Cape Breton that the federal government felt it necessary to intervene.

DEVCO was established to take over the mines and to provide jobs and new industries outside the mining sector. (At about the same time, the Nova Scotia government was forced by circumstances to establish a provincial Crown corporation to take over the Sydney Steel Plant).

Mr. Pearson issued a statement in December, 1966 which explained the government's decision to opt for a public corporation. He pointed out that DEVCO was a solution to a potentially disastrous social problem on the Island. It was clear that nothing but public ownership on a massive scale could deal with the problems of so many affected Cape Breton individuals, their families and their communities in lieu of the sudden, dramatic cessation of production in the coal industry.

Allan MacEachen was publicly acknowledged to be the father of DEVCO. Tom Kent would become its widely respected second President and social conscience, establishing a pension plan for the miners, among a host of measures widely applauded for their farsightedness. I was very fortunate to serve with Tom as Vice President and Executive Secretary of the Corporation during those challenging days.

As with medicare, DEVCO was part of the infrastructure of a political culture of respect for people. We believed that individual Canadians had to be masters in their own houses. We believed that, in Canada - unlike most other countries on the face of the planet - "if you come back broken we would see that you mend." In that way, the lovely *Song of the Mira* - the river that all Cape Bretoners love - is as well a tribute to the vast, compassionate Canadian nation of which it is such a beautiful part.

3. A Road Less Travelled

The island of Corsica is a long way from Cape Breton. But in 1977 I found myself in attendance at my first Liberal International Congress (LI) in this lovely and historic place. The decision to apply for full membership in LI had been made in 1975, the year I assumed the Presidency of the Liberal Party of Canada.

Membership in the organization had been strongly recommended by my predecessor presidents, Senator Gildas Molgat and Senator Richard Stanbury who had taken an early and very useful interest in the affairs of Liberal International. I spoke to Prime Minister Trudeau several times for his thoughts on the value of our representation in such an organization.

The enormously respected Trudeau led the most successful Liberal party in the world, and was then in the seventh year of his tenure. He felt that Canada could make valuable friends at LI and perhaps serve as a moderating force on the European liberal parties, regarded at the time by many Canadians as considerably farther to the right than our own.

I might point out that of all the middle powers on the world stage, Canada has the broadest range of contacts and influences. We belong to more multilateral clubs than any nation on earth. Canadians are known to be proficient mediators and consistent keepers and makers of the peace.

Some of the reasons for this internationalist instinct can be found in the accidents of history and geography. We have found ourselves wedged between the superpowers at the northern end of the world, which may be reason enough in the nuclear age. Pierre Trudeau once referred to another. The fact that we "sleep with the elephant" means that we feel each "twitch and grunt" of our great neighbour to the south.

Lester Pearson had spent long years in the corridors of international diplomacy before becoming Prime Minister of Canada in 1963. He had always argued convincingly over the decades that Canadian foreign policy had to remain focused on multilateralism because our security could not be centred exclusively on the benevolence of the Americans. If Canada was to escape from permanent inferiority, he argued, it must find security in organizations in which Canadians themselves contributed.

Mr. Pearson was part of a generation of idealistic, yet pragmatic multilateralists who understood that peace was a long journey and that there were no shortcuts to freedom. They mapped out the back roads and the high roads travelled by generations of peacekeepers and their blue berets yet to come. Those roads led to Cyprus and Sarajevo; to Suez, Haiti, Namibia and Cambodia. But whatever roads they travelled, the blue berets were to become a symbol of hope in countries where hope had been forgotten; where terror and ethnic hatred were commonplace, and often all semblance of organized life and society had disappeared.

Over the decades peacekeeping has evolved into new experiments with peacekeeping partnerships which include the military, civilian police, government and non-governmental agencies dealing with human rights and humanitarian assistance, diplomats, the media, as well as organizations sponsoring development and democratization programmes. Canada's Lester B. Pearson International Peacekeeping Training Centre (the Pearson Peacekeeping Centre) in Cornwallis, Nova Scotia, is playing a pathfinder role in the further understanding of peacekeeping partnerships and has become a mecca of knowledge - an international university - vital to the education of the blue berets of the future and the peace and security of the global community at large.

I believe that if Mr. Pearson were alive today, he would be astonished to learn that Canada has played a role in nearly every United Nations mission since its inception. Perhaps it is true that the very size of the multilateralist commitment of Canada abroad is due primarily to the Canadian urge to escape from the feeling of inferiority that he had clearly identified. In many ways, this accounts for the easy familiarity with the world which distinguishes so many of our citizens. Maybe it is a part of what being Canadian really means.

Liberal International was founded in 1947 at Oxford in the same spirit of pragmatic, yet idealistic institution building which was so much a part of the immediate post-war period. One of the original founders was a Canadian economics professor and RCAF veteran, Huntley Sinclair, who married and settled in England after the war. He would become the anchor of Liberal International in all ways, spiritually, philosophically, and practically.

Huntley Sinclair personified the intellectual commitment and compassionate idealism so typical of the spirit of Liberal International. My knowledge of and exposure to international problems was still extremely limited at the time of that first Congress. I listened to a whole series of informed and enlightened colleagues in Corsica, saying little. Huntley was a big influence in expanding my horizons.

At subsequent Congresses, I was privileged to serve with a host of distinguished statesmen from countries around the world. The wise and erudite Senator Giovanni Malagodi of Italy was for many years the heart and guiding light of Liberal International. Adolpe Suarez, the former President of Spain, was a leading proponent of democratic principles in his home country, and tried very hard to expand that influence in Latin America.

Otto Graf Lambsdorff, a past President of Liberal International and a former Minister of the Economy in Germany, is a passionate activist and has been committed to Liberalism as a stepping stone in helping to advance the process of democracy throughout East and Central Europe.

Fritz Bolkestein, leader of the VVD, the Liberal Party in the Netherlands, is a former minister of government who many believe will one day be Prime Minister in his own country. I have grown to know and appreciate Fritz for his logical mind, keen insights, and desire to cut to the chase to get the job done.

Sir David Steel, immediate past President of LI, has been another outstanding force in the organization. His keen journalistic and communications skills mix with a lifetime dedication to compassionate idealism. Always at the cutting edge in British politics - over 30 years a Member of the House of Commons - he remains in personal life a passionate Scot, whose books on his beloved border country of Tweeddale display a loyalty and love of tradition which make him such a delightful friend and colleague.

This international collegiality has worked in unforeseen channels for me on many occasions. When I first met Brian Atwood, now Administrator of the US Agency for International Development (US AID), he was Director (later President) of the then recently established National Democratic Institute (NDI) in Washington. Brian and I became close friends and eventually I would be best man at his wedding to Liberal International's highly regarded Susan Johnson.

It was Brian who would call me in late 1985 with a request to serve on the combined National Democratic Institute for International Affairs - National Republican Institute for International Affairs (NDIIA-NRIIA)[5] observer team then being organized to monitor what would become the dramatic Philippine elections of February, 1986. This would be the first and most critical of all the elections I observed.

All of us who met under the umbrella of Liberal International learned from one another and formed bonds of trust. We developed linkages which enriched us not only as private citizens of our home countries, but as citizens of the world. In 1994, my friend Steingrimur Hermannsson was instrumental in organizing an LI congress in Rekjavik. A former Prime Minister of Iceland, Hermannsson, now Governor of the National Bank in that country, has a quiet, firm approach with excellent judgement.

I felt Prime Minister Chretien could only benefit from attending the Congress. As it turned out, the reaction of the delegates to the arrival of the leader of the most successful Liberal party in the world was overwhelming. Mr. Chretien has taken a keen and extremely influential interest in Liberal International ever since he attended his first Congress in Lucerne, Switzerland in 1991. In the decade of the 1990s, many wonder about the continuing significance of Liberal beliefs and ideals.

Jean Chretien was able to show them that there was room for a Liberal ideology in today's world, and that dedication to the well-being of individuals could still blend with the interests of a free market economy. Representatives from the emerging democracies present in Iceland were able to see that Liberal politics still meant politics from the bottom up.

During the spring 1995 Turbot war with Spain, Canada found it useful to have European friends with whom we could speak, and who we could count on to understand the Canadian position in the matter. The Minister of Fisheries and Oceans at the time, Brian Tobin (now Premier of Newfoundland), displayed great good sense and eloquence in his handling of the affair. He had a number of influential and understanding friends in European capitals who had, due to some linkages provided by Liberal International, an easy acquaintance with, and sympathy for, our arguments in the matter.

It was probably also ludicrous to them that some Spanish officials would argue that Canadians did not understand international law, while, at that very time, Canadian military and civilian peacekeeprs were serving in Bosnia, attempting to keep the peace in Europe's backyard - in Spain's backyard.

The collegiality of forums such as LI has been beneficial in many ways. During the Madrid Congress of 1985, I was thousands of miles away from home when my son-in-law, George Barrett, called from Nova Scotia to tell me I was a grandfather for the first-time. George is married to one of my daughters, Eileen. As I reflected on baby Maria Kathleen's birth so far from home, I knew I did so within the global Liberal family. I felt encouraged to announce spontaneously to all assembled my joy at her birth, and at the same time my concerns about the world's children.

I wondered aloud if the children of the world would face the same animosities, the same injustices, the same unfairness, the same prejudices and the same fears as were prevalent in our time. I thought of our role as custodians for the next generation of our citizens. I thought of the beautiful expression of Canada's Haida nation from the Queen Charlotte Islands in the Province of British Columbia: "we do not inherit this land from our ancestors," they say, "we borrow it from our children." I then suggested in assembly that we should consider the establishment of a human rights committee. With the help of many people, it came into being and Canada became the host country to an extraordinary human rights conference in 1987.

In so doing, LI became the springboard, not only for an international gathering of some of the most fiercely dedicated human rights activists, writers and political leaders in the world, but it became as well a springboard for the strengthening of the consciousness of my fellow Canadian citizens as well.

As LI has grown to include representatives from many of the new emerging democracies, I have felt the meaning and significance of these forums intensify.

They have had so much to teach the more mature democracies in attendance. In many ways, they are best placed to teach us about freedom. In this way, they keep the collective conscience of Liberal International alive. Most of them understand through personal experience that democracy requires sacrifice and hard work from the bottom up. They know that indifference, intransigence and paralysis are the gravest threats to freedom. They know that citizens who fall victim to these tendencies pay with the ultimate price of failure. They pay with the very existence of democracy itself.

I speak with first-hand experience because my own country has become a target. In the aftermath of the enormously unsettling referendum held in the Province of Quebec in the autumn of 1995, Canadians agonized over the precipice they had so narrowly avoided falling over.

Canada is a multicultural federation which in many ways is a microcosm of the planet. It is a country which has been built on a vision and a dream based on tolerance, justice, cooperation and compromise. In Canada, we have people newly-arrived from virtually every country of the world. But some leaders of the regions and provinces in the federation now claim that cooperation cannot be possible because every gain for one region means an equal loss for another region.

To put it another way, these are voices which add to the rhetoric but contribute nothing to the solutions. "We want more," the voices say, "always more. What is more for us is less for you. What is less for us is more for you."

Such individuals have a zero-sum concept of Canada which is rooted in attitudes and ideas which consider compromise and cooperation - the glue of our federation - to be impossible.

As I looked over the wonderful assembly of Liberals from across the world who gathered this past June for a Congress in the Netherlands, I thought of the many who had worked for democratic rights and freedom in their home countries. I couldn't help thinking as a Canadian, as a citizen of one of the most fortunate countries in the world, that maybe we should invite some of them to conduct a speaking tour in my country - and perhaps other established democracies where the citizens believe that freedom is a gift which they have a right to - but no responsibility to defend.

I thought that we should invite Nicaraguans, Cambodians, and Slovakians; all those who had fought the good fight- from Croatia, South Africa, Paraguay and the Philippines. Then they could tell Canadians, some of whom have lost the commitment and the spirit of tolerance and the idea of strength through diversity, about the real meaning of what happens when people lose their vigilance and will to defend democracy.

Then I thought of the thousands of people who wait in immigration offices around the world seeking access to Canada. These people believe that the red maple leaf flies over a vast and wonderful country which covers one-fifth of the globe.

They want to come to Canada to find peace and freedom and compassion and respect for the rights of the individual. For these are the values which bind all Canadians, whether they be from Quebec or Ontario, from Saskatchewan or Nova Scotia. These are the values which make up the national soul. How ironic it was, I thought to myself at that assembly in the Netherlands, that Liberal International had helped me better to understand and appreciate my own country. Liberal International has been a source of strength and continuity, particularly in the present decade of radical change and transition, a time in which many of us feel, justifiably, that contradiction and unpredictability are the only certainties in life.

People of different political persuasions, of course, have found their own common ground and source of inspiration in the highly commendable work carried out by the "Internationals", such as Socialist International, the International Democrat Union, and the Christian Democrat International. The leaders of these Internationals have been known to meet together periodically, because no matter what their domestic political differences, their global objectives are always the same; the worldwide promotion of justice, tolerance, fairness and freedom, the cause of human rights.

Much of the universe has been transformed in our time; yet, a great deal of that transformation is only on a technological plane. The forces of globalization and the internet have interconnected the lifestyles and the ideas of the world's citizens in a web of tiny arteries. All signs seem to point at the development of a single global civilization. Yet underlying the vast international communications web lies another reality.

Hatreds founded on ancient antagonisms, ethnic and racial intolerance, secessionism and terrorism continue to plague us. They are fuelled by the increasing, horrific poverty of the vast majority of our global population and the unconscionable, escalating inequities between the very rich and the very poor.

In the general celebration of the genius of the world economic revolution, we tend to shunt aside the massive problem of human responsibility. The technological revolution has meant absolute progress and generated tremendous hope for the future, but the current threat to jobs has translated into a huge human toll. The global restructuring of industry has led to hardship and desperation - a sense of powerlessness - in the lives of far too many of our talented and creative citizens. Comparatively speaking, Canadians have been protected from some of the worst consequences of this dramatic transformation. I think it can be fairly said that it is because of our social programmes that we have been spared the huge gaps between rich and poor which haunt developing and developed countries alike.

Some people still wonder if the competitive marketplace might permanently exclude large portions of our working population. They fear the instability and chaos, the threat to family life - particularly when children are involved - which is a by-product of joblessness. Young people are especially hard hit by the rapid transition to what many view as the new and ruthless economy.

Even acknowledging technological progress, the facts remain stark, blunt, and undeniable. We are a civilization which has shown too little responsibility for the underprivileged and undernourished of our time. The President of the Czech Republic, Vaclav Havel, put the problem simply in an address at Harvard University in 1995. "Our conscience must keep up with our reason, otherwise we are lost," he said.

It is in forums like Liberal International where our conscience does keep up with our reason. I understood from the time of the first Congress in Corsica that it is in such assemblies where the international conscience of man, what I would regard as the real barometer of progress, is shaped and monitored and renewed.

In these forums we have drawn together in a spirit of intellectual honesty and a commitment to a better world. This kind of idealism may be a road less travelled, but as the American poet Robert Frost once wrote, it is the road less travelled that will make all the difference. He was right. But in some ways, the road map is a matter of inspiration. That, and a lot of help from your friends.

PART TWO
THE DAWNING OF DEMOCRACY

In the aftermath of the historic dismantling of the Berlin Wall on November 9, 1989, Eastern Europe rang out with the optimism and exuberance of a new frontier; the kind, one would imagine, that permeates all societies experiencing great moments in time.

While on a flight to Budapest to observe the March, 1990 Hungarian elections, I happened to read one of Vaclav Havel's wonderful comments on the changes engulfing the communist bloc. The playwright came through in the then-President of the old Czechoslovakia as he beautifully encapsulated the spirit of the times after the crumbling of the darkness. "It was a drama so thrilling, and tragic, and absurd", he wrote, "that no earthling could have written it."

Vaclav Havel was right about our times. They are thrilling, they are tragic - and yes, they are absurd. But while there is much horror in the world, there is also much to celebrate.

We hear continuously that there is no place to hide in our shrinking world from the forces of hypernationalism, of hatred and desperate poverty which surround us. But we must remember also that there is no place to hide from the global reach of education and the rich burgeoning of citizen participation across the planet.

Something very significant has happened over the past decade. The voices of ordinary people have begun to demand change from the bottom up. So while the times are thrilling and tragic and absurd, they are also times of great hope as the people begin to take the lead.

As an international observer of many elections over the past decade, I have been privileged to see people power at work. The crumbling of the darkness[6] and the end of the Cold War has meant that a country's democratic legitimacy and not its bloc allegiance has become the critical factor in determining whether or not transition governments take front-row seats on the global stage. Elections are the launching pads of civilian societies without which there can be no real liberty of the human spirit. Because elections are the catalysts to the advancement of the democratic values which anchor pluralist systems and institutions, they are therefore "defining moments" in the collective political lives of transition states.

The need to protect and secure these defining moments is urgent because democracy doesn't just happen.[7] In Part Three of this book, we will look at the meaning and significance of the observation process, as well as the kinds of democratic craftmanship needed to nurture pluralist institutions into being.

Elections are the launching pads to the dawning of democracy. It is this recognition which has led to the wave of internationally monitored elections in our time. That wave parallels an unfolding global reality; that the growth of a new law on earth is palpable and that the new law of democratic governance will result in a better, fairer, more tolerant world in the future.

I believe that world is in the making as Part Two, "The Dawning of Democracy", makes clear. Chapter Four, entitled "The Soul of our Foreign Policy", examines the evolution of international norms and understandings among states with respect to democracy and the rights of individuals which have emerged in our time. We will look at some of the new thinking on humanitarian intervention, as well, taking into account the fact that "...it now matters to people and groups around the world if the internal affairs of countries violate the rights and safety of their citizens..."[8]

The development of civilian societies and the shift to pluralist institutions is a very frustrating and painful process, as we will see in Chapter Five, "A New Law on Earth" and is beset by many obstacles. Much depends on the political will and commitment to democracy shown by the transitional leadership in the critical days of the dawning of democracy. If they break trust with the people, the defining moments will be lost.

As will be made clear in Section 6, we can't just love them and leave them; the Western democracies have very great responsibilities to assist democratic development after the elections. Countries like South Africa and Mexico face tremendous challenges in the wake of historic elections held in April and August of 1994, respectively. A fragile peace presently holds in tragic Bosnia after the controversial elections of September, 1996. The international community cannot disregard the will and commitment and courage shown by so many in the difficult transition to democracy by abandoning them to the whims of authoritarian leaders, to unconscionable social and economic inequity, or to the violence of unrestrained ethnic and racial conflict.

4. The Soul of Foreign Policy

If anyone is associated in the public mind with sowing the seeds of freedom, it is former President Jimmy Carter. He has become the most visible and influential international election observer. The *Washington Post's* Mary McGrory once praised President Carter for the unique "moral imperative" fuelling his dramatic initiatives on behalf of human rights, good governance and democratic development around the world.

President Carter, by his personal example, has kept that spirit alive and well over the years. He has continually reminded citizens of the world that indifference and pessimism are the great enemies of our time. A speech given at the Rice University convocation in the spring of 1993 illustrated his commitment to the values which he has brought to all his work in the international arena.

Carter spoke of the permanent things in life as he recounted the story of Paul's biblical conversation with his young friend, Timothy. Paul told Timothy that the permanent things in life are those things we cannot see, such as truth, compassion, justice and love.

In the declining years of the twentieth century, such simple truths serve us well. There are many who feel that the uncertainties of the present have led to the idea of communion with others for the sake of the common good. The difficulties of our time have made that biblical conversation very significant.

Those of us who have had the honour to serve with President Carter in the cause of democratic development have recognized that moral imperative as the driving force behind all of his global engagements, as McGrory so well understood. The settlement in Haiti which led to the return of President Aristide on the 15th of October, 1994, is only the latest example of Carter's crusading spirit in politics.

The historic threads of American idealism and liberal internationalism have discernably embellished his vision of an activist America committed to the advancement of world order and freedom. It was the same Jimmy Carter, after all, who announced in his Inaugural Address of 1977 that human rights was to be the soul of America's foreign policy. This was a highly controversial policy in the United States at that time and would later be rejected in many of its aspects by President Ronald Reagan.

Nonetheless, in spite of the domestic criticism, the dynamism of the new thrust in policy would make waves in the Western liberal democracies, particularly as debate began to rage over the evident contradictions in bilateral trade/aid relations with developing countries. Set against an increasing popular consciousness with regard to the protection of human rights, governments began to concern themselves with mapping out the fundamental ingredients of foreign policy with a human face.[9]

In Canada, over the course of the last decade, conscience began to square off with commerce in determining government policy. As the authors of one of the first foreign policy reports in our history to deal with the controversial debate put it:[10]

> The effective promotion of human rights internationally faces many challenges and paractical obstacles. It is rejected in some quarters as unacceptable interference in the affairs of sovereign states. We insist, on the contrary, that the behaviour of governments, like that of individuals, is subject to universal values. It is not interference to pass judgement on a government's conduct and to adjust relations with that government accordingly. Actions such as terminating aid or trading relations are exactly the opposite of intervention in the internal affairs of another country.

The debate over interference quickly began to centre on our foreign aid budgets. Canadians had begun to believe that matching aid to human rights was simply a matter of common sense. This conviction was widespread throughout the country as it had become increasingly clear that, in some cases, our aid was serving more to prop up bad regimes than to promote development.

Human rights had moved to the front and centre of Canadian consciousness during the Mulroney years. During this period, the government began to play a major role in building international pressure against apartheid. As the Code of Conduct for Canadian companies operating in South Africa was strengthened, voluntary disinvestment became commonplace as many business leaders began to recognize that the South African game was "no longer worth the candle."[11] At that time, Canada introduced more than two dozen sanctions designed to isolate the apartheid regime which would be developed by the Commonwealth and the United Nations.

South African President de Klerk announced the revocation of the ban on all political organizations and released Nelson Mandela and other political prisoners in February, 1990. This historic decision shook the world. Canadians took great pride in Mandela's subsequent visit to Canada in June of that year and his stirring address to the Members of both Houses of Parliament.

In many ways, that address symbolized the long history of Canadian involvement and concern over human rights issues. But Prime Minister Mulroney's clear interest in the subject helped speed up the momentum already evident throughout the country.[12] Ultimately, it was his government's contributions to the course of human rights policy direction in Canada which may be chalked up by the historians of the future as Brian Mulroney's finest hour.

Another means of interference in the course of the global advancement of the cause of human rights through our foreign policy commitments was then seen to be the development of a Canadian facility for election monitoring. In August, 1988, the Parliament of Canada adopted a law creating the International Centre for Human

Rights and Democratic Development. The International Bill of Human Rights was the heart and soul of the centre's mandate. The general idea behind its establishment was to help strengthen practices and build institutions which would protect the basic rights and freedom of individual persons as outlined in the international statutes.[13]

In this respect, programmes of technical assistance as well as the expertise needed to build enduring electoral institutions and procedures in countries across the globe were seen as vital components of the Institute's overall mandate.

In the fall of 1994, a Special Senate - House of Commons Joint Committee reviewing Canada's Foreign Policy continued to uphold the paramount place of international rights and freedoms as central to our overall foreign policy. The Allan MacEachen - Jean Robert Gauthier report hailed the traditional values of human rights, good governance and democratic development as universal values which anchored Canada's political tradition both at home and abroad. The then Foreign Minister, the Honourable André Ouellet, and the former Minister for International Trade, the Honourable Roy MacLaren, responded to the review recommendations on behalf of the government of Canada:

> The Government regards respect for human rights not only as a fundamental value, but also as a crucial element in the development of democratic and prosperous societies at peace with each other... development assistance is a constructive way to address human rights, democracy and governance issues. As one of six priorities for ODA, assistance in this area will support such activities as peace and reconciliation initiatives, human rights education, widening access to legal remedies, strengthening legislatures and judicial systems, and increasing the capacity of organizations and other representatives of civil society to participate fully and effectively in decision making in their countries.[14]

The evolving policy orientation of the government of my own country illustrates the increasing commitment to democratization around the world. As well, this reflects the understanding that democratic development is a process which requires the continuing assistance of outside governments to the growth of pluralist institutions in emerging civilian societies.

I believe we have come a long way in our appreciation of how best to conceive and construct democratic societies which are harbingers of hope for a more peaceful international community in the future. Over the course of the last decade, international concern with regard to questions of basic civil and political rights and freedoms has spiralled, signifying a quantum leap in the global consciousness of these issues.

It will be remembered that the United Nations had earlier taken action against the apartheid regime in South Africa and the unilateral declaration of independence in Rhodesia, measures which had been considered exceptional at the time and taken largely because of Third World pressures over racial discrimination. The notable absence of any collective pressure from the mature Western democracies reflected the minimal consciousness with regard to human rights and freedoms which existed only a quarter of a century ago.

It became increasingly clear to the international community in later years, however, that repression and electoral fraud led to instability and were therefore threats both to regional and global peace and security. Central America provided some striking illustrations of this. General Noriega's refusal to accept the results of democratic elections in Panama led to his capture and subsequent imprisonment as part of the controversial invasion of the country by the United States in 1989. Anastasio Somoza's repeated efforts to rig elections in Nicaragua led to a revolution in that country in 1979, with Somoza agreeing, in July of that year, to go into exile in Florida. The savagery of the Haitian military in what many observers had begun to describe as a "failed country" led to international action to restore President Aristide in October, 1994.

Negotiations on defence-of-democracy mechanisms which involved forms of outside intervention became increasingly common in regional forums such as the Organization of American States. Thinkers and scholars began to emphasize specific phrases from the Preamble of the United Nations Charter, such as: "We the peoples of the United Nations", and the affirmation of "faith in fundamental human rights." Some analysts went as far as to suggest that the people, not their rulers, are the real bearers of sovereignty. At the same time, recurring attempts were made to reconcile these important beliefs with the traditional notion of the defence of sovereignty so explicitly endorsed in article 2(7) of the same Charter.

Yet, in spite of the contradictions of the Charter and all of the global discourse which has emerged on rights and freedoms, an international consensus has begun to emerge on what constitutes legitimate rule. New concepts on humanitarian intervention and global collective action have paralleled this evolving understanding on people-derived government.[15]

It was in Latin America where regional initiatives first began to reflect emerging international norms. The 1991 Santiago decision taken by the Organization of American States was a dramatic pledge to take action in the defence of democracy when it was threatened in the Western Hemisphere. The Santiago Commitment provides that in the event of: "any sudden or irregular interruption of the democratic institutional process" in a member state, an emergency meeting of OAS Foreign Ministers will be convoked within10 days to decide on a collective reaction.[16]

In the Haiti, Peru, and Guatemala coups which followed, "...the OAS foreign Ministers have not only condemned the overthrow as illegal and called for a prompt return to democratic rule, but have resorted to economic and political sanctions to back up their demands."[17] This was the first effort by the OAS to respond to the widespread revulsion of so many Latin Americans directed at the dictatorships of then recent memory.

Similar trends were at work in Europe. The Conference on Security and Cooperation in Europe (CSCE) on the Human Dimension held in Moscow in 1991 was of great significance. The assembled European states, the USA and Canada, all members of the CSCE, were unanimous in their declaration that:

> ...commitments undertaken in the field of the human dimension of the CSCE are matters of direct and legitimate concern to all participating states and do not belong exclusively to the internal affairs of the state concerned.[18]

When the United States government castigated the attempted coup against the established Soviet government in August, 1991, it referred to the commitments to domestic reforms made by Soviet leaders at the time of the Helsinki Accords of 1977, which addressed questions of European human rights. No one at the time seemed to be too concerned that this was undue interference in the internal affairs of another state.

In the spring, 1992 issue of *Foreign Affairs*, the Russian Foreign Minister, Andrei Kozyrev wrote:

> Wherever threats to democracy and human rights occur, let alone violations thereof, the international community can and must contribute to their removal ...Such measures are regarded today not as interference in internal affairs, but as assistance and cooperation in ensuring everywhere a most favoured regime for the life of the peoples - one consistent with each state's human rights under the United Nations Charter, international covenants, and other international instruments.[19]

It would appear that the international community is gradually reaching consensus on the legitimacy of democratic regimes. We might recall that in its last year of existence the Soviet Union joined in the remarkable document of the Copenhagen meeting of the Conference on Security and Cooperation in Europe which stated that: "the will of the people, freely and fairly expressed through periodic and genuine elections, is the basis of the authority and legitimacy of all government."[20]

Pursuant to the same document signed in 1990, the member states of the Conference took upon themselves the obligation to facilitate the presence of international observers to all national elections in their respective countries. In December, 1991, the General Assembly approved a resolution which called upon the Secretary General to establish a focal point "...to ensure consistency in the handling of requests of Member States organizing elections." Only three states dissented from this resolution and James Jonah, then Under-Secretary for Political Affairs became the focal point.

Shortly thereafter, a small electoral assistance unit (EAU) was founded in the secretariat at the United Nations. The EAU has detailed six categories of responses to any member state requesting assistance:

- organization and conduct of elections by the United Nations (e.g. Cambodia);
- supervision of the elections (e.g. Namibia);
- electoral verification (e.g. Nicaragua, Haiti, and Angola);
- coordination of observers (e.g. Ethiopia, Burundi, Lesotho, and Malawai);
- follow and report (e.g. Romania); and
- technical assistance (e.g. Romania, Guyana, and Albania).[21]

As we will see, the huge costs involved in the long-time observation processes in South Africa, El Salvador, and Mexico - all elections held in 1994 - would lead to new efforts at electoral coordination, and, particularly, the training of domestic election monitors.

But for now, we can see that the immediate ramifications of the CSCE document issued in Copenhagen combined with the decisions at the UN to make election verification a top priority had an extraordinary meaning for our time. Together, they signalled an evolving global understanding of the limits of sovereignty and the need to support humanitarian intervention in the defence of democracy and human rights. UN Secretary-General Boutros Boutros-Ghali took note of these developments in his report, "Agenda for Peace", concluding that: "The time of absolute and exclusive sovereignty .. has passed."[22]

In the new, more intervention-minded global community, requests for international election monitors became increasingly routine. Much of the international community has drawn together in concluding that those governments who deny their citizens the right to free and open elections and good governance are violating a principle that is fast becoming an integral part of the conscience of mankind.

Specifically, the recent surge of international election monitoring has presented huge challenges to traditional notions of state sovereignty. Observers from abroad, equipped only with a badge certifying that they are entitled to watch and report on voting procedures, are in fact taking a big leap in the international consciousness of man. They are doing so by the seemingly simple act of crossing the boundary which separates international from domestic politics.

My experience has been on the practical side of this great historic transition. I have been fully aware in the many countries I visited that the practice of election observing deeply involves outsiders in the domestic cultures of countries across the globe. The electoral monitoring system has an important spin-off effect. It means that outsiders are brokers of democratic value systems. This is true whether mediation is at the request of the state authorities involved, or simply through the dissemination of influence associated with the very presence of observers from other countries.

There is legitimate and profound debate on the pros and cons of assistance to democratic development throughout the international community at present. I believe we cannot afford to let democracy fail because of the consequences of that failure for all of us.

I believe a truly democratic world would pursue international politics very differently than it has in the past. I am not certain that a democratic world would lead to the elimination of war, but I think it would mean a much lower tolerance level for conflict. There is strong evidence that democracies seldom fight with one another.

That in itself should be a very interesting and positive signal to the international community.

The links between democracy and peace are strong and compelling. A civic culture provides a climate of seeking peaceful means to settle differences. It also provides for the domestic and external institutions essential to shaping values and attitudes which are crucial to diminishing the risks of future conflicts. I believe that strengthening democracy is an urgent requirement. I know there are many who are less convinced. Some might ask, and with great justification, will a democratic Russia translate into a peace-loving state? Will a democratic Russia mean the country will shun war with other states?

My own experience has convinced me that the probable answers to both these questions are yes. At the very least, the probability is so great as to pose another question. If the international community fails to invest adequately in the process of democratic development, do we not collectively risk a much greater problem? I need only mention one; the loss of human lives.

That is why I believe our assistance to the development of civil and political liberties and free, fair electoral systems - all part of the process of democratic development - has become the soul of our foreign policy. In this, I refer to the foreign policy of individual nations, as well as that of the broader global community. That assistance is the engine of an evolving new law on earth.

5. A New Law on Earth

One of the great paradoxes of the 1990s is the side-by-side existence of the forces of order and enlightenment and the forces of chaos. Many might wonder if ethnic extremism and separatist secessionism, all virulent forms of nationalism, stand as the wave of the future. I do not think this. I believe that in today's world, to quote one classical writer on the subject, "nationalism is a form of speech which shouts, not merely so that it will be heard, but so that it will believe itself."[23]

More and more it seems to me that the extremists are working at opposite ends of a new global trend towards integration and enlightenment. The development of huge, hemispheric trade blocks and the parallel growth through a vast web of communications circuits of what could be conceived to be a single global civilization seem portentous enough that the forces of integration will win out in the end. So too does the spread of the democratic ideal in countries which only a few years ago seemed outside the solar system of political pluralism.

We live in an age which future historians will record as one in which there was a struggle for open, democratic politics and free-market systems. It will be these developments, rather than the failure of communism which will be highlighted as having produced some of the most historically significant reverberations of our century.[24]

James N. Rosenau is the author of the well-known "turbulence model" which identifies the global patterns at work behind the recent waves of democratization. I had the pleasure of his company in observing the 1993 elections in Paraguay. As a consequence, I am now able to associate his compassion and sense of fun with the analysis of a highly respected scholar. [25]

Rosenau starts with the assumption that the international information culture has generated a "world authority crisis" in our interdependent world. The authority crisis generates the waves of emotional and psychic encouragement which lead to the integration of ideas and peoples.

Lester M. Salamon summarizes the spin-off effect this way:

> A striking upsurge has taken place in organized volunteer activity, in the formation and increased activism of private, non-profit, or non-governmental organizations in every part of the world...people are forming associations, foundations and other similar institutions to deliver human services, promote grassroots development, prevent environmental degradation, protect civil rights... "an associational revolution" now seems underway at the global level that may constitute as significant a social and political development of the latter twentieth century as the rise of the nation state was of the latter nineteenth.[26]

The communications revolution and the internet accelerate the avalanche of news about the virtues of democracy and the failings of authoritarianism. The vast web of communications circuits which binds us and which has so radically transformed our ability to grasp images of life virtually anywhere on the planet means that ideas, information, and communication have become a force far more potent than tanks and automatic weapons.

Recent events lead us to think of dramatic evidence to the contrary; the ability of the Chinese government to crush dissent at Tiananmen Square through the crude application of ruthless oppression is only one such example. But these kinds of regimes can only repress ideas and information and the unalterable wave of democratization for so long. Dissidents around the world understand the power of the digital revolution. As China continues to add each year as many new phones as we have in total in Canada, it is clear that technology itself will be the new Trojan Horse; the vehicle of human rights and freedom which the old authoritarian regimes will find impossible to restrain or oppress or cast into exile.

The power of the communications revolution has led to explosive developments. Even in countries with deep authoritarian traditions, such as those in Latin America, demands for accountability and popular participation in the processes of government have transformed political cultures from the bottom up. In today's world, the simple acceptance of authority has become a thing of the past.

The growing emergence of internationally shared norms on questions of human rights and democratic institutions is a parallel development of great significance, as we have seen. Unfortunately, the global community is still in the early phases of a collective understanding with regard to defence-of-democracy mechanisms which will ensure vulnerable experiments in political pluralism do not fail. I refer here to democracy with the very minimal characteristics I would regard as essential to a pluralist system. These are factors such as free and fair competition for power, elected civilian control, accountability, representativeness, and legal guarantees for rights of conscience, expression, organization, and assembly.

The emergence of democracy around the globe is always the by-product of a combination of causes which vary from country to country.[27] Sometimes the process starts from the grass roots, as I saw it happen in the Philippines in the historic 1986 elections. In that remarkable country, over 500,000 volunteers worked on election day, defying threats and violence, to ensure that the world at large would see the full reality of the defeat of Ferdinand Marcos at the polls.

In other cases, the process of democratization has begun as the result of strategic arrangements among pro-democracy forces in transition states. While most of the negotiations which produce those convergences are matters which take place within the domestic context of states, the mediation of individuals and groups from foreign governments and non-governmental organizations is often a critical factor.

I have seen much of this kind of activity in sensitive transition states on the eve of democratic breakthroughs. I consider the initial invention of democracy - because invention it was - in Paraguay, 1989, in this light. That is not to say that the will to democratize did not exist within that country, because it was very much evident amongst critical sectors of Paraguayan life and society. The problem was that there, as was so evident in many other countries, the electoral system had been unfairly manipulated against local opposition groups.

As a result, distrust and discouragement were primary obstacles to the necessary strategic consensus between the principle parties, the kind of consensus so vital to the holding of elections which are in themselves the first steps in the process of democratization.

As we will see, the mediator role played by international election monitors has often helped draw excluded groups into the electoral consensus. Such participation has therefore legitimized processes in countries which would otherwise have been doomed to failure.

The actions of international monitoring teams have often been essential in ensuring that fledgling democratic governments will achieve the consensus necessary for the implementation of often tough economic and social reforms.

We can't say there is any linear or rational evolution in the growth of democratic systems. Some democracies abort as soon as they emerge; others erode more than they consolidate.[28] And many are only partly free. In its Comparative Survey of Freedom for 1995, Freedom House listed 114 countries as democracies, yet it also classified one-third of these as only partly free because of the attacks on political liberties and basic human rights which characterized their political landscapes.

The problem of discerning levels and stages of freedom has led to a whole barrage of new terms in the expanding vocabulary of democracy. These range from expressions like "competitive semi-democracies" and "restrictive semi-democracies" through to the more familiar term "authoritarian democracy", for example.[29]

Samuel Huntington, the father of some of the most important work on the so-called "third wave of democratization," gave some interesting examples of authoritarian democracy in a recent essay and followed up with a thought-provoking question. In writing about President Fujimori's famous April, 1992 executive coup in Peru, at which time he banned political organizations and imprisoned politicians and censored the media, among other things, Huntington noted:

> that he(Fujimori) ...used his authoritarian power to break the influence of the terrorist Sendero Luminoso(Shining Path), restore law and order, stabilize the currency, promote foreign investment, achieve the highest rate of economic growth in Latin America, and win overwhelming re-

election in what was generally considered to be a fair vote...after Fujimori's coup, Secretary of State James Baker immediately attacked it, saying, "you can't save democracy by destroying it." But perhaps Fujimori did just that.[30]

Democratic Consolidation

Over the past decade, democratic regimes have gradually taken hold throughout the international community, even though the levels of freedom vary from country to country. In many instances, the most that can be said is that there is now more pluralism in politics and civil society than before. But no matter how we categorize them, we can say that the international community is now faced not so much with the question of the addition of new democracies, as it is with the consolidation of recently established democracies such as those in Russia, South Africa, and Mexico.

The consolidation process is a complex one and really lies outside the parameters of this book. Nevertheless, a few thoughts are offered. First, a consolidated democracy is one in which pluralism becomes the only game in town.[31] Pluralism isn't just about institutions and rules, we must remember. It is also a state of mind - for example, the cherishing of the value of the democratic ideal and procedures - even in the face of severe economic crisis.

It must be emphasized that no consolidation can occur without the growth of a citizenry with full confidence in their political institutions. Democracy becomes truly stable only when people come to value it widely, not solely for its economic and social performance, but intrinsically for its political attributes.

It takes root when real citizens start to develop and by real citizens I refer to people who understand that the deepening of democracy is an on-going process and there are no short cuts to freedom. Real citizens are people who understand that there are rights as well as duties and responsibilities which are all a part of membership in a civilian-based society.

The development of a free, lively, and critical civil society is a factor which is vital to democratic consolidation. So, too, is the rule of law and the accountability of all political leaders to it. The impartiality of the judiciary, police and civil service is crucial to the building of public trust which is the unseen engine of transition.

In South Africa, two notable events took place in 1995 which proved the President himself constrained by the judiciary. When the President dismissed Winnie Mandela from her post as a junior minister in the government, the Supreme Court found the President had acted unconstitutionally and reversed the decision. In a second case, the Supreme Court rejected President Mandela's proclamations overriding decisions by the Western Cape province and declared them invalid. In this sense, the citizens of South Africa became increasingly aware that the principle of accountability, so essential to the development of a real tradition of liberal governance, was alive and well in the critical first months and years of this most remarkable transition.

The glue which bonds future civilians with their own unfamiliar representative institutions is trust. The leaders of a particular country must mediate a domestic agreement amongst many different ethnic groups and classes with regard to the legitimacy and value of democratic institutions. Much depends on the moral behaviour of politicians in the new democracies.

As we look back throughout history, particularly to ancient Greece, we read of Aristotle reflecting upon the fact that the number of people involved in the "ruling" was not nearly as important as the motivation of the people who rule.

It was clear that the rulers must rule for others, not for themselves. He saw that the people, the "demos", would become a mob if rulers were not altruistic, working for the good of all people. The worst setback any new democracy can experience is the loss of public trust in the leaders of the transition.

I think of one case, Albania, where the great hopes generated throughout the international community in the days following the exhilarating elections of March, 1992, have been succeeded by deep disappointment in the wake of the 1996 elections.

Much of the concern and consternation expressed by governments and pro-democracy NGOs alike has been focused on the behaviour of Doctor Sali Berisha and his governing Democratic Party in the period up to and during the May 26 and June 2, 1996 elections.

I first met Doctor Berisha during the Bulgarian elections of October, 1991. We were co-leaders of a 75-member delegation from 23 countries assembled to monitor the election in that country. At that time, he encouraged me to visit Albania for the forthcoming spring elections. Doctor Berisha feared that the Commissars, the old style Communists, would try to rig the elections again. Unfortunately, I could not go.

I followed the events in tiny Albania with great interest, communicating several times with Doctor Berisha before and after the elections. I was, at the time, highly doubtful about the prospects for democratization in that country.

Little was known about Albania, a country significant mainly as an isolated and seemingly impregnable Stalinist-like fortress led by Enver Hoxha. As Europe's poorest country, it had become a totalitarian wasteland, far removed from the mainstream of Gorbachev-style reformism. As such, outside observers felt Albania to be a highly unlikely candidate for democratization.

Yet the victory for Berisha's Democratic Party in the March elections was only a harbinger of what was to come. On the night of his triumph, Berisha announced joyfully to 60,000 jubilant supporters that the long night of communism had ended.

At the same time, he was aware that the "commissars" of the old communist regime had been replaced by new, in many cases, more deadly enemies. Post-election Albania was besieged on all sides by starvation, economic ruination, and disease. In fact, Berisha inherited a country on the verge of collapse. In the first few months, Albanians were nearly completely dependent on humanitarian aid from abroad for survival.

The new President's confidence and optimism paralleled the extraordinary courage of the Albanian people in those difficult early years. Astonishingly, much of the infrastructure for a pluralist democracy and a market economy was constructed under the auspices of the new government.

The poor and marginalized people of Albania courageously voted for freedom and stand on the threshold of a new age. Time will tell if Albania can successfully make the transition to a full-fledged democracy. But that will depend very much on the political will of Doctor Berisha himself. Unfortunately, according to reports, it is feared that that will may have considerably weakened in the few short years he has held power.

The elections of May 26 and June 2, 1996 seem to point to this unhappy development. The National Democratic Institute observers recounted widespread electoral irregularities, together with examples of violent government reaction against protestors on May 28, actions which cut off the freedom of expression and assembly crucial to a pluralistic democratic society.

The Helsinki based International Federation for Human Rights recorded significant human rights violations before, during, and after the election. The group referred to many examples of government manipulation of the media, intimidation of opposition politicians and independent journalists alike. It also suggested that, on election day, ballot stuffing, multiple voting, voter list manipulation and police intimidation were commonplace. Many agreed with the Helsinki group's recommendation that new Albanian elections should be held.

I come back to the issue of trust and the important principle that rulers must rule in the interests of the citizens rather than themselves. In practical terms, those in power, no matter how many, must be constrained by a constitution which sets the parameters of their power. We cannot speak about the people being the decision makers in a system, unless we work as well on the constitution and the laws which will determine voting and other procedures.

Since 1990, most of sub-Saharan Africa's 45 states have experienced transitions from authoritarianism to democracy, the fate of these transitions running anywhere from total disaster to some relative success. Still, there are grounds for hope as the politically committed, well-educated members of civic and opposition groups courageously pursue the democratic ideal. These democrats are mired in incredible political difficulties within their own homelands, but their immediate agenda must consist:

> ...of establishing the conceptual and institutional foundations for popular government...here the relevant issues are the same ones addressed by the European and American pioneers of democracy, whose words resonate in the discourse of African democracy today. The real challenge, of course, is adapting those original ideas to local conditions. It is no accident that the transitions to democracy in Namibia, South Africa, and Malawi came in the wake of realistic and lengthy constitution-making processes that took stock of those countries' social complexities.[32]

Deepening Democracy

I think most of us understand that real democracy evolves over time and goes far beyond the formal trappings of democratic political systems and processes. Real democracy assumes many diverse forms and to succeed must become a process indigenous to the particular historical, social and cultural values and traditions of individual states.

Real democracy goes far beyond the concept of multipartyism and the holding of elections. As we have seen, if democratic consolidation is to occur, the important elements of accountability along with genuine popular participation of citizens in the political and economic decision making process must be present in a nation's consciousness.

But real democracy is a process and is constantly restoring itself as people-derived institutions proliferate and popular participation deepens. This is a truth that citizens of the more mature democracies can often be lulled into forgetting. The struggle for democracy is never finished.

The collapse of communism in our time has meant the defeat of a vast body of ideas and assumptions which was for many decades the mainstay of our great historic rival in the Cold War. But the end of this ideological confrontation has already begun to cause much soul-searching in the established liberal democracies. I think it is fair to say that we have all become more conscious of the needs for change in the way our own systems work.

There are those who believe that the politics of the 21st century are likely to be characterized, in part, by broad new understandings about the nature of the democratic process or perhaps even "a radical change in the process by which the democratic idea is put into practice."[34]

A great deal has been written of the disillusionment and malaise souring public opinion in the Western democracies, and the commensurate broad distrust of political representatives regardless of ideology.[34] This malaise has been well depicted as a kind of "moral crisis". It must be remembered that the new democracies cannot escape the turbulence and uncertainty afflicting the more mature models. The course of change and transition in the Western democracies will, to a large extent, influence and determine the evolution of pluralism in other regions.

So, too, will the appeal of alternative models. The Islamic path is one of these, which by the very nature of its religious foundations, cannot claim a general global audience.

But Asian authoritarianism clearly does. The remarkable economic growth combined with nondemocratic systems of government which characterizes countries such as Malaysia, Indonesia, and Singapore illustrates the tremendous appeal of this model. No other democratic country, except for Japan, has sustained the eight percent or higher growth rates that these countries have achieved under authoritarian rule.[35] Clearly, a strong case can be made for the East Asian model, including the social and cultural benefits of the Asian values of order, community, and discipline. Indeed, the stability and order of such regimes is often compared favourably by their proponents with the license, unchecked individualism and disrespect for authority which seem to coincide with the deep sense of alienation sweeping civilian societies in the Western democracies.

Prime Minister Mahathir of Malaysia and Senior Minister Lee Kuan Yew of Singapore typify the most influential proponents of this world view. Yet while authoritarian rule may provide good government for a decade, or even a generation, it cannot provide - and throughout history has never provided - good government over a sustained period of time. It lacks the institutions for self-reform: public debate, a free press, protest movements, opposition political parties, and competitive elections.[36]

Although some authoritarian governments, like that in Singapore, have been highly successful, many others have been unmitigated disasters, characterized by economic ruination, gross corruption, and domestic violence. On the subject of leadership, it might be somewhat gratuitous to observe that many authoritarian leaders are simply not good people.

Overall, these kinds of regimes suffer from a number of important weaknesses, but the most important, in my opinion, is the lack of feedback mechanisms, one of the greatest advantages of pluralist systems. Generally, politicians concerned about re-election are reluctant to let their people starve.

In this sense, the recent democratic election of Boris Yeltsin as President of Russia is of greater significance than perhaps many appreciate. With at least the rudimentary underpinnings of participatory democracy now in place, it may, if we compare the situation with the Peoples Republic of China, be Russia's turn to take the Great Leap Forward.[37]

As Thomas Friedman has so well put it, the tortoise, Russia, has in this respect passed a major speedbump in its competition with what many analysts had always regarded as the hare - the People's Republic, so widely noted for its spectacular economic growth rate. The speedbumps he referred to are the critical feed-back mechanisms, now in evidence in this former totalitarian country.

Clearly China has a huge speedbump waiting for it down the road. As the country grows more prosperous, its people will demand a less arbitrary system because it is only through participatory government that that country will reach the next stage in its economic growth. As Friedman observes, "no-one, least of all investors in China, knows what will happen when it hits that speed bump."

The idea of democratic succession is unknown in communist systems. The fact that China's 92 year old paramount leader, Deng Xiaoping, is the most influential decision maker in that country in spite of the fact that he holds no official postion in either his country's party or its government, clearly illustrates the conundrum these kinds of systems face when questions of succession emerge, as they inevitably must. The plethora of worrisome questions posed to all the ousiders now attempting to penetrate the China market is self evident.

So in many ways, when Friedman advises "bet the tortoise", it is because of the elementary, but still essential notions of participatory democracy now in evolution in Russia which may make those bets a lot safer in the long-term.

Therefore, in this brief survey of the alternatives to political pluralism, I must find myself in full agreement with Winston Churchill's famous observation: "Democracy is the worst form of government - except for all the others."

I return to the question of the malaise and uncertainty which haunts so many mature democracies. Democratic governments cannot forget that their models will influence the consolidation process in transition states around the world. The course of renewal and revitalization of pluralist systems in the West is therefore integrally linked with the future success of the fledgling democracies of our time. We must return to the basics. I believe that, for example, the popular need for civic education in the Western democracies has never been greater.

The strengthening of civil society and the development of a real citizenry with a conscious understanding of their rights and responsibilities will, over time, prove to be one of the most important challenges to all democratic governments, whether they are old or new, developing or developed.

International peace and security very much depend on the deepening of democracy. Even in regions of extreme turmoil such as the Middle East, the cautious and formative steps we are currently seeing in terms of assistance to the growth of functioning civilian societies is a source of hope for the future.

The Palestinians are currently striving to achieve at least a modicum of sovereignty as well as the infrastructure conducive to the support of pluralism in the years to come. They turned out in large numbers for the January 20, 1996 first-time elections in Gaza and the West Bank for a new Palestinian Council and, separately, a President.

The Islamic Hamas movement and radical secular groups boycotted the election to protest the compromises Mr. Yasir Arafat, long-time leader of the Palestine Liberation Organization, made with Israel over questions of territory and security. But in spite of that fact, most Palestinians were determined to cast their ballots. They understood that the elections imply only partial sovereignty. Although they bring the people closer to their own state, the full corner has yet to be turned.

Palestinians know the path ahead is long, frustrating, and dangerous. Israel's deep anxiety over the need for secure and defensible borders is only one of the better known obstacles to self-determination. Less well understood are the often overt divide-and-rule policies pursued by Arab governments which claim to be their "brothers." The denial of citizenship by some Arab governments to the Palestinans dispersed throughout the Middle East is only one of the more obvious examples of this kind of tactic.

So although the recent elections imply a partial increase in sovereignty for this divided people, history has taught them that there are no shortcuts to freedom. The elections were just one more signpost on the long way home. Nonetheless, they were a critical defining moment in time because Palestinians had caught a glimpse of the possible.

International observers helped secure the defining moment. Their complaints about Israeli security measures in East Jerusalem, which appeared to intimidate Palestinians from voting, led to an easing of security. Palestinians voted for democracy, but from the squalor of the refugee camps it is no wonder that many would find it difficult to begin to think about the rights and responsibilities of citizens. The infrastructure for an evolving civic culture is yet to be designed. The aid package of $1.3 billion (US) put together in the weeks prior to the election by over 50 donor nations and NGOs is a step in the right direction. But much more must come.

I believe that the growth of democracy in our time will correspond with the evolution of tolerant, civilian societies and will be the catalyst to peace in the future. In societies torn by civil strife and conflict, the task of deepening democracy assumes urgent proportions. Seemingly simple solutions, such as those which encourage popular participation on as many levels as possible, can often become the only means of inspiring trust.

In Northern Ireland the painfully incremental and frustrating search for peace continues in the wake of recent terrorist bombings which shattered the peace limbo of 1995. The litany of 25 years of strife and over 3,200 deaths has haunted the land of Ulster causing many outsiders to wonder if a spirit of tolerance can ever take root in that troubled land.

I attended a conference on crime in Belfast early in 1995 which was organized by Liberal International's David Steel and the Alliance Party of Northern Ireland's John Alderdice. Delegates from 23 countries ranging from Israel to the Netherlands were in attendance.

I participated in a BBC open-line talk show as part of my visit to Belfast. In response to questioning about my view of the troubles, I spoke of my belief that peace was a process and that it was essential for its adherents to persevere, in spite of all the frustrations, intimidation, and fear that often made the ultimate objective appear to be out of reach. I spoke of the many courageous individuals in countries across the world who had made democratic transitions work; often in spite of incredible obstacles. "Don't disengage", I told listeners on another broadcasting station. "Never give up."

The deepening of democracy is an on-going challenge and everything depends on the commitment of a citizenry to the renewal and continual revitalization of the institutions of political pluralism. I spoke at the conference of the process at work in my own country. In a way, I was not surprised at the high level of interest shown by the delegates in the Canadian government's new commitments to work in partnership with the first nations, our aboriginal peoples.

That partnership has taken the form of community policing, in which local people decide how they will be policed and by whom. This community-driven approach will ensure that the police force will reflect the culture and beliefs of aboriginal peoples. It has become one of the building blocks of democracy in my own country, a deepening of the democratic practice in Canada.

In Northern Ireland, where the operations of paramilitaries have impeded the process of peace over the decades, such community- driven approaches could, of course, have important implications for the future. The deepening of democracy must work from the bottom up. In one of the world's most tragic cities, Belfast, the armed camp of Northern Ireland, this is particularly true.

The process will be aided by the tolerant and constructive leadership of individuals such as the then Lord Mayor, Hugh Smith, who said simply in an address to us: "All we want is to live in peace like other ordinary citizens in peaceful areas of the world." The housekeeper in the hotel where I was staying echoed the sentiments of many. "God, I hope the troubles are over," she said.

No matter what the country, democratic values must be continually revitalized. Civilian society is in a state of permanent reconstruction as the needs and interests of the inhabitants change over time. All citizens, whether it is the Lord Mayor or the housekeeper, are essential participants in the process.

But no matter what challenges lie ahead, there is a very simple reality to keep in mind. The revitalization of democratic systems is the responsibility of all citizens. This continuing commitment demands hard work and sacrifice from the bottom up.

The symphony is always unfinished. But no matter what the country, no matter what hybrid form democracy assumes around the world, it promises a better life for all those citizens who have a stake in attaining it, preserving it, and renewing it.

Of course the challenges are much greater for the citizens of the new democracies, because they have yet to attain that stake in a better life. One thing is certain. We can't ensure them that stake if we love them and leave them.

6. Don't Love Them and Leave Them

Just before the spring, 1990 elections in Germany, a small group of foreign observers were invited to East Berlin by the Federation of Protestant Churches. The purpose was to meet with the parties contesting the election. I attended in the company of a number of my colleagues from Liberal International, including the former President of Spain, Adolpho Suarez, and former Prime Minister Hermanson of Iceland, as well as Count Otto Lambsdorff of Germany, then President-elect of Liberal International.

It was shortly after the Wall had come down. I remember taking a chunk from the Wall as a souvenir in the company of Brian Atwood. There were many names at the Wall of those who had died in vain attempts to escape to the West. One of those was 20 year old Chris Gueffroy, an East German waiter who had been shot as he climbed the Wall, seeking to flee to West Berlin in February, 1989.[38] Gueffroy was believed to be the last of about 200 people killed seeking to flee to the West. It all seemed so senseless.

Brian and I had served on many missions together, but we found ourselves particularly moved by the words spoken at the meeting that day by an East German.

> I am 42 years of age. I was born free. But immediately after my birth, I was no longer free and for 42 years I was told how to live my life. Now I am told that was all wrong. Here, we know nothing about elections; we know nothing about democracy; we know nothing about the free market. You will have to help us.

Many of us in that room reflected deeply on the long-term commitments sought by so many of those in transition states. The publisher of ABC Colour in Paraguay once reminded me of our obligations in this regard.

His was the largest tabloid in Paraguay and it had been suppressed during the Stroessner years. But after the military coup and the exile of the former President, ABC Colour was back on the streets.

The day after the election he held a reception at his home for our delegation and some members of the government. On the way there, I was surprised to hear him say that he felt the elections had gone very well. The Colorado Party had, after all, won 73 percent of the vote in an election which was by no means fair. He then qualified his remark: "I was afraid there might be a lot of bloodshed."

He went on to praise the role of the observers, but insisted:

> Don't love us and leave us. President Rodriguez has promised a new constitution, electoral reform, and a new code of human rights. You must monitor the situation on a continuing basis to ensure he lives up to all his promises.

The election is only the beginning, as my Paraguayan friend so well pointed out. The Western democracies must think about parallel commitments to the long-term institutional development of election systems. Our expectations of successful electoral transitions must match our collective will to follow up.

Perhaps even more importantly, we need only look at the evolution of our own Western democratic traditions to know that the sanctity of a secret ballot indicates the singular stake a citizen has in the governing process of his or her country.

It is difficult to imagine a genuine institutional development of free, fair election systems in countries when the vast majority of the people do not, due to the obvious factors of homelessness, hunger, and general destitution, see themselves as having such a stake.

Peace, democracy, and development are inseparably linked. This is all a parallel process.[39] In the case of South Africa, where so much hope has arisen in the wake of the remarkable events of 1994, it is easy to forget that our commitments to freedom and peace in that beautiful country must last far beyond the elections.

After the Elections: South Africa

I recently spoke with one of my Canadian friends who had named her new baby son Mandela. I reflected with some irony that it had only been a few short years since a group of us (among them Archbishop Ted Scott, the Hon. Roy McMurtry, and former Member of Parliament Howard McCurdy) had had some difficulty in raising money in the Canadian business community for a democratic education fund in South Africa. The effort was prompted by a request to External Affairs Minister Joe Clark from Mandela himself shortly after his release from prison in February, 1990.

So today, as Mandela's winds of change sweep across South Africa and the long journey of national reconstruction begins, hope emerges, cautiously, from the despair of a long dark night. For all the baby Mandelas born in the aftermath of the historic 1994 elections, South Africa's quiet miracle parallels their own.

The road ahead will not be easy. As an informed observer pointed out, post-apartheid South Africa faces two imposing challenges: the first is to form a peacefully united country, and the second is to reconstruct virtually every aspect of economic life in that country - distorted as a direct result of apartheid. "Ending apartheid and forming a new government will require a complete reimagining of the nation, of what it means to be South African."[40]

A 1993 World Bank report illustrated the magnitude of the challenge presently facing South Africa by comparing it to the reconstruction of post-war Europe, or the reunification of Germany in the 1990s. In a sensitive article written on the eve of the elections, Nelson Mandela did not attempt to minimise the extent of South Africa's economic crisis.[41]

In this, Mandela elucidated a clear and solid vision for a new South African foreign policy. Issues of human rights would be central to the conduct of international relations and a pillar of global engagement. A reconstructed South Africa would dedicate itself to the principle that just and lasting solutions to the problems of humankind can only come through the promotion of democracy worldwide.

But first, of course, Mandela faces the monumental challenge of instilling real democratic traditions and values at home. South African novelist Andre Brink summarized the situation candidly in recounting his own election day experiences: "Here I've been waiting for six hours; some of these people have been waiting for 30, 40, 50, 60 years. The country has been waiting for three and a half centuries."[42]

So while the seeds of freedom have been sown and a democratic dawn has risen out of the long South African night, the road ahead remains perilous and uncertain. At present, the most we can say is that South Africans have caught a glimpse of the possible; the awareness of a life, a country, and a humanity we share, as Brink so wisely put it. But that glimpse has captivated and inspired South Africans and given them hope.

Archbishop Scott pointed out in a recent conversation that much of the common concern for the well-being of South Africa has been generated by the presence of Mandela himself. Scott was part of the Commonwealth group of Eminent Persons which visited Mandela in prison on two occasions. He reflected upon the great personal honour it was for him to be able to attend and celebrate Mr. Mandela's inauguration.

The Archbishop recalled that Mandela had always had an admiration for Western democracy and the value and dignity of every human being. The imagery of the Marxist guerilla concocted by former white regimes was never reflected in a serious examination of Mandela's speeches and writing over the years, he told me.

Mandela always viewed himself as a South African nationalist and, he reminded the Eminent Persons group on one prison visit, South African nationalists come in more than one colour. Scott said that Mandela had always had a realistic view of the frustrations of the white community in South Africa.

The fears of white South Africans were understandable. Over just a few decades, the white community had dwindled from approximately 40 percent of the population to 14 percent, forecast to be 9 percent by the year 2 000. As the Archbishop pointed out, Mandela's refusal to demonize all whites could be seen in the tremendous respect shown him by his prison guards.

Scott recalled that one of the guards wept openly over Mandela's departure at the time of his release. Now, a long way from his prison cell, the new President symbolizes the humanity that all South Africans share. The presence of that same prison guard on the platform at the time of his inauguration was a striking visual image of Mandela's vision of a multi-racial society in which minority groups will feel secure.

Many observers across the globe were overwhelmed at the rapidity of the transition in South Africa. Even more so, and considering the long history of violence in that country, it is truly amazing to witness the consensus that has been forged, and the positive changes in attitude which are so apparent.

The government has worked hard to keep the people informed of, and engaged in, the evolving policy process. Mandela has conducted "people's" forums in the townships to discover at first-hand the needs and grievances of the residents. His government has been widely applauded for both a stable and responsible approach to the economy which, it is hoped, will generate new wealth to overcome the social and economic legacy of apartheid.

A new confidence is apparent after the first period of democracy in South Africa. This suggests that future political problems can be overcome. The temporal expectations of South Africans have been shelved for the time being as the population has shouldered the tremendous strains of democratic transition with remarkable patience and sacrifice. The poor have not revolted and the whites have not left the country. This is a triumph for the Mandela government. But all this must be seen as a race against time.

Development must be seen to be equitable by all South Africans or the spirit of compromise and the will to work together will begin to unravel. A politics of inclusion must be matched by an economics of inclusion. The South African miracle must not be permitted to fail.

And a miracle it is. I recall very well my first visit to the continent in attendance at a Southern African Development Coordination Conference (SADCC) held in Zambia in 1984. The host was Kenneth Kaunda. None of us in attendance would have believed in their wildest imaginings that the pariah state, South Africa, would, in the course of only a decade, be so dramatically transformed.

At the time SADCC was established in 1980, the founding members had the objective of creating a trade bloc which reflected the intractable conflict between South Africa and its independent members. The nine founding members were Angola, Botswana, Lesotho, Malawi, Mozambique, Swaziland, Tanzania, Zambia and Zimbabwe. Namibia joined in 1991 after gaining its independence two years previously.

My mission was to announce, on behalf of the Government of Canada, that SADCC had become a priority for Canadian development assistance. Canada's average annual disbursements of $25 million were to be targeted over and above our existing assistance programmes in individual SADCC member countries over the ensuing five years.

I made the announcement with great pride, because, comparatively speaking, this package was the largest yet offered by any country in the international community. As well, I told the assembled delegates that Canadians shared their sense of frustration and impatience with South Africa's then illegal occupation of Namibia. The protracted delays in the implementation of Security Council Resolution 435, and the military hostilities then ongoing in the absence of a settlement, aggravated the situation.

The speeches of the day rang out with denunciations of the evil of apartheid, and of the white supremacist regime which many of us felt lay at the crux of most of the region's problems. I fully believed that, even on the most optimistic note, it would be decades before a democratic transition would take place in South Africa.

I did promise the delegates, however, that Canada would continue its efforts and exert any influence possible until Namibia was free and joined its neighbours as a full fledged member of SADCC. Again, as a conference delegate in Zambia in 1984, I could not imagine that I would be part of the process of democratic transition in Namibia within five years.

It was difficult not to be caught up in the spirit of SADCC at its birth. Its founders believed they could force a realignment of economic relations among its members. They felt they could change the pattern of asymmetrical economic relations with South Africa to which they had been linked as junior partners.

But the centrality of South Africa's economy within the region proved to be too much for their collective resolve. Rather than disengaging, they tended not only to retain but to deepen their bilateral commercial links with South Africa over the ensuing decade. The realities of the power equation in the southern part of the continent dictated defeat for the early hopes of the founders. South Africa remained the centre of the solar system and the SADCC planets continued to rotate dutifully in their assigned geopolitical orbits.

Along with this, South Africa's continuing policy of destabilization throughout the 1980s severely undermined the efforts of the member states to coordinate regional development, thus ensuring the perpetuation of the junior partnership role which the creation of SADCC had been designed to eliminate.

By the end of the decade, the SADCC countries had become keenly aware of the limitations of the organization, the most important one of which I believed was to pin its development strategy almost entirely on foreign aid. In August, 1992, the member states made the significant decision to become a market based economic community - a decision which some have argued was a tactical move to head off marginalization in the then foreseeable post-apartheid South Africa.[43]

At the 1992 summit, the members:

> expressed the hope that a democratic South Africa would join the SADCC family of nations soon in order to enable all of the region's peoples to join hands in building a new economic order in Southern Africa based on balance, equity and mutual benefit.[44]

Only two years later, that hope became a reality as the dawn of democracy broke in the chaotic, yet spectacular April elections of 1994. As South Africans begin their own internal reconstruction it seems only a matter of time before a genuine regional economic community develops on the continent, with the former apartheid state in a leadership role which is both inspirational and constructive. If the South African miracle fails, the flickering light of democracy on the continent will die.

The efforts to foster participation and consensus building on that continent must be sustained by global efforts of assistance. Hungry people are angry people. Latin America's "lost decade" of the 1980s proved that young, democratically elected governments cannot survive gaping inequities and overwhelming economic pain. Yet poverty and inequity remain the greatest enemies of democracy in our time.

The world cannot become a fairer or safer place until we come up with a formula for assuring sustainable growth and at least the promise from wealthy nations to deal fairly with the Third World, and the over one-billion people on this planet who are hungry.

Unhappily, the disparities between North and South seem to be widening and worsening. We know that we cannot afford to fail in coming up with formulas for fairness and yet the facts remain immutable. The developed world retains its corner on wealth and power. Formulas for fairness continue to elude us.

The net transfer of billions of dollars from South to North over the past decade provides convincing proof that much of that assistance has been counterproductive.

Today, the process of globalization is creating even wider inequality between the wealthy and the poor, the winners and the losers, across the traditional divide between north and south. The world economic revolution has ensured that:

> the ominous combination of a growing gap between the majority of the Southern and Northern countries as well as the existence of a privileged minority in a "global north" and a marginalized majority in a "global south" ...(one of the worst sets of problems being)...most of the "global South" - some 45 percent of humanity who reside mainly in the 140 poorest countries of the Third World - is locked in poverty and left behind as the richer strata grow.[45]

The perverse income inequalities of our time are best reflected in the dramatic growth of the numbers of billionaires over the past few years as those who are already wealthy cash in on the opportunities presented by the digital revolution, and the spread of free market policies around the world. Broad and Cavanagh have calculated that there are now 358 billionaires worth $762 billion, which is estimated as the combined income of the 2.5 billion of the world's poorest.[46]

As they point out, the impact of accelerating economic integration on the concentration of wealth has been most pronounced in Mexico. In 1987 there was just one billionaire in Mexico. By 1994, there were 24 who accounted for 44.1 billion in collective wealth. This exceeded the total income of the poorest 40% of Mexican households. As a result, the 24 wealthiest people are richer than the poorest 33 million people in Mexico.

After the Elections: Mexico

Yet, as the gap between the rich and poor widens in that country, Mexicans are at the same time caught up in a painstaking movement towards democracy. But it is clear that because of the unconscionable and worsening inequities in Mexico the task of strengthening democratic institutions in that country will be monumental. Still, in many ways, the elections of August 21, 1994 marked a critical defining moment in the history of this sadly beautiful country. Maria Sol Martin Reig, a Mexican lawyer who addressed the annual meeting of the Canadian Association of Latin American and Caribbean Studies in November, 1994, put it this way:

> This memorable day was the culmination of several events which included: 1) the participation of nine candidates for the presidency nominated by their corresponding political parties (three of whom had well-founded aspirations of winning the election); 2) a number of substantive and formal constitutional reforms on electoral matters; 3) an active involvement of civic groups having the double role of supervising the presidential campaigns and denouncing irregularities in the actions of the candidates as well as those observed during election day; 4) a mass

media dedicated to the production of political-electoral news; and 5) a plethora of prestigious national and international observers whose role consisted of attesting to the normalcy, transparency and validity of the elections, or, if it were the case, the errors and fraud in the voting. All the foregoing can surely be considered a first in Mexican history.[47]

Edward Broadbent was one of many international observers who watched Mexicans vote. At the time President of the International Centre for Human Rights and Democratic Development, Broadbent concurred with most foreign observers who made the distinction between a clean vote count, which did occur largely due to the monitoring actions of local civics groups, and a fair and free electoral process, which decidedly did not occur.

Still, observers generally considered them to be an improvement on the notoriously unfair, unfree and corrupt elections of the past. But significantly, Broadbent worried openly in his analysis of the results about what he called "...the deeply inequitable and authoritarian nature of Mexican democracy."[48]

Naked poverty remains oppressive reality for the vast majority of the population. The furthering of democracy will entail the filtering down of the country's dramatic economic progress to Mexico's poorest citizens.[49] Social development for all of the country's regions is fundamental to strengthening and accelerating the process of democratisation.

But the will to proceed beyond elections and accelerate the process exists, and it was recorded by observers on August 21, 1994. Many believed chaos and rioting could take place as Mexicans went to the polls in massive numbers. But the citizenry showed impressive maturity and came to the rescue of what had become a great impasse for the government. In this, they showed a civic spirit critical to the resolution of the institutional crises plaguing them.

But for now, the politics of poverty haunt a nation, poised so precariously on the road to democracy. Economic crisis has strained Mexico's meagre social services. Four out of 10 Mexicans of working age do not have jobs. An estimated 40 million people out of a population of 90 million are undernourished. To compound the pressures, President Zedillo is under pressure from international organizations, such as the IMF, to initiate further structural reforms.

The plunging peso crisis of early 1995 revealed many painful truths about the nature of Mexico's economy. But it may have had a silver lining in some respects. It shook the long dominant Partido Industrial Revolucionario (PRI) to the foundations, forcing the government to sign an agreement with opposition leaders to democratize the country more fully. Political scientist Alonso Lujambio put it this way:

> The foreign investors don't care about democracy; they care about stability... They would be perfectly happy if you could achieve that with an authoritarian government, but you can't anymore. Democracy is the only way and I think Zedillo is starting to understand that.[50]

Another silver lining can be seen from the perspective of international cooperation; the international community moved quickly with a $50 billion aid package. In some ways, there was really no other choice. Mexico has become an integral part of the North American market - and its two developed trade partners have a vested interest in the stability of their developing neighbour to the south.

Mexico's course of democratization and development has been followed with great interest in Canada. The North American Free Trade Agreement (NAFTA) means much more than tariffs and trade. The larger objective from the time of its signing in 1992, was to harmonize the policies of the three countries on such matters as environmental standards, anti-trust legislation, agriculture, telecommunications, immigration, and government procurement.

Once primarily domestic issues, these now have major international implications in an age of increasing interdependence. In this sense, the issue of harmonization of standards will become vital to the future of Mexican democratization. The big challenge to its NAFTA partners will be to ensure that harmonization means a thrust upwards for the only developing country which is a full party to the agreement and a better, more equitable distribution of the benefits for Mexicans of all regions and classes.

Mexicans and South Africans have recently experienced historic elections. Now the course of democratization can begin. The challenges ahead are formidable. Poverty and inequity remain the most important and perverse of these.

Nonetheless, in spite of the enormous challenges to the existence of these fledgling democracies, the defining moments in the collective consciousness of Mexicans and South Africans have taken place. Those moments must be preserved in time so that the gigantic task of building fair societies can begin.

After the Elections: Bosnia

Nowhere does that task appear more gargantuan than in Bosnia and Herzegovina. The September 14, 1996 elections passed more peacefully than many had predicted with about two-thirds of the electorate casting ballots. They were flawed, as expected. The ruling parties dominated the media. Many Muslims were effectively disenfranchised when they tried to vote in the Serb-controlled half of the country. Observers generally agreed that the elections were considerably less than free and fair. There were major problems with the electoral list, based on the 1991 census which had been taken before the huge wartime displacement of the population. Opposition politicians were regularly threatened, and in some cases beaten.

Though they were flawed, the fact that the elections were brought to a successful conclusion was due in large part to the presence of the over 50,000-strong NATO-led multinational peace Implementation Force (IFOR), and their civilian counterparts representing the Organization of Security and Co-operation in Europe. The massive IFOR and OSCE presence, along with that of dozens of UN agencies and non-governmental organizations, was all part of the post-Dayton international commitment to the reconstruction of a multi-ethnic Bosnia with shared institutions; in short, the global effort to put that tragic country back together again.

The dramatic Dayton Accord of November 21, 1995 ushered in a paper peace and was the result of fortuitous timing which made the United States role as a helpful fixer imperative to all the Bosnian factions - all for different reasons. The July, 1995 fall of helpless Srebrenica to Bosnian Serb forces - the savagery of which was played out in full view of the global audience of CNN - was without doubt one of the final events which stood to stiffen Western spines and resistance to any further attacks on the United Nations Protection Force (UNPROFOR) safe areas. The subsequent Dayton Accord was celebrated by a world worn out by the barbarism and atrocity of the 42 month conflict.

Its provisions were worked out in debate which was agonizing, delicate and painfully complex. The Bosnian government in Sarajevo was able to gain its objective of a single autonomous sovereign state. Two sub-states with considerable autonomy made up the federation; a fact particularly true in the case of the Serb dominated Republika Srpska, and less so with respect to the Bosnia-Croat Federation. The Accord also called upon all the parties to aid in the investigation and prosecution of war crimes and banned all those indicted or convicted from holding public office.

The post-Dayton period saw a flood of global assistance aimed at improvising the ceasefire and the military provisions of the Accord, as well as the reconstruction process which implied a vast process, some examples of which included preparations for the September elections, human rights monitoring, as well as the return of thousands of refugees and internally displaced peoples. The assistance "flooded into Bosnia like a vast, imperial expedition...the country's war-damaged infrastructure literally sags beneath their weight."[51]

A former Prime Minister of Sweden, Carl Bilt, was the international community's principal viceroy on the civilian side of the herculean efforts to reconstruct the envisioned multi-ethnic federation. The elections were viewed as the first step in developing a constructive engagement between ethnic factions which have been involved in some of the most terrifying violence of our time.

The standards established at Dayton for the 1996 elections were high. For example, the Accord encouraged Bosnia's refugee and displaced populations to vote in their pre-war constituencies because the signatories did not want to appear to be condoning ethnic cleansing. But the attempts to re-create Bosnia's prewar ethnic diversity, in theory highly admirable, were negated by the reality of three highly-segregated communities increasingly subject to the appeal of nationalist parties. As the pre-election campaigning began, those parties concentrated on strategies for majoritizing their respective ethnic populations; in effect by trying to concentrate their own communities geographically, thus impeding any prospects of, or movement towards, integration.

Fear was another principal factor as the election date loomed. The slogans of the Serb Democratic Party (SDS) were emphatically secessionist; some analysts believed that the SDS was planning to bring Radovan Karadzic, twice indicted for crimes against humanity, out of hiding with a flourish after an anticipated electoral triumph among Serb voters.[52] The international press was filled with stories of the estimated 20,000 Muslim voters who braved heavily guarded checkpoints and the menacing enmity of former neighbours to cross into Serb territory and cast ballots for regional governments, a joint Parliament for the whole country, as well as a joint presidency comprising one Muslim, one Serb, and one Croat. Those who defied the ethnic cleansing laws, and took up the invitation to violence implicit in going into the other side's neighbourhood usually gave the same reason for doing so. They often just wanted to see their old homes, their old neighbourhoods - maybe find an old friend with whom to drink a treasured and last coffee.

But ethnic cleansing had been too successful. The wounds from the war that had killed over 200,000 people were graphically displayed in the corridors of barbed wire and the checkpoints manned by thousands of peacekeepers brandishing automatic weapons, all backed up with tanks. But in spite of the huge military presence, many potential voters were told by the authorities that their individual safety could not be guaranteed. It was no surprise that so many displaced persons returned to their minibuses and went back over the so-called "interethnic boundary lines," becoming part of the many disenfranchised voters observed by international mediators.

But even in this bitter and painful place, glimmers of hope can be found after the elections. There is a small chance that the three- man presidency can nudge the various factions towards some measure of co-operation. Though the votes were cast largely along ethnic lines, cautious hope can be derived from the relative success of Mladen Ivanic who won almost a third of the Bosnian Serb votes for the presidency, and thus perhaps loosened the anticipated stranglehold of hard-core Serbian nationalists within the SDS. Many unknowns hang over the unwinding of future events. But the most important of these is surely the resolve of the international community to stay engaged in the process and give peace a chance.

A lengthening of the NATO commitment and timetable for a continuing presence for another two years beyond December, 1996 is surely one of the most important examples of international resolve needed as new country-wide governmental mechanisms are forged. These institutions must be made to work in order to begin the gigantic task of healing inter-ethnic tensions in a country just emerging from hell. Maybe in this sense, a form of peaceful co-existence can last out the long dark night and edge slowly, so slowly, into the dawning of democracy.

The engagement in Bosnia must hold. We can't love them and leave them.Without our continuing intervention, the critical defining moments of the last few months will slip away in time.

But now we will look at the significance of those defining moments in the lives of the evolving citizenry of transition states. International election observation is only one of the many forms of assistance to democratization; a process which, to be effective, must begin in the early phases of the pre-election process of those countries experiencing the dawn of democracy. It is in the months prior to the historic voting day that the seeds of freedom must be sown and the germination of civic societies must begin. That process begins in the hearts and minds of voters who need outside support to undertake, not only the social and economic movement towards democracy, but, more importantly, the psychological conversion to the rights and responsibilities which freedom entails.

PART THREE
THE SEEDS OF FREEDOM

As we have seen, the process of democratization is part of the evolving belief system of much of the international community, no matter what its form, no matter how restrictively or how broadly it has been applied. The current global democratic revolution of our time has had a significant impact. One of its most important byproducts has been the principle that those governments which deny their citizens the right to free and open elections are violating a fundamental norm of the conscience of mankind.

International election observing was rare prior to the massive third wave of democratic transition. This was particularly observable in Eastern Europe, Latin America and parts of Africa over the last decade. The opinion of the international community was that this kind of activity was illegal interference in the national sovereign domain of states and was admissible only in the exceptional circumstances of decolonization. Until the past decade, electoral assistance tended to be provided by the United Nations to the African trust territories in the process of achieving their independence from colonial rule.

More recently, Nicaragua and Cambodia experienced elections following the end of long civil wars and domestic upheaval. Those critical defining moments required substantial support from the outside world. But more frequently, observers were called upon to mediate the transformation of political systems from one party or authoritarian rule to multi-party structures. As new political beginnings swept the former Eastern Bloc countries, as well as Central and South America, thousands of election observers supported pluralist processes in places where democracy had yet to be invented.

Finally, in countries like the Philippines in 1986 and South Africa in 1994 - both countries where domestic tensions were so great that the results were certain to be rejected by substantial segments of the population - observers were called upon to certify the reliability of election results to prevent increased violence and bloodshed.

In Part Three of *The Seeds of Freedom*, I want to develop some of the broad strokes which serve as an intellectual prelude to the actual case studies of election observers at work, or, as I call it, democratic craftmanship, which follows. In Chapter Eight, "Defining Moments", we will look at the meaning of elections in the lives and thought processes of first-time voters, as well as the collective experience which the international community has acquired over the years.

In "An Assault on Discouragement", I will highlight some of the less under-stood aspects of the observation process, which, among other things, helps to culti-vate trust among the major competitors. The lessons we have learned in this area are all part of the continuing, incremental understanding of the many forms of conflict resolution in our time. International election observing is critical in alleviating the psychological discouragement of first-time voters, haunted by intimidation and fear.

Finally, I will trace some of the UN's new chapters in the electoral observation and verification field, ventures which have contributed to new forms of peacekeep-ing partnerships in countries like Namibia and Nicaragua and Cambodia. These provide continuing and convincing evidence of the truth that if the United Nations did not exist, it would have to be invented.

7. Defining Moments

In March, 1990, I arrived in Budapest as part of an international observer team then assembling to monitor the historic elections in Hungary. I remember former United States Vice President Walter Mondale's fine leadership and his natural good humour being that much more so as we walked together through the chaos, the colour, the charm, and the antiquity of the city. My friend Brian Atwood and I, just prior to leaving the city for our assigned sites, talked about the infectious atmosphere of good will and energy which flooded the streets. We both felt we were very lucky people to be able to once again participate in such a momentous exercise.

I felt the reverberations of the drama as a number of us set out to watch the people of Miskolc cast their first ballots. I had particularly wanted to go to that area, because it had great relevance for me. It was a small steel and coal district and therefore had much in common with the resource based economy of my native Cape Breton. We all felt the excitement as we came closer to the Czechoslovakian border.

The election posters throughout the country captured the poignancy of what had become a very significant moment in time for all Hungarians. I remember one in particular. It was a visual image of a conversation between a young man of voting age and his grandfather. The young man said: "Grandpa, this is my first vote." The grandfather replied: "Yes, I know, and this is my first vote in 45 years."

It was in Miskolc where I witnessed the well-known civility of the Hungarian people. Elderly gentlemen on their way from church to the polls unfailingly tipped their hats to the ladies. In their hands they clutched what appeared to be a treasure of monumental importance - the little piece of paper which certified that they were entitled to vote in a free election.

In the many transition processes I have monitored, one thing stands out clearly. That is the collective will of ordinary people, in spite of all the frustrations associated with first-time elections, to carry on tenaciously and cast a secret ballot.

Long journeys of up to 12, 14, 16 hours or more to polling booths in the developing world are common. Intimidation by brutal governments is, in many cases, a terrifying certainty faced by far too many of the world's voters. Administrative bungling, sometimes deliberate fraud, and institutional chaos complicate the process. Illiteracy and conditions of soul-searing poverty are visible reminders that the lot of the poorest of the poor has not improved in our time.

But all observers will testify that such conditions do not detract from the joy and elation seen in the faces of the thousands who wait patiently in lineups worldwide to put their personal mark upon a secret ballot. The symbolism is very clearly understood. The act of casting that ballot represents their individual entitlement to partici-pate in the construction of a better life for themselves and their children.

Centuries ago, Thomas Jefferson summarized the conviction behind that sense of entitlement when he argued that that government is the strongest in which every man feels himself a part. In many emerging democracies today, ordinary people have come to believe this timeless truth, and have cast the ballots which they see as vital to the full assertion of their human worth.

My friend, Chris Edley, Jr., a Harvard Law Professor, who was part of a delega-tion I led to the magnificent transition exercise in Namibia, once wrote of the "mar-vellous devotion to democracy" he saw in that country. In that arid land, part of one of the most bitter power struggles of this century, people of conviction and courage actually willed the transition to take place.

All of us who played a role in the monitoring of that election understood that the real victory lay with the Namibian people themselves. As their spirit and will forced sorghum to grow from the dust, so too did their spirit and will force the seeds of freedom to grow from a terrain noted mostly for repression and fear.

Like Tom Paine, the great pamphleteer-patriot of the American revolution sev-eral centuries ago, they believed they had the power to start the world over again. The birthday of a new world was at hand. Voting, in a word, was a means of their empowerment. And that freedom from powerlessness is the elusive spiritual ingre-dient which makes democratic transitions work.

Elections are turning points in any political system, but in transition states they are not simply turning points in ideas on governance. Rather they are central to the creation of civilian society itself, and the belief systems around which people-de-rived governments can be constituted.

When the defining moments are lost, so too are the vital belief systems funda-mental to the whole course of democratic development. But successful elections can have implications which go far beyond the historic day in question.

Rosenau and Fagen put it this way:

> The downfall of Marcos in the Philippines, the peaceful transfer of power in Nicaragua, the tumultuous transfer in Panama, and the circuitous transfer in Haiti were defining events for each of these countries, but they were also part of a cumulative process whereby citizens, NGOs, publics, and officials everywhere have acquired the value orientations, the technical capacities and the political will to contribute their share to future elections in the developing world.[53]

Therefore the learning process within transition states becomes internationalized as a direct consequence of the electoral experience and evolves into a cumulative process of support for democratic institutions around the world.

We must remember that the entire electoral operation demands the skills and the expertise of a vast infrastructure of civilian volunteers to bring the process to a successful conclusion. Poll watchers must be trained. Institutes of civic education must be available to dispense information on basic issues such as the meaning and significance of the secret ballot. Social scientists and computer specialists must create the procedures which assure an orderly processing of basic informational and electoral data.

Elections generate a broad-based network of citizens committed to the process of democratization. For example, in many transition states the coercive role of the authoritarian state parallels the often passionate commitment of opposition groups within the body politic. The presence of scientific evidence is often the quintessential factor in ensuring the acceptance of election results because it is independent of the biases of key actors in the electoral process.

The international use of "quick counts" in volatile races provides an example of the kind of technical expertise critical to the monitoring process and the acceptability of the results. Quick counts technically entail a random sampling of election results in statistically significant numbers of polling sites that actually enable observers to project or confirm the results of an election. As a means of overcoming mass scepticism about announced results, they help diffuse distrust, therefore providing the critical legitimacy to govern, the first big step in the foundation of democratic institutions.

We will see concrete examples of the importance of the quick count below. But for the time being, the main point is not so much the centrality of the scientific proof in the final acceptance of the results, but the creation of a cadre of citizens trained and committed to its usage.

When Paraguayans monitor elections in Bulgaria, and Filipinos monitor elections in South Africa, they implicitly export this expertise and contribute to the collective global understanding of the democratic process. In this sense, elections are truly defining moments, not simply in the life of a nation, but in the evolution of a new law on earth.

But the global democratic revolution cannot be sustained without multi-faceted efforts of assistance, whether it take the form of the simple provision of electoral materials, such as ballot boxes, ballot papers and computers - or the more complicated involvement of outside observers in improving a transition state's electoral law.

Electoral assistance can be provided to strengthen political parties, as well to further the development of democratic institutions. In some cases, such as the provision of election supervision, a term used by the UN, a more dramatic form of intervention is implied. UN supervisors are able to interfere directly if the officials of the host state charged with implementing the elections don't comply with national directives. The enormous scope of the UN conflict resolution mandate in Cambodia translated into a very costly electoral mission in that country. As the UN drew up the law, appointed the electoral commission and local committees, registered the voters, carried out the election, counted the votes etc.

But whatever its form, such outside support for the democratic process is vital to the establishment and continuity of political pluralism in states all around the world.

That assistance can have dramatic implications, for:

> ...irrespective of the degree to which the outcome is tainted by fraud, apathy, or violence, and quite apart from who wins and who loses, an election is the one moment when all citizens engage in the same behaviour...with the result that their society undergoes a collective experience that reaffirms or alters its prior course.[54]

The long-term observation process is one of the steel girders which support the collective transformation and the new political beginnings of societies across the planet. Contrary to popular opinion, this is an activity which goes far beyond the immediate events of election day. An experienced observer outlined the major features of the long-term process this way:

- mediating on election law issues;
- reviewing administrative arrangements for the electoral   process;
- assisting with the development and implementation of civic education programmes;
- supporting and evaluating voter registration processes;
- assessing the fairness of the election campaign;
- analyzing issues such as media access and fairness;
- reviewing the complaint adjudication process;
- observing the integrity of the balloting process on election day;
- conducting independent vote counts;
- investigating post-election complaints; and
- facilitating the transition process.[55]

The idea of watching other people vote means, in fact, a sustained observation effort which is often complicated by incidences of what I like to call "invited intervention." We will see many examples of the "brokerage" role of observers below.

But, as we start to reflect upon the significance of international election observing, we must not lose sight of the principal objective and the long-term strategy to achieve it. No matter which international mission is involved - from the United Nations, nnon-governmentalgovernmental organizations, or as part of bilateral assistance from donor nations - the central objective is the same. The election observation process empowers people to believe they can be architects of their own destiny. Where there is no belief, there is no conception of liberty. If people feel isolated and discouraged, the opportunity for liberty is lost.

An observer commenting on the Guatemalan elections of 1985 put it this way: "... an election won't guarantee that democracy will flourish...but it has emboldened vast numbers of people across the rigid stratifications of a poor and frightened polity to believe there is a better way to live".[56]

The seeds of freedom spring from the hearts and minds of everyday citizens. All the craftsmanship which goes into the electoral observation process revolves around one principal strategy. Loosely defined, this can be seen as all those actions which together serve as an assault on discouragement. It must be remembered that the seeds of freedom flourish in a spiritual dimension. Ultimately, it is in the souls of men and women where the struggle for democracy is won or lost.

8. An Assault on Discouragement

For most people, election observers are understood to be those individuals who play a role in advising home governments on the degree to which foreign countries are developing in a democratic fashion. What they say about their experiences, for example, about the legitimacy of a foreign government's claim to office, will impact upon the kind of bilateral ties Western governments will establish or sustain.

Besides the actual legitimation of the "fair and free" in a given election process, observers give psychological support to opposition parties, voters, and domestic civicsgrou
ian intervention which are beginning to transform world politics.

The reports of observer missions document many cases of these forms of intervention. The questions arise usually within the context of the form and the timing of the invitation. For example, did the observer mission draw the problem to the attention of local authorities, using gentle pressures which can evolve into forms of conflict resolution. Or did the electoral officials in the transition state actually request the participation of outsiders in delicate affairs of state?

When touchy questions concerning state sovereignty have come up, common sense has normally been our guide. If a problem arises which threatens the series of bargains at the heart of delicate election processes, we have generally not hesitated to approach the responsible officials, or, in some cases, the heads of state themselves.

More frequently, our teams have been called upon by the respective governments of transition states to advise on questions such as the drafting and/or revision of electoral legislation. We have rarely failed to take up the challenges put to us. We have advised and revised in efforts to promote a free and fair environment in which all the principal participants could compete. When it became obvious that gross unfairness existed prior to electoral contests, some qualified observers have not been hesitant to point this out to key officials. Almost always, they have been requested to provide detailed drafts of suggestions to keep elections in motion.

The monitoring process usually includes a variety of confidence building measures. Some may be as simple as the provision of needed election materials. Perhaps more sensationally, international election observers frequently assist in quick counts in high risk races in efforts to defuse the political instability associated with potentially explosive results. But whatever task presents itself, observers must be prepared to serve as mediators in easing suspicion and distrust.

Often, small scale yet critical acts of reassurance prove to be all that is needed. The more dramatic cases of personal intervention, exercised by well-known observers like President Carter, are generally the exception. Yet, in some cases, only personal intervention is the key to ensuring that confidence is maintained in the electoral process itself. The 1993 Paraguayan presidential elections provide an excellent case in point.

I co-chaired an international delegation with President Carter and former President Rodrigo Carazzo of Costa Rica. The advance team organized a luncheon for the three presidential candidates on the day of the election. All of us believed that this would be essential to the hoped-for peaceful acceptance of the final results by all parties. When President Carter asked us how we were able to carry off such a feat, we answered simply, "we used your name."

This is only a small example of the kind of magic the Carter name carries in sensitive processes as the one then unravelling in that country. Just after our meeting with the candidates, however, we encountered a problem which provoked nearly universal apprehension that the elections could be aborted.

The phone lines into SAKA, a consortium of local non-governmental organizations providing thousands of poll watchers on election day - were cut in the morning after the polls opened. This meant that the announcement of the Paraguayan quick count would be delayed. No one expected the delay to be more than a matter of hours, but because of the volatility of the atmosphere, nerves started to wear thin as time passed.

Many feared the election would be stolen. Others felt that the wire-cutting incident signalled the ill will of the authorities, particularly the Paraguayan military. It was widely speculated that the armed forces would not tolerate a peaceful transition in the event of a Colorado Party loss.

Immediately after the luncheon, we drove to the residence of President Rodriguez. President Carter was the first to inform him that the lines had been cut. Rodriguez acted at once, although resolution of the problem took longer than we had hoped. As it was, the quick count appeared to confirm a victory for the government, dispelling most doubts.

But that did not mean the end of our involvement. The following day, in spite of the general knowledge that the governing Colorado party would win, Carter organized three separate meetings with the major candidates in the election, speaking with them each individually. The meaning was clear. It was his way of ensuring that Paraguayans would continue with the transition process in spite of the legacy of oppression and distrust in that country. But for that to happen, the three leaders had to be encouraged to work together for peace, trust and unity in the wake of the electoral exercise.

Carter instantly understood this and did not hesitate to use his own personal powers of persuasion when they were needed. But there have been many examples of the extraordinary implications of his intervention over the years. During the Dominican Republic's 1990 elections, President Carter appeared on television to explain procedures which he had helped negotiate with the government and the major parties in the electoral contest. He told the people of that country that the results of the bargaining would prevent violence from erupting over any potential allegations of electoral fraud. This was an act of confidence building which sustained the difficult election process.

The historic Haitian elections of 1990 provide another case in point. The atmosphere in the country was visibly charged with apprehension and fear. Haitians dreaded a repeat of the murders and assassinations of the 1987 elections which had been cancelled due to the violence and savagery directed by brutal military forces against voters and election officials alike.

On election day in 1990, an international observer delegation led by Carter and the Prime Minister of Belize, George Price, encouraged fearful Haitians to remain waiting in line at polling stations throughout the country. But fear was not the only factor. In the general chaos, polling booths in a number of regions had opened late. This had caused many prospective voters waiting in long line-ups to feel that they would have no hope of casting a ballot. Carter and Price explained to the people that the polls would remain open after hours to accommodate all Haitians. This intervention was of great importance, as many discouraged voters had begun to leave. In fact, it may have been critical in ensuring that the real voice of the people was heard. Father Jean-Bertrand Aristide was sworn in as President of Haiti on February 7, 1991.

In political cultures marked by intimidation and fear, observer groups have often been instrumental in carrying difficult electoral processes through to successful conclusions. During the Bulgarian elections of 1990, for example, international election observers persuaded the government to allow an independent vote count to proceed.

As we will see below, the Bulgarian Socialist Party won only 47.15 percent of the popular vote in the fiercely contested elections, certainly no overwhelming percentage. The opposition United Democratic Front's (UDF) frustration at the results was undeniably high, as they had won 37.84 percent. The parallel vote count organized by the non-partisan Bulgarian Association for Fair Elections proved to be the critical confidence building measure because it was the means by which the opposition UDF was convinced to accept the ruling party victory.

In fact, this was the principal factor in ensuring a peaceful transition. As was the case in Paraguay, this election monitoring organization received technical and financial assistance from the National Democratic Institute.

The monitoring process in Bulgaria prevented an outbreak of violence and bloodshed in that troubled country. In fact, the independent count was a powerful deterrent to open insurrection. It provides a striking example of the role of domestic observers in assaulting discouragement, the most powerful and debilitating of all the forces impeding the progress of democratic transitions worldwide.

Such mediating activities must be undertaken with extreme sensitivity to local conditions. The appearance of a multiplicity of non-governmental organizations on the world stage has proven to be a complicating factor in this regard. Some of them have engaged in the monitoring of international election processes as offshoots of special agenda projects.

Later, we will look at the mandates and composition of a number of international observer delegations. But, for the time being, just a brief list of some of the major NGOs illustrates the large potential for outsider involvement in states undergoing difficult transition exercises. They include:

> The Inter-Parliamentary Union, party institutes, international labour and business organizations and groups like the Council of Freely-Elected Heads of Government ... or the International Human Rights Law Group that has considerable expertise on constitutions and electoral procedures. Among the international party institutes that have played the most important roles are: The Christian Democratic International, the Socialist International, the Liberal International, the National Democratic and International Republican Institutes for International Affairs...[57]

One of the big challenges for the international community is to devise linkages to facilitate the necessary cooperation between the many different monitoring agencies and institutes involved in all the varied phases of the electoral process. The United Nations imaginative new chapter in brokering democratic development has paralleled much useful and creative thinking throughout the international community on better ways to support democratic development in the near future.

9. Brokering Democratic Development

The UN's New Chapter

The subject of United Nations reform has become more urgent as a new century approaches. Much international scepticism about the continuing relevance of the world organization abounds; some of it is warranted. Critics point to the increasing lack of credibility of many UN agencies, as well as to the obvious failure of the present composition of the Security Council to reflect adequately the reality of world economic power.

The failure of the United Nations to mediate complex international disputes, most dramatically in the former Yugoslavia, has led more and more concerned international citizens to write lengthy articles on why the UN has fallen short.[58]

I believe there is a huge gap between what the UN can realistically do, and the perennial popular expectations of what the international organization should do. There is also a tendency to dwell upon failure. This is a common propensity of much of the international media. It is rare that one reads about success. Rather, United Nations achievements appear as lonely orphans in the columns and editorials of the popular press.

Too many critics take the attitude that the reforms required are too costly, the challenges are too great, and the political and institutional obstacles to change are too deeply imbedded. They say, "why bother?" Conventional wisdom seems to tell us that the UN should be able to make instantaneous changes, as though it was in the business of assembly line production.

I have always believed that the UN remains a reflection of the hopes and aspirations of the civilized world, and is in constant need of reform and revitalization as are the member states which comprise it. If we were to tolerate the failure of the United Nations, we would be tolerating the failure of all humankind. And I think not only of grief-stricken humanity, but as well of the people who live in developed countries in the more favoured parts of the world.

If we fail to find ways to improve the lot of the poorest of the poor, we fail only ourselves. If we fail to provide security on the other side of the world, we only endanger the limited security we have here. The United Nations, in spite of all its problems, is a symbol of hope. Hope is the last thing that any of us in this difficult and dangerous decade can afford to surrender.

I have been privileged to witness some remarkable instances of the involvement of the United Nations in areas of peace-building and peacemaking. It is a new and challenging development in the history of the global organization. Because I have monitored elections in proximity to United Nations teams involved in peace-building efforts, I can say without question that in this area alone, success is no lonely orphan.

Election observing is part of the broad umbrella of strategies to construct peaceful societies. In fact, the task of international monitoring is often referred to as civilian peacekeeping. Because of the vital links between democratic institutions and international security the United Nations has developed a series of responses to those states requesting international election assistance.

The historic Namibian and Nicaraguan elections were held respectively in 1989 and 1990. These were momentous times and the decisions made in both countries were to be of great significance to many influential players in the international system. As a result, thousands of UN officials, as well as election observers from across the globe, poured in to watch some of the most controversial elections in recent times.

As a non-governmental observer, I represented the National Democratic Institute in Namibia, and Liberal International in Nicaragua. United Nations officials worked in close proximity to our own teams, and I had ample opportunity to see the evolution of collective new approaches to peace-building in both countries.

UN officials worked around the clock to draw both of these tense and complex electoral exercises to climactic conclusions. United Nations assistance was provided on a number of levels ranging from human rights monitoring to the movement of refugees. Yet, even with all the outside assistance, the challenges were daunting. For example, in war-torn Nicaragua, where no front line really existed, the challenges of brokering democratic development appeared nearly insurmountable.

As is well known, the elections in that country were some of the most widely observed of the last decade. Due to the significance of the outcome to the international community, it became essential to provide enough missions to visit as many of the sites as possible in the volatile electoral climate. This accounts for the fact that 2,578 accredited observers from 278 organizations were in that country on election day, along with 435 observers from the OAS and 237 UN monitors. It is estimated that 1,500 members of the international press were also present.[59]

The sheer volume of missions involved exemplified the intense international concerns over the future of that unhappy country. Nowhere was that intensity more evident than in the United States, where the very mention of Nicaragua generally resulted in cries of selective moral indignation from every part of the ideological spectrum.

For example, the Heritage Foundation and the Council for Inter-American Security viewed all Sandinista sympathizers as "the Left's Latin American Lobby" or the "Revolution Lobby". On the other side of this divide was the Washington office on Latin America and the Council on Hemispheric Affairs.

No matter what the political complexion of the beholder, most Americans presumed to know what was right for Nicaraguans. The well-known external assistance provided to the Contras by the US was only one example of United States involvement which complicated an already disastrous domestic situation. The economic deterioration due to the structural effects of a decade of war and an astronomical 33,000 percent inflation rate had propelled that nation into bankruptcy and impoverished the people. The unpopular military draft had provoked widespread loathing. The trade embargo and the halt to international aid and loans had, by election day, substantially aggravated an already desperate situation.

Democratic transition in Nicaragua was a byproduct of a complex series of negotiations on many levels. The date of the elections was only the first in a series. President Daniel Ortega agreed to advance the then-foreseen November, 1990 target date set for the elections to February of that year, in exchange for regional backing to a plan for Contra demobilization. In the San Jose agreement of late 1989, he got such a deal, although many observers felt at the time that it was flawed because no precise deadline was set. Nonetheless, a symmetrical arrangement was established between the Contras and the Salvadoran rebels. This was something which the Nicaraguan government had refused to accept in the past.

President Ortega then invited the UN, the OAS and other independent observers to monitor the election process. It was widely believed that the precedent-setting invitation was proffered because Ortega's party, the FSLN, was confident they could secure an easy victory at the polls.

The President calculated that an electoral win would force US withdrawal of support for the Contras. A free, fair decision - guaranteed by election monitors from abroad - could result in a renewal of loans from the international community and lead to the economic recovery so essential to continued Sandinista control of Nicaragua. The presence of the OAS and the UN would give the administration the legitimacy of international law.

All my political instincts told me that the appearances inside Nicaragua were deceiving. The conversations I had with people on the streets and back roads led me to trust my gut feelings more emphatically. It seemed that a majority were voting for the United Opposition and consequent change.

Further, I was certain that the polls had to be inaccurate. Polling was new to Nicaraguans and they generally associated the pollsters with the government, a likely enough fear in that country. Naturally, many would announce their support for the Ortega forces, but in doing so, they rendered the whole process unreliable. The size of the Sandinista rallies was also a red herring. A conversation I had with the leader of the opposition forces, Violetto Chomorro, two days before she was elected President, convinced me that my earlier suspicions might be accurate. She claimed that Ortega was packing the rallies by trucking in workers and supporters from isolated regions of the country in government vehicles.

So while Ortega's defeat caught even veteran analysts by surprise, it confirmed a theory that I held upon my arrival in Nicaragua, and recounted to veteran Canadian newsman Joe Schlesinger. If you want to get the most accurate reading on who is going to win an election, ask the taxi drivers.

Nicaragua's Sandinista government was probably the first "revolutionary government" to give up its power freely after internationally acclaimed fair elections.[60] The efforts put into ensuring that the democratic transition in Nicaragua stayed on course were monumental, but were obscured by the spectacular final results. It is important to remember that without the presence of international observers and their involvement at all levels of the pre-election phase, some of the most significant elections in history would not have been held. Put simply, they served as brokers of national reconciliation.

Robert Pastor summarized the situation this way:

> ...external groups did much more than just observe the elections; they mediated the rules of the political game...the observers became the surrogates for a free electoral process. They assisted all parties despite their deep suspicions, to participate in the election and to accept the results, permitting the first peaceful transfer of power in the nation's history.[61]

The UN operation itself began seven months before the elections were held. The UN Secretary General appointed a highly regarded former US cabinet officer, Mr. Elliot Richardson, as his personal representative. UN officials actively engaged in mediation efforts between the ruling and opposition parties to ensure the resolution of conflict on many levels. They were present at most of the rallies organized by political parties during the campaign. They took on and successfully carried out the enormous task of registering 90 percent of all the eligible voters on the first four Sundays in October, 1989.

In fact, the achievements of the registration campaign were such that the UN operation in Nicaragua has been considered by most analysts to be a model for future international activities in this area.

The UN used a parallel vote tabulation which served as an accurate projection of election day results. This was of essential importance because it encouraged the parties to accept the results. The international organization remained on-site in the critical days and weeks following the elections, thus ensuring a smooth transition.[62]

In a March 22, 1990 letter to the Secretary General, Elliot Richardson made the connection between the future of democracy in Nicaragua and the need to ensure free and fair elections - the defining moments which would ensure the peace and stability critical to a successful transition.

> ...attention should be focused on the decision taken early in ONUVEN (the acronym used for the UN mission in Nicaragua) history that responsibility for verification of the electoral process demanded more than merely recording the process, more than monitoring, and could not stop short of actively seeking to get corrected whatever substantial defects had been discovered. The very fact that the future of Nicaragua literally depended on the fairness and freedom of the elections would have made a purely passive role for ONUVEN morally unacceptable: a comparably important decision [was] to make a judgement before election day as to whether or not, despite its deficiencies, the electoral process was on balance sufficiently fair so as to assure that voters would be able to exercise a free choice. It had to be recognized, of course, that the election might be close, and in that event, not to have done this, to have waited instead until after the vote had been counted, could have greatly complicated the effort to render a final verdict.[63]

When President Carter arrived in Nicaragua in December, 1989, he stated that the Nicaraguan people were determined to participate in free and fair elections.[64] That was true. It was ultimately their decision to find solutions to the devastation produced by war and economic blockade which was the stuff of the democratic transition.

But in Nicaragua, as well as in many other countries, political will had to be brokered well into the final phases of the process. In many ways, the most critical hours of election day are the final hours. Defeat may be inevitable for ruling parties which have been accustomed to long and uninterrupted tenures of office. In the end, I watched in fascination as President Carter played a vital role in helping to negotiate a peaceful acceptance of defeat by Ortega. Throughout the tense and anxious hours of election night, by his personal intervention, he aided in the attainment of a comparatively smooth transition to the Chamorro regime.

Violeta Barrios Chamorro governed this desperately poor country for six years. Nicaragua is the hemisphere's poorest nation after Haiti. The tragedy of a civil war which took over 50,000 lives, lives on in the hearts and minds of a polarized population. Over 70 percent of 4.6 million Nicaraguans live in poverty. And yet, in the October 20, 1996 elections, former Marxist guerillas and right wing supporters of the old Somoza regime stood peacefully in long line-ups to cast ballots rather than shoot bullets at one another.

In these elections, Nicaraguans voted for democracy. While accusations and fierce rhetoric from the camps of Daniel Ortega on the left and the former mayor of

Managua, Arnoldo Aleman, on the right, proliferated in the weeks prior to the election, little violence actually occurred on the day at hand. The people waited calmly on election day under a tropical sun, mixed with drenching showers. There was a marked lack of political tension or fear in the air. International observers reported serious logistical problems and administrative glitches, such as delays of voting materials throughout the country. But the will to hold fair and free elections far outweighed the difficulties caused largely by inexperience as Nicaraguans went to the polls.

The Carter Centre recounted one instance of a nation's commitment. The sight of over 300 mules used to distribute late-arriving materials in areas where heavy storms and torrential raid had wiped out roads was a moving, visual testimony to the determination of the people to get on with the future.

Delays and chaos did mar the voting. But when outgoing President Chamorro called this "a beautiful process", there were hundreds of international observers who would have agreed with her. The beauty of it went far beyond the realm of a technically fair and free election - it lay in the quite courage of the people, in a land for so many decades awash with guns, to begin the process of building a civic society and, in so doing, to find peace.

Much will depend on the spirit of tolerance generated by the new President, Arnoldo Aleman, who defeated Daniel Ortega in a close contest. Aleman prospered under the Somoza regime and was later jailed by the Sandinistas. In order to forge ahead with reconstruction, Aleman must first make clear that his priorities lie in healing the wounds of the past.

Nicaraguans have made their choice, freely and it should be respected. But the foreign community must be vigilant as well, that there is no return to the dark Somozoist past, with its corruption, violence and disdain for ordinary people.[65]

The UN and Civilian Peacekeeping: Against All Odds

As we have seen, the presence of the blue berets in the February 1990 elections in Nicaragua opened a window of opportunity which led to the dramatic developments of October, 1996.

In the case of Namibia, the experiment with democratic institutions has been an astonishing success. In that country, the magnitude of the UN operation was equally unprecedented.

The mandate of the United Nations Transitional Assistance Group (UNTAG) was to facilitate political reconciliation in a country imprisoned by geopolitical rivalry and the long arm of the white supremacist regime of South Africa. UNTAG had to help negotiate the terms of the electoral process and generate the political will to carry through a democratic transition in an atmosphere fraught with distrust and suspicion.

The UNTAG operation was one of the finest illustrations of the new activist orientation of UN operations in the challenging and murky terrain of peacemaking. It has been said that Namibia changed forever the role of the UN in election assistance, a role which, prior to 1989, had been regarded as too sensitive for the international organization. Over $700 million would be spent in organizing the constituent assembly elections for the 1.5 million Namibians who were to make the transition to one of the most successful democracies in Africa.[66]

Since that watershed election, there has been much debate within the international community on the whole question of peacemaking and the big questions which arise with regard to traditional notions of state sovereignty embodied in Article twoof the Charter.

We are seeing a gradual evolution beyond the terms of the Charter on a "de facto" basis. In El Salvador, for example, human rights monitors, prison specialists and criminologists exemplify some aspects of multi-functionalism and the evolving leverage necessary to put peace on a faster track[67]. It is clear (and the spin-off from the UN success in Iraq has hastened the process) that governments are now giving responsibilities to the UN which they would not have given years ago.

The enormity of the 1992-93 Cambodian operation provides more evidence that if the UN did not exist, it would have to be invented.

As soon as the 1991 Paris peace accords on Cambodia were signed, the Security Council dispatched the first peacekeeping contingents to the country to monitor the ceasefire and prepare estimates as to the size of the final UN contingents. As in Namibia, the 20,000 UN personnel had administrative, military-security functions as well as those related to election-monitoring. In the same fashion, the UN took responsibility for the return of 350,000 Cambodian refugees then living in Thailand.[68]

The United Nations Transitional Authority in Cambodia (UNTAC) has been the subject of much debate. But even though the very high expectations associated with the UNTAC mission had to be adjusted, one cannot underestimate the importance of its presence in Cambodia.

It represented not only, in a conspicuous way, the interest of the world community in the future of a small Southeast Asian state, but an outside, generally neutral presence whose sole aim was to permit Cambodians to exercise their right to self-determination.[69]

This was a gigantic presence and elections were to be only one of the operations the United Nations was committed to. A fact finding team of electoral experts was sent in immediately to design the logistical plan for the upcoming elections of May, 1993 as well as scramble to organize a massive voter registration programme. The team was led by Ron Gould of Elections Canada, our Deputy Chief Electoral Officer, and one of this country's most experienced election observers.

Cambodia was a vast wasteland destroyed by 25 years of war. From May, 1992 to June, 1993, the multi-functional UN team lived with lawlessness and tropical disease in a country where all semblance of organized life and society had disappeared. Its members also lived with the daily terror of impending, murderous attacks by the Khmer Rouge which had reneged on their earlier commitments made in Paris, and were again stepping up their savage attacks on villages.

A Canadian district election supervisor for the UN mission recorded a scene which was commonplace for all those who served in Cambodia:

> As I came down the steep bank towards the boat, I noticed the crowd of children by the water's edge. They were not making much commotion, but obviously there was something of interest in the water...The corpse was the bloated remains of a man who had suffered greatly before his death. I could see his hands were tied above his head to a pole; he wore a black shirt and pants, but his chest and genitals were exposed, revealing bloody gashes and what looked like burns. The face was pulp. I remember thinking afterwards how matter-of-fact we were that morning...although the situation was shocking, we behaved as though it was all in a day's work.[70]

In spite of the terror and the general societal breakdown, the voter registration programme was a huge success as over 4.5 million Cambodians, close to 100 percent of the estimated voter population were registered. When the historic elections were held, Cambodians turned out in droves. 85 percent of the registered voters cast ballots and said no to the men of violence in their country.

Against a backdrop of a river of mud, in which voting materials had to be transported on oxen or in pony carts, one of the most dramatic enactments of human courage in our time took place. One of the observers described it this way:

> Against all the odds, the voters came by the thousands - rowdy soldiers, saffron-robed monks, ancient women bent double, young girls, families. They waited in the rain before the polls opened at 7am, having slogged through mud and rain, waded across lakes, and trudged or bicycled for miles in the dark. They came in large numbers all day the first day, and the ballot boxes filled to bursting.[71]

Against all odds, the people responded to and reinforced the credibility of this expensive, frustrating and dangerous United Nations exercise.

When we look at the record over the past decade, it becomes evident that the United Nations has entered an extraordinary new chapter in its 50 year history. But while there is much to celebrate, it is clear that the record is mixed.

As Larry Garber, the then Senior Associate for electoral processes at NDI pointed out:

> Somewhat fortuitously, the UN was not involved in the difficult cases of Cameroon, Ghana, Senegal and Togo ...where election results were contested by some or all of the losing parties. Thus, the question remains - would the UN publicly criticize and implicitly delegitimize a member state because of a flawed election?[72]

Nonetheless, the UN has brokered a series of important democratic transitions. The world organization has been a central vehicle in the assault on discouragement, often occupying the same terrain as prominent personalities like President Carter, non-governmental organizations, and, of course, donor states. But whatever the source of their respective mandates, election observers are democratic craftsmen who inevitably find themselves confronting the same problems.

PART FOUR
DEMOCRATIC CRAFTMANSHIP

Election observers who have reflected upon their respective journeys to the other side of the world may give some thought to J.R. Tolkien's enchanting tale about the "Hobbit" and the saga of Bilbo Baggins.

Bilbo was a comfort-loving Hobbit from the Shire, whose repose was destroyed by adventure and whose personal evolution involved the discovery that his quiet life of certitude was, in fact, illusory in the real world outside. Traditional Hobbits scolded him as he set out upon his dangerous quest which worked up to a dramatic finale, war.

We are a plain quiet folk, they said and have no use for adventures. Nasty, disturbing uncomfortable things! Make you late for dinner! I can't think what anybody sees in them.

Fortunately, Bilbo ignored their counsel. For the many global adventurers who have been part of observer missions across the world, his saga is in many ways theirs. As we will see, such missions tend to destroy repose and quiet lives of certitude.

In the world outside the ideological universe of John Locke, most of our assumptions about liberal democracy are unknown. As we attempt to mediate the value systems of one world into another, the imperfections of our own systems become even clearer. No one who has really thought about the significance of election observing in the contemporary world can fail to acquire very substantial amounts of humility.

The fact that there is no certitude about the impact of democratization on transition states is only one of the many causes for reflection. Election observing can be nasty, uncomfortable and disturbing. It can, as the plain, quiet folk warned Bilbo, make you late for dinner - if you have dinner at all.

Indeed, the very presence of election monitors in transition states is often the subject of heated conjecture. I believe that it is almost always better to observe elections than to stay on the sidelines. We will look into this subject; one which always provokes much debate. Measuring democracy is, in itself, nearly as complicated a question. The problem of determining the free and fair is full of imponderables.

Election observers are always faced with the difficult task of deciding whether fraud or chaos have caused elections to go askew in transition states. We will explore some of the difficulties which often arise in trying to ascertain the difference.

10. To Observe or not to Observe

It has become a common international practice for transitional countries to request electoral assistance from donor states and non-governmental organizations to observe contentious, first-time elections. While these requests normally emanate from the governments of transition states, in some cases, opposition parties have also requested outside mediation in order to turn the attention of the international community to tension-wracked races in which the probability of intimidation and fraud would be extremely high.

The historic October 5, 1988 plebiscite in Chile provides an ideal illustration of the potential of a united, determined opposition to unseat a powerful authoritarian foe.[73] At the time, General Augusto Pinochet's expectations of another eight-year presidential term were rejected by the voters. Pinochet, who by means of a military coup, had seized control of Chile from democratically elected Salvadore Allende on September 11, 1973, had expected the plebiscite would endorse the political institutionalization of his military regime. In the interval leading up to the dramatic events of 1988, the dictator presided over a period of economic recovery in his country. But the end result of the plebiscite was an astonishing political redemocratization and a release from the darkness of human rights abuses which characterized the Pinochet regime.

The pro-democracy forces understood that the brutal dictatorship could not be directly unseated and replaced. Between 1982-89, the opposition forces which would form into the Concertacion de Partidos por el No - which mobilized votes against retaining Pinochet in the Presidency and therefore unleashed the transition- had learned important lessons which would culminate in the restoration of democracy and the presidential and parliamentary elections of December, 1989.

During those years, the social and cultural opposition that predominated during the first decade of military rule began to be overshadowed by social mobilizations and protests, and afterwards by more politically oriented goals. Chilean opposition leaders learned much from such international examples of democratization as the elections in the Philippines and Argentina, the transition in Spain, and the plebescite in Uruguay, among other cases. The key lesson, perhaps, concerned the need to stay unified and work within existing institutional channels.[74]

They did so both domestically and internationally, with powerful results. Non-governmental organizations such as the National Democratic Institute were important mediators in the process of bringing the previously fragmented democratic opposition together on common ground, often in conferences hosted outside their country. This allowed the Chileans to reaffirm a common purpose. Many of the signatories to the National Accord were also part of the Movement for Free Elections (MFE) which launched a massive voter registration drive in preparation for the plebiscite. They received tremendous support and expertise from the international community in carrying out that critical process.

Throughout that fateful day, the watchful eye of the global community focused on Chileans. Observers from many countries recorded the new, strong voices of the people in a country where the brooding presence of the military establishment had always been feared. When the people voted a resounding "no", the darkness lifted.

Invitations from opposition groups such as the Concertacion de Partidos por el No are far less frequent than those from host governments, however. The most common reason for issuing such invitations is that:

> Governments whose legitimacy is questioned are turning to the interna-
> tional system for that validation which their national polis is yet unable to
> give. They do so to avoid the alternative - persistent challenges to au-
> thority by coups and countercoups, instability and stasis - and to enable
> themselves to govern with essential societal acquiescence. What they
> seek is legitimation by a global standard monitored by processes of the
> international system.[75]

Upon receipt of an invitation to observe an election, a Western government or non-governmental organization must decide on whether the evident obstacles to any potential free and fair election are such that it is or is not worthwhile to accept.

Larry Garber is one of the world's best known election observers. Both as practitioner and theorist, he has played a pathfinder role in our understanding of democratic development. I have had the good fortune to work with Larry in many of the missions I have led or participated in. His analysis of electoral law and procedures and human rights is complimented by a deep understanding of the historical processes and political cultures of the many countries in which NDI operated. My missions often sought his expertise in complex processes such as the pre-electoral phase of the movement towards Namibian independence in 1989.

As a senior policy adviser to NDI at the time, Garber sent us draft resolutions to deal with the then serious problem of South African induced intimidation in the former German colony of South West Africa. His thinking would be essential to the demands made by our delegation for changes to the electoral law in that country (see Section 18) and the adoption of an election system which considerably levelled the playing field, hence encouraging the maximum participation by the Namibian people.

His *Guidelines to International Election Observing*, written in 1984, has become a bible to all those involved in what was, at that time, essentially a new frontier. In *Guidelines...*, he outlined criteria useful to decision makers who were then involved in arriving at the difficult decision of whether to comply with the invitation of a host country to observe, or not.

An organization should consider the following factors before determining whether to send an election observer mission: has there been a request for observers from the host country; has the organization been monitoring political developments in the host country for a period of time; does the election represent a transition in power from a colonial or non-democratic government; have there been prior instances of fraud or manipulation in the electoral process of the host country; is there a debate surrounding the legitimacy of the election; and is the election occurring in a country where there have been serious allegations of human rights violations?[76]

Such questions are clearly paramount in the calculations of policy makers who are considering the substantial allocation of resources which the support of democratic transition implies. The request for observers is an important consideration because if there is no invitation, observers have no freedom of movement or access to information in the transition state, not to speak of the potential for a serious breach in relations between host and donor governments. Invitations should also be timely. Observers should theoretically be accorded the opportunity for long-term monitoring in order to observe the real nature of the electoral playing field. In fact, the UN insists on receiving invitations four months before the registration of voters in order to assemble its verification missions.

The decision to send electoral assistance and observer missions should theoretically only be made if the political environment accords with at least a nominal societal consensus. Basic political rights should be in evidence; donor states must wrestle with the difficult question of whether minimal political freedoms exist in the host country. Other questions include: do the voters have the right to be adequately informed in order to make their decision? - can the observers work with local civics groups and monitors? - do they have the freedom of action within a certain country which allows them to render a fair judgement with regard to the electoral process?

These questions should be answered in the affimative before monitors are dispersed. But, in spite of the guidelines, Western governments and NGOs have observed elections in which there have been prior instances of fraud or manipulation. As well, missions have been dispatched to countries where there have been serious debates over the legitimacy of the electoral processes themselves, and where more or less serious allegations of human rights violations have arisen.

Often, authoritarian governments have staged only minimally free elections as showcase models of their commitment to the democratic process. Western decision makers have been entirely conscious of the very limited will extant in some states to make transitions work. Yet, the decisions have been made to observe such elections as transitory phases in democratic development.

While the cynics might wonder at the significance of such "five second exercises in democracy",[79] it is difficult to make a strong case for the fact that such elections should not have been observed at all. In many cases, such as the Guatemalan elections of 1985, the unexpected has happened. A number of Western governments, including my own, made the decision to observe the elections with the full knowledge that terror was a daily fact of life inside the «Guatemalan death masque.»[78]

It was an established fact that the Guatemalan military presided over one of the most violent political cultures of our time. Astonishingly, they also presided over elections "...which offered the Guatemalan people a fair, honest opportunity to express their political preferences", and, which "overall ...went smoothly".[79] Louis Lavoie, then the Director of Operations at Elections Canada and author of a summary report on the election could not hide his surprise at the results:

> I am now convinced that such an exercise was not a myth but a reality; while I was somewhat sceptical at the start, I now admit that what I saw was real and was contrary to what I might have expected, given the past history of elections in Guatemala."[80]

When Vinicio Cerezo, the first civilian president of Guatemala in 20 years, stood to give his inaugural address in January 1986, he spoke of his belief that democracy would be restored. "We are a people who were thrown out of our house, and today we return",[81] he said.

Cerezo knew all about hopes betrayed. He rose to leadership of the Christian Democrat party in Guatemala after many of its members had been assassinated or had disappeared. He himself survived three assassination attempts perpetrated by the efficient apparatus of political terrorism which existed at the heart of this bureaucracy of death. Unfortunately, Cerezo would leave in disgrace. The accusations surrounding his departure proved to be tragic in light of the hope he represented for the future of his country.

We must remember, however, that Cerezo won an overwhelming victory in Guatemala only because the military stood in abeyance. Prior to the election, the general consensus had been that no popular vote would be tolerated and that the government of General Megia Victores would never voluntarily hand over power.

In fact, elections were held, and the military did what no one had considered possible. The generals tolerated a return to civilian rule. The Guatemalan military understood the problems in store for any government presiding over a country wracked by chaos. It was this practical understanding that dominated their actions; and was certainly not due to any newly conceived fascination for democratic institutions.

But did this mean that outside governments should have waived their discretionary power to watch Guatemalans vote?

The Executive Summary on the elections prepared by the National Democratic Institute put it this way:

> the elections marked a first, but very important step towards the transition to democracy, and an alternative preferable to a reformist military coup or prolonged armed confrontation between left and right. In conducting an election that was procedurally correct, Guatemala made important progress toward the goal of civilian rule.

Stated differently, the election marked progress in increasing meaningful political participation by the citizenry. As such, those five seconds were of vital historical importance in time because ordinary people had been encouraged to believe there is a better way to live.

I referred to this phenomenon as a process of emboldenment. The fact is that without the presence of observers, the perennial problems of fear and intimidation may have proven to be too much for most Guatemalans. It must be remembered that terror had been the grim reality of daily life in that unhappy country.

Unfortunately, the path of democratization in Guatemala has been tortuous. The hopes that had been raised on the election of Vinicio Cerezo were not to be borne out, even though elections were held in 1990 and the rudiments of a democratic system seemed to survive.

In 1993, another coup brought the roller coaster ride which symbolized the course of Guatemalan democratisation to a wrenching halt. This time, it was President Jorge Serrano Elias, elected only two years previously, who was ousted by a combination of military, business, and opposition leaders. His main claim to fame was that the political, economic and social policies he had pursued had alienated nearly everyone in the country. The United States and the OAS then vociferously called for a return to democracy. Alarmed by the threats posed to Guatemala's economy, a strange coalition of moderate and left-leaning politicians called the National Forum for Consensus began to mobilize opposition to the military junta.

The Forum included eminent personalities such as Nobel Prize winner Rigoberta Menchu and human rights ombudsman Ramiro de Leon Carpio. This was a sign that, in spite of appearances, undercurrents of belief in civilian society and democratic institutions remained important features of the political landscape.
When President Serrano Elias was forced out of the country by the military high command in May, 1993, Congress elected de Carpio as his successor. The challenges to his administration were formidable. He did not contest the January, 1996 elections - the closest elections in that country's history - in which the Guatemalan people chose a new President, Alvaro Arzu Irogoyen.

The new president has pledged to supervise the "reincorporation of Guatemala back into the democratic countries of the world."[82] But his slim victory has been dramatically undercut by the fact that General Rios Montt and his right-wing Guatemalan Republican Front took nearly half the vote. The General and his party won that vote on the promise to institute the same iron fist that marked his bloody and repressive tenure as Guatemala's strongman in 1982-83.

It is imperative that President Irogoyen set in process the reforms necessary to dismantle the structures of privilege and inequality responsible for the continuing civil war in that country. UN statistics tell some of the story. 85 percent of Guatemala's 11 million people live in poverty, 70 percent in a state of deprivation regarded as extreme. It is now imperative that the outside world support the new president with massive assistance. If another coup seems in the offing, the Organization of American States (OAS) membership must actualize their commitments to the defence of democracy in that unhappy country - where the struggle has been so courageously waged over the last decade by the ordinary people who deserve the better life a vote for democracy promises.

Over the years, our support to the electoral process in countries such as Guatemala has been a critical factor in keeping the belief in the democratic ideal alive. So when it comes to the big decision as to whether or not to observe elections in adverse circumstances, I draw on my own experience as a guide. Very simply, I have learned that it is always better to observe than to sit on the sidelines.

11. Don't Sit on the Sidelines

I was first asked to be a member of the Philippine Election International Observer team by Brian Atwood, at the time the President of the National Democratic Institute for International Affairs (NDI). He wondered whether I would consider going in the event NDI sent an observer team to the 1986 elections.

While I was excited at the prospect, I had to have the answers to two questions. First, I wanted his assurance that an advance NDI team would conclude that an outside observer contingent could play a meaningful and worthwhile role in the forthcoming elections. The fact that most analysts at the time felt they would be highly volatile made this a question of much more than peripheral interest.

Further, I wanted his pledge that our mission would have the wholehearted endorsement of the principal parties. President Marcos' support would be expected to be half-hearted, of course. But for Corazan Aquino leader of the opposition forces, as well as the COMELEC (Commission on Elections) and NAMFREL (The National Citizens Movement for Free Elections), the presence of international observers would be absolutely essential.

Early in 1986, Brian Atwood responded with affirmative answers to both questions. Soon we were on the long road to Manila by way of New York. Atwood and myself were joined on that flight by the colourful John Hume, leader of the Social Democratic Labour Party in Northern Ireland.

When Hume, who has played a major role in the dramatic unfolding of events in Northern Ireland, appeared on the plane, I was curious as to why he had come all the way from Heathrow to JFK en route to Manila. I though it seemed to be a long and circuitous venture, and Hume agreed.

Two hours out of New York, Hume turned to Atwood in some exasperation and said: "Brian, why did you take me all this way?" - to which Atwood replied with his customary grin, "because I wanted you to get to know Al Graham." Hume took one hard look at me in disbelief. We then proceeded to toast the future of our mission, not, in any way anticipating the drama of the events yet to come.

In fact, we were to get much more than we bargained for. Unbeknownst to us at the time, our international observer delegation played a crucial role in the final outcome in the historic February, 1986 elections.

In spite of the mounting catastrophe all around him, the ailing President Ferdinand Marcos had called for "snap elections" on November 3, 1985. At the time, the insurgency of the Maoist New Peoples' Army and the violent activities of Muslim separatists throughout the Philippines had reached crisis levels. The Marcos regime had become increasingly corrupt; the autocrat himself ruling an impoverished country which the Marcos family and close associates looted at will. The voices of opposition critics were regularly silenced by Marcos loyalists such as the infamous General Ver, Security Chief and Armed Forces Chief of Staff.

The brutal assasination of Benigno Aquino at Manila airport on August 2, 1983 had provided only one of the more horrible examples of the actions of a desperate regime which had become increasingly brutal as the waves of widespread anti-government protest grew. When Aquino had returned to the Philippines after years of imprisonment and exile from his homeland - before he stepped off the plane and before his feet touched the soil of his beloved country - he was shot in the head at close range by security officers, in full view of journalists. A military commission would be established in 1984 to investigate the crime, but eventually, what came to be known as the Aquino trial would end with the acquittal of the suspects, most of whom, like General Ver himself, would be reinstated. The verdict, announced in December, 1985, would lead to protests all across the Philippines. The verdict would be condemned by the highly-regarded Cardinal Sin and many others. On December 3, 1985, Aquino's widow, Corazon announced her candidacy for the "snap" elections, at the time only two months away.

Marcos had decided to hold elections in a display of arrogant disregard for opposition gathering around his increasingly isolated regime.

The US administration was clearly putting pressure on the dictator to ease the climate of American opinion swayed by such fervent Marcos critics as Senator Edward Kennedy and New York Congressman Stephen Solarz. Solarz was at the time investigating the huge, secret investments the Marcos family had made overseas and became a powerful voice behind the allegations that the President had stolen billions of US aid dollars that had been directed to his impoverished country over the years.

The United States had considerable strategic investments in the Philippines, notably the Clark and Subic Bay air and naval bases which were vital to American security interests in the Pacific. Although President Reagan had full knowledge of the deteriorating conditions in the country and the ground swell of domestic opposition to his friend, Ferdinand Marcos, he had as well a stubborn conviction that the dictator should remain in power. An election would have the advantage of disarming his many critics in the United States. In the fall of 1985, the CIA Director, William Casey put the case for elections to the beleagured President. Marcos concurred with this counsel. Ironically, both Reagan and Marcos believed that Marcos could win the February elections.

The 26 million voters of the Philippines turned out to vote on February 7. Sterling Seagrave portrayed the events of election day this way:

> Poll watchers reported extraordinary harassment and intimidation, the
> theft of voter lists and ballot boxes, and the flying of voters from district
> to district to cast multiple ballots. Most foreign observers saw and heard
> about widespread fraud, vote tampering and violence by Ferdinand's
> followers. One of my colleagues spent a night in an army 'safe house' in
> one of the outlying provinces and found it stacked from wall to wall with
> fake ballot boxes loaded with bogus ballots, waiting for army distribution
> on election day...Ferdinand had spent $430 million to buy votes. This
> forced the Central Bank to raise interest rates by 50 percent. Nearly half
> a billion dollars failed to buy him the election, even when backed by
> 200,000 soldiers, 1 million bogus ballots, and subverted computers...[83]

In spite of the fraud, the fear, and the vote-rigging, Cory Aquino and her supporters remained resolute. NAMFREL's extraordinary mobilization of 500,000 volunteers, posted at all polling places to prevent tampering - was an example of people-
power which moved the world.

But it must be remembered that without credible outside observers and the
important ability to outline to the international community the sheer magnitude of
the electoral abuse which took place in the Philippines, the pressure on Marcos to
leave the country would have been far weaker. As well, there would have been much
more violence and widespread bloodshed throughout the country. (See section 15.)

I recall vividly the night the computer operators walked out of the central
COMELEC counting headquarters. They had been ordered by Marcos-backed officials to enter phoney returns in their computers from polling centres around the
country. The returns would have indicated that Marcos was winning. In fact, the
opposite was true.

NAMFREL was then showing in its quick count that Aquino was ahead by a
wide margin. The operators themselves were independent and proud of their profes-
sion. They were ashamed to be dragged into a web of deceit. They proved to be
unwilling conspirators as their subsequent walk out amply demonstrated.[84]

Word spread quickly to the Hotel Manila where our delegation had reassembled
from around the country. In the early morning hours, we were asked to go to the
Baclaran Redemptorist Church. There we found the operators huddled together
telling their story to the assembled observers and the media.

We were there to listen. But our presence proved to be fortunate, providing life-
saving protection from the Marcos loyalists who roamed the streets and back alleys
in search of anyone who might threaten their stranglehold on Philippine power. The
move by the technicians was bold, dramatic, and decisive. It provided the kind of
factual evidence needed to convince skeptics in Washington and elsewhere that the
election was fraudulent in the extreme.

Senator Richard Lugar, Chairman of the US Senate Foreign Relations Committee, had been sent by President Reagan as a personal envoy to observe and report. The Senator did suspect the worst, but none of us really knew this at the time. As it was, he played an important role in helping to convince the President and his administration of the vast fraud perpetrated by the Marcos regime.

But independent international observers who had seen the cheating and the vote-buying and the intimidation at first-hand were in a better position to witness the dastardly deed. It is important to remember that while Senator Lugar reported directly to President Reagan, members of the international delegation were responsible only to the international community.

Of course many of us were shocked to hear President Reagan's first pronouncement on the situation. The President stated that democracy was still alive in the Philippines, much to the consternation of all those on the ground who were aware of the travesty of the situation. The President added that there had been fault on both sides. He expressed the hope that Marcos and Aquino would get together soon to resolve their respective problems.

I couldn't believe my ears. I had been one of the first from the international community to say that the election had been rigged. In a *Globe and Mail* interview, I outlined the many instances of intimidation and vote-buying which went far beyond even my imagination, concluding that "now, it looks like they (Marcos) are just trying to decide how many votes they need to win."[85] I added that Marcos had to go before there could be peace in the Philippines.

For these reasons, I wondered out loud whether I had been in another country, perhaps observing another election.

A letter from a friend encouraged me to believe that I was not. M. Ronalda MacLellan, a native of Cape Breton was then serving as Second Secretary at the Canadian Embassy in Manila. She was quite candid in her comments.

10 March, 1986
Manila, Philippines

Senator Alasdair Graham
The Canadian Senate
Parliament Hill
Ottawa, Ontario
Canada

Dear Senator Graham,
    Now that the Marcos regime has fallen, I couldn't resist writing to report on the impact of your comments made in Canada on election fraud here in the Philippines. Your timing could not have been better.

    Reports of your statement reached Manila on the heels of President Reagan's now infamous press conference in which he suggested an Aquino-Marcos power-sharing arrangement. The Filipinos were both stunned and sent reeling by the White House remarks when reports of your blunt assessment came through on the wire. In response, the local alternative press and Radio Veritas spotlighted your comments. For almost a day you grabbed the headlines and provided a moment of relief to a then gloomy situation. You were one of the very few foreigners, at the time, to *publicly rail against the Marcos regime and I know that it was very much appreciated by the Filipinos.*

    While, of course, your comments were not the decisive factor, *you should know that at a time when the Filipinos anticipated a whole repertoire of international support, only a selected few, yourself included, were able to provide a ray of hope to a seemingly deteriorating situation.*

    Although it was understood that you were not representing the Government of Canada (unfortunately, I might add), I must say I was proud, indeed delighted, that a Canadian Senator had the gumption and integrity to speak up. Thank you.

M. Ronnie MacLellan

It wasn't easy to convince President Reagan, but, to his credit, he eventually became a believer. He then sent a long-time friend of Marcos, Senator Paul Laxalt, to convince the disgraced President that he would have to live in exile. The ensuing events are now a matter of history.

But for now, the case of the Philippine elections exemplifies the vital importance of international observers in countries where inequity, fear, and brute force dominate the electoral landscape. I learned a great deal from my experience in that country, probably the most important being the strength of the human spirit in conditions of extreme adversity.

Much more on this subject will be recounted later. But for now, the message is perhaps a bit more basic. No matter how volatile and difficult a particular electoral process may be predicted to be, it serves no one's purpose to sit on the sidelines. Had we done so on the eve of the elections, President Marcos could very conceivably have snatched victory through fraud and continued to govern with impunity.

But we must not forget that when transition processes are as challenging as they have been in the Philippines and so many other countries, the mandates of the international observer missions must be clear.

If not, the impact of our assistance becomes negligible. And in some cases, it can become both counter-productive and dangerous to all the parties.

12. Have Some More Democracy

Over the past decade the reports of observer teams have become significant to Western governments as a means of determining their bilateral relations based on the legitimacy of a foreign government's claim to office.

As we have seen, the role of such international missions has evolved substantially, so that often observers act as brokers of democratic development. Because of the advent of these new forms of humanitarian intervention, it has become more important than ever that the mandates given to observers be clear and non-threatening to all parties involved in transition exercises.

Mandates differ from mission to mission. In some cases, they are limited in scope. A team may visit country-X only briefly as a representative of the will of a particular Western government to show support for the electoral process. I have always felt that the most impartial observers are those who do not have the responsibility of reporting back directly to their home governments. But no matter what the sponsorship, most observer units do not observe the entire election campaign.

It would be unfair to criticize such missions unduly. They have served as a means of deterring fraud in some countries. But the brevity of their service in transition states does not really allow them to determine the true nature of the situation or the full extent of the equities and inequities present.

In some cases, the term "electoral tourism" best illustrates the kinds of problems associated with observer delegations that fly into an area one or two days before an election, staying only long enough to call a news conference. The 1984 Panamanian presidential elections were labelled free and fair by observers who stayed only long enough to watch long lines of voters and then left the country in euphoria shortly after the polls closed. Genuine surprise was registered in international capitals several days later when cohorts of General Manuel Noriega stole the election.

Election observer missions should have substantial mandates. Long-term observation is clearly the most desirable. This allows for an analysis of the electoral process, which includes such practices as the monitoring of the electoral law, the registration process, and the government's public information policy. Only long-term observation guarantees a fair assessment after the election is held. This kind of deployment "...during pre-election flare-ups between the local political rivals offers the option of placing at the latters disposal mediators who are impartial but also acquainted with the situation."[86]

The costs of long-term observation are enormous, but the international community is presently experimenting with new approaches which augur well for the future. The concept of an international institute for electoral cooperation and assistance was endorsed in Stockholm in 1994. A small working group consisting of Sir David Steel of Great Britain, Ambassador Bengt Save-Soderbergh of Sweden, and Sir Shridath Ramphal, former Secretary General of the Commonwealth have been active in developing the International Electoral Institute Commission.

The institute's role will be to coordinate electoral bodies with different mandates. The founders believe that observation should be global in scope, taking a long-term approach to issues of elections and democratic development. In all of this, the pathfinder role played by the National Democratic Institute in preparatory and follow-up work has proven to be a model for the global community.

Another approach is to put much more emphasis on local civics groups and observers. The experience of the United Nations explains why. In 1994 alone, the UN mounted three enormous missions, in El Salvador, South Africa, and Mexico respectively. In El Salvador the 3,000 UN observers were joined by an equal number of observers from donor states and NGOs. In South Africa, the UN sent in 8,000 observers; 12,000 more joined them. The costs were staggering and it is small wonder that the UN Election Assistance Unit (EAU) began to re-think its electoral assistance policy.

Mexico became the forum for a whole new approach leading up to the August, 1994 elections. The UN received a request from that country to support a massive election monitoring programme organized by Alianza Civica, a network of domestic civics groups. The 80,000 trained observers ensured that the elections were the cleanest ever in a country where notions of democracy barely existed. Together, as one, the civics groups persisted in giving the registration lists transparency and carefully watched the polls the day of the elections. The 80,000 have now become a permanent resource in that country.

Electoral observation is becoming more global in scope as international coordination increases. But, unfortunately, many electoral processes are still plagued with what Cedric Thornberry, who directed the office of the Special Representative of the United Nations during the Namibian transition, once called "do-gooder" delegations. By these he meant, as he so well put it: "all those who had pre-written their press releases before leaving their own home countries."

Troubled Namibia was particularly over-run by these types of delegations. I recall both Louis Pienaar, the South African appointed Administrator General of Namibia, and Martii Ahtisaari, the UN Special Representative, now President of Finland, complaining that the country had been flooded by observers focusing on their own agendas. Most often, these reflected open support for the South West African Peoples' Organization (SWAPO).

This became a major problem for the authorities in that country because the political process was so delicately conceived. As we will see, it was essential to maintain the cooperation of South Africa in order to keep the elections in Namibia on course. The white supremacist government had been a deadly enemy of SWAPO over the decades preceding the historic vote of November, 1989. Careless observers were therefore in great danger of unhinging a very carefully negotiated series of bargains between the parties.

As it was, independent observer delegations proved to be critical to the successful unfolding of the elections in that country. It is true, as Cedric Thornberry pointed out, that independent observers could often say things that UNTAG could not because the UN was restricted by the terms of the Charter.

For example, my NDI delegation, a non-governmental mission, called for changes to the draft electoral law and encouraged UNTAG to move more aggressively in the struggle against intimidation. Generally, such efforts were successful and contributed overall in a positive way to the process. This didn't just happen. A great deal of rigorous advance work had been done by NDI representatives before the arrival of our team. We were able to maintain an attitude of impartiality which added to the credibility of our presence in that country.[87]

Because of this, my delegation was viewed as a realistic and helpful fixer. We were therefore able to assist in brokering a more level playing field, hence removing some of the distrust from the process of democratic development. But it must be remembered that such an activist role could only be undertaken with extreme discretion. It had to be coloured with a profound understanding of local political conditions.

But some observer missions took sides openly upon arrival. They therefore threatened the very fragile strategic bargains which had to be continually reworked during the months preceding the elections. Those which did openly announce their support for SWAPO during the electoral contest were generally very critical of what they felt to be the limited effectiveness of the UN vis-à-vis South Africa.

Such observer teams became a source of embarrassment to the other international missions working so hard to bring the Namibian elections to a successful conclusion.

I recall speaking to a group of observers (most of them fror the first time) in a Montreal airport about to depart for Namibia, was to approach their delicate role with an attitude of total independence. Leave your biases at home, I told them. Just tell the truth.

In fact, I was simply repeating the counsel that had been given to me earlier by a very courageous woman. I will never forget the circumstances in which I heard this.

At the conclusion of the 1987 elections in the Philippines, I was invited to a press conference with Mrs. Aquino and some members of her cabinet. Ken Wollack and other members of our delegation were present as well. Wollack, now President of the National Democratic Institute, is a long-time democratic activist with a domestic and international reputation for honesty and good judgement.

Before we began, I asked the President in private if there was anything special she wanted me to say. "No, just tell the truth," she said.

Unlike the fraudulent 1986 elections which led to the downfall of President Marcos, the 1987 elections were significant for irregularities so minor that they might be found in any democratic process in any industrialized country. After the election, however, Umberto Enrile, former Chief of the Armed Forces in that country had charged that we were just tools for Aquino, and further, that the Aquino forces had been guilty of manipulation and fraud. Needless to say, the 1987 results disproved all this.

There is no doubt that the truth is sometimes hard to tell in contests where bitterness, fear and intimidation are present. I felt the heat in the 1986 snap elections as I have pointed out above. But the reality is that no observer can fail to ignore the cardinal principle of such international involvement - what an observer group says, how that group communicates the message and how it exercises influence has serious ramifications.

When observer delegations operate from private agendas, the consequences can be disastrous, as they are often taken seriously by transition government and election officials. I have heard too many conversations reminiscent of the lecture given by the self- important March Hare to Alice at the tea party in Wonderland.

The subject was tea but could just as easily go this way: "Take some more democracy", the March Hare said to Alice very earnestly. "But I've had nothing yet", Alice replied in an offended tone, "so I can't take more".

Much damage can be done to the whole cause of democratic development when missions are poorly selected and briefed.

Fortunately, cumulative experience is teaching most donor organizations and states that contradictory mandates and evaluations can severely damage the credibility of all missions engaged in the observation process. Cooperation is essential. In many elections of the past, the rigours of the process have led to a *de facto* accommodation of interests and strategies.

In the Nicaraguan elections of 1990, the OAS, the UN and The Council of Freely-Elected Heads of Government had a number of problems in cooperating with one another; nonetheless a kind of tacit division of labour did come into play for:

> ...while Carter's high level group tried to resolve the main problems by dealing directly with President Ortega and Mrs. Chamorro ...both the OAS and the UN had the funds and the personnel to assemble large missions. The OAS deployed its groups to every region and its comparative advantage was in working out problems privately with the FSLN and UNO at the regional and national levels. The strength of the UN team lay in its analytical skills and its diplomatic approaches at middle levels in Managua. UN reports of campaign problems were invaluable for all of the observers.[88]

In conclusion, we are beginning to see elements of cooperation on this new frontier. It has become clear to most election monitoring organizations that competition should be the preserve of the candidates and political parties directly engaged in the electoral process - and not the preserve of the observers themselves. The greatest injury sustained is that to democratic development itself.

The mandates for our observer teams must be clearly elaborated in the future as the demands on all our countries for a sustained, experienced and active observer presence will grow significantly. As our peacekeeping capacity abroad begins to assume the dimensions of peacemaking, the challenges facing the liberal democracies will multiply.

But for now, let us continue our examination of election observers at work. The problem of determining what is free and what is fair in elections around the world would seem at first glance to be a relatively simple one to solve. Nothing could be further from the truth, however. Once again, we are faced with more questions than answers.

13. The Problem of Determining the Fair and the Free

Election monitors must often determine in very difficult conditions whether political frameworks conducive to the holding of free and fair elections really exist. Some of the factors which influence their analysis are relatively straightforward, such as the specific provisions of a country's Electoral Law.

But when it comes to questions like the evolving political culture of a transition state, which tends to be as much a part of the consciousness of a nation as the air the people breathe, the situation becomes considerably more complicated. International observers must write up and reflect upon their conclusions within the broad spectrum of beliefs which make up that political culture. First-time elections are only part of a broad process of change. In order to record and monitor democratic development within a particular country, observers must take care to do so within the framework of ideas and traditions which serve as the infrastructure of the national consciousness.[89] No experienced observer can be insensitive to the larger questions that arise in attempting to measure levels of freedom in countries where the seeds have just been planted.

How do we begin to measure abstract notions such as conviction? How do we begin to estimate the evolving empowerment of people?

As an Atlantic Canadian, I sometimes like to compare the experience of democratic development with the sea itself. As we mediate our value systems into other social and political cultures, as the two different worlds meet, the waters shift and churn and ebb. The currents seethe with colour, with light and with darkness. All these elements are scarcely visible - before, as rapidly, they disappear.

I have often felt a sense of illusion in monitoring first-time elections, as I have felt it when I watched the waves break on the shores of my native Cape Breton. In all the countries I visited, I have come to realize that most of our assumptions about liberal democracy are only fleeting appearances, as with the sea-foam capping Atlantic breakers. They are forms which generally have little to do with the realities of life on the other side of the world.

For example, Western human rights instruments, such as the UN Declaration of Human Rights provide no workable tools for observers operating in African countries where one-party systems have traditionally stood as the rule, and also as an alternative to tribal warfare.

In the former Eastern Bloc countries, democratic exercises in the form of multi-party elections have been carried out, but political cultures susceptible to the sustaining of such democratic exercises are still very much in their infancy. It is well known that an election can appear to be fair and free in a repressive political culture.

As I have noted above, election observers agreed uniformly that the August 21, 1994 elections in Mexico were clean, but not fair. The process was not fair because the ruling party, the Institutional Revolutionary Party (IRP), which has ruled Mexico for the past 65 years took customary care to slant the whole process in its favour. Domestic monitoring groups, along with observers from the Carter Centre's Council of Freely Elected Heads of Governments described the massive use of state resources to promote PRI candidates, as well as the large resource disparities between the PRI and other parties. They recorded as well the evident bias favouring the PRI in terms of television and media coverage in general.

While there was an absence of contrived election-day fraud, the fact remained that the electoral process itself was by no stretch of the imagination free and fair.

Democratic forms can co-exist with authoritarian reality as any experienced observer knows. Technically, all the accoutrements of a modern electoral system may be in place in a given country. Yet failure to weigh the political intangibles, such as political will, a key factor in bringing any electoral process to a successful conclusion, can lead to highly inaccurate assessments.

The election system in a particular country can be flawed; yet if the parties want a free and fair election this will happen in spite of the systemic defects. The converse is also true. The determining factor in any transition is the general wish to proceed to a fair conclusion. Political will is the lifeblood of any democratic transition.

In 1996, if all goes well, over 18 African countries will hold national elections. In line with the pro-democracy wave which swept across the continent in the early 1990s, it is anticipated that the people will turn out in numbers which should shame the citizenry of the more established democracies. Very few, if any, of the new governments will be elected in first-past-the-post, multi-party style elections. The fear of multipartyism as a trigger to Africa's endemic tribalism is a realistic one. A winner-take-all attitude could inevitably lead to civil war in a number of countries.

Everything now depends on the quality of leadership on the continent. Nelson Mandela's wisdom has brought about a politics of inclusion in South Africa. It is now critical that responsible political leaders across the continent emulate this wisdom and include as many groups as possible in the process of government. This principle is far too important to be left solely to the whims of newly elected leaders. The politics of inclusion must be constitutionally enshrined and this will demand a revolution in thinking that goes well beyond the ballot box.

Democracy must develop in partnership with the distinctive traditions and cultures indigenous to the continent. One analyst summarized the situation this way:

> Quick fixes and shortcuts, or the attempted mimicry of inappropriate
> foreign models, would be exercises in futility. The new African demo-
> cratic, transformational ethic cannot be developed by others on behalf of
> the African people, but only by Africans themselves, acting in light of
> their own values, perceptions, concerns, and aspirations. Only the people
> can drive the process forward.[90]

The task of introducing multi-party democracy in sub-Saharan Africa is beset
with difficulties and much of the Western press paints the prospects for democratization in rather grim, improbable terms. Over the past few years, multi-party elections
in Kenya, Cameroon, Ghana, Cote d'Ivoire, Togo, and Ethiopia - to list only a few -
were all deeply flawed. The deepest fiasco of all was probably the Nigerian military's
1993 annulment of that country's fairest election in history and the subsequent dis-
graceful actions taken in putting Moshood Abiola on trial for treason in the summer
of 1994.

Outside observers have tended to conclude that these flawed elections are better than none at all, and have generally endorsed them as at least a start, albeit
imperfect, on the road to democratic governance. However, many of the autocratic
rulers endorsed by outsiders have tightened up their repressive regimes and the
opposition parties have warred among themselves, showing a marked inability to
rally behind pro-democracy banners.

I think it would be a mistake to overlook what has become a growing circle of
well-educated and politically committed civic leaders in countries throughout the
continent. As Michael Chege put it:

> ...their faith and belief in the continent's capacity for better government
> is unshakeable. These pioneering democrats - whose numbers, though
> small, are growing - include members of the Campaign for Democracy
> and its many allies in Nigeria, pro-democratic lawyers and clergy in Kenya,
> tough-minded opposition legislators in Ghana's Hawa Yakubu-Ogede
> and Kenya's Martha Karua, and trade unionists, religious leaders, aca-
> demics and independent journalists in Ethiopia, Senegal,... Kenya and
> elsewhere...all of them belying...the portrayal of African leaders as a be-
> nighted lot. The social texture and goals of pro-democracy coalitions
> throughout the continent are similar to those of the movement that
> broke the back of apartheid in South Africa - a fact that has not been lost
> on the enemies of the open society elsewhere on the continent."[91]

These courageous leaders of civic associations are gaining a new lease on life
from the many pro-democratic international NGOs that are now providing them with
direct assistance. Multilateral and bilateral donors are refusing to accept national
borders as sacrosanct and are now giving aid to local pro-democracy civil associations on the continent. This is often direct assistance and it avoids the pitfalls of past
aid disbursements which often were channelled through the state, with predictably
disastrous consequences.

We must also consider the fact that new information and communications technologies present dramatic opportunities to civil society as pro-democracy leaders attempt the monumental task of sowing the seeds of freedom. I believe the prospects for a continuation of this process are propitious, if for no other reason than that Africans understand only too well the costs to them of the failure of democracy.

In this critical year, when so many elections will be held in Africa, the international community will again be deluged with observer analysis as to whether or not some of the processes could be regarded as free and fair.

In attempting to do so, the observers will again be beset with complex questions. How does one apply Western standards of free and fair election practices to countries in which only a partial opposition is tolerated. Or, as one observer asked, can we say that "a semi-competitive election is better than none at all?"[92] Based on my own experience as an election monitor, I would reply that the answer is clearly, yes.

In the 1989 Paraguayan presidential elections, the opposition parties almost withdrew from the process. There were solid reasons for their frustration. The odds in that country were tilted heavily against them. The independent and opposition press had been suppressed for years and if it operated at all, according to the government of the day, it did so illegally.

This was only one example of the many inequities which the fledgling opposition parties in that country faced.

In spite of the circumstances, we encouraged Domingo Laino to stay in. Laino, the leader of the Authentic Radical Liberal Party, had been for years a front-line fighter in the cause of democracy and human rights. His discouragement and frustration became more evident as the campaign got underway.

Our delegation reasoned that the democratic engine was warm and the wheels of democracy were moving, no matter how slowly. We told Laino that even the 20 percent he could gain in the general voting would qualify his party for seats in the Senate. We also warned him that if he did not participate, he could set the process back a long time. Laino did stay - in spite of the fact that the ruling Colorado Party was heading for an overwhelming victory, eventually winning 73 percent of the vote.

The 1989 election was a classic example of a semi-competitive election. Those of us in the country at the time kept up a continuing vigil. We all had our credibility on the line because we were asking candidates like Laino to stay in and support, by his presence, a basically unfair process. But the first step had to be taken.

Part of our role developed into encouraging Paraguayans to believe that the seeds of freedom would grow and that we would continue to assist in nurturing them. We were not just there to monitor a five- second snapshot.

To conclude, the assessment of free and fair elections is only part of the task of observer missions. More important, observers must attempt to measure the nature and extent of progress towards democratic development.

That includes ascertaining degrees of political repression, evaluating the plurality of political parties and assessing the inequities of the playing field. It means sizing up the political will of the authorities in question to genuinely move towards democratic practices. It also implies distinguishing between pre-meditated fraud on the part of the governing authorities, and the normal chaos which is due to institutional weaknesses in transition states holding elections for the first-time.

In many of the countries I visited, the task of distinguishing between fraud and chaos has greatly complicated the work of the missions involved. It is to this question we will now turn.

14. Fraud or Chaos

First-time elections are often tumultuous occasions for developing countries. Many times, the enormous costs involved outstrip the resources of poor governments. As well, the basic skills essential to democratic elections are usually lacking in such countries. They require the interaction of an enormous infrastructure of trained personnel and equipment. Elections are only improved as a nation's familiarity with the process is enhanced.

One need only think of the daunting challenges involved in putting together the large infrastructures needed to maintain accurate registries. It is a simple point, but it needs stressing nonetheless, that vital statistics are often missing in the Third World.[93]

Our support in supplying election materials and logistical assistance, to cite only a few examples, often makes a critical difference in such countries. In one of his earliest election reports, Ron Gould of Elections Canada showed how critical outside assistance turned out to be in the case of the Honduran elections of November 24, 1985.

In Honduras, the US Agency for International Development (AID) had provided nearly 100 percent of the funding, but as Gould emphasized in his report, Honduran officials were responsible for the distribution of the monies. US AID advised Honduran electoral officials in the dynamics of voter registration and "... a large proportion of the $5 million provided by the US AID for the voter registration system was used to purchase the hardware and software and to set up the very sophisticated computerized registration and vote recording system".[94]

AID supplied the ballot paper and the indelible ink needed for marking voters' fingers - a useful means of dispelling accusations of fraud and a very common technique in elections held throughout the developing world. The Agency paid the construction costs for ballot boxes and purchased signing machines which were used to stamp the votes as valid. As another example of the depth of outside support for the Honduran electoral process, US AID also provided funds which covered the costs of international election observers.

The kind of electoral assistance seen in Honduras has been replicated in countries around the world and has often been essential in keeping difficult processes on track. But in some cases, local governments do not have the necessary skills to ensure logistical plans are carried out.

The 1984 elections in El Salvador were well documented by international observers and were considered to be, in lieu of the tragic history of that country, extremely significant to the international community. After a long period of authoritarianism, the country has come a long way along the road of democratic development. The extraordinary peace-building efforts of the United Nations in contemporary El Salvador have already been mentioned.[95]

The violence and political murders which characterized daily life in El Salvador led most observers to believe that a peaceful transition would be inconceivable. It is rather astonishing to note that when the elections were held, observers found that the problems they saw were not the result of premeditated fraud, the logical and antici- pated source of difficulty. Rather, as one observer recounted, they stemmed from simple practical causes which she labelled "administrative disaster."

> The problems in March 1984 were due to the following factors: the politicization of the Central Election Commission (CCE); the setting up of an election system so determined to avoid election fraud that it was complex, cumbersome, and rigid; the lack of financial support from the government of El Salvador; the late passage of the electoral law; the Salvadoran government procurement regulations which slowed delivery of election equipment and materials; the many problems with the regis- try list; the ineffective dissemination to the voters on the changes in the system and where to go to vote; the problems in the timely delivery of election materials to the polling sites; the insufficient number of national polling places for voters outside their home districts; the polling sites not being equipped to handle large number of voters; and the power out- ages caused by the guerillas the night before the election....
>
> Was the election free and fair? Some 150,000 voters were prevented from casting their votes because of the problems mentioned. The total vote was 1.4 million. Some fraud and intimidation was observed by others. I did not see fraud. What I saw was administrative and logistical failure.
>
> My conclusion is that despite the failures in the election system, the vote reflected the will of the people.[96]

This kind of commentary was duplicated in many of the reports of the period. Salvadorans lived in one of the most savage political cultures of our time. However, when they went to the polls in one of their earliest elections, observers saw only institutional weakness at work. They did not see ill intent, which was in itself an astonishing commentary on the determination of the Salvadoran people to get on with the future.

In country after country that determination and commitment has been evident to observers. This resolute sense of entitlement is visible even in countries where mass murder, disappearances, and torture have been daily occurrences. It was the driving force behind the quiet courage displayed by thousands of Salvadorans in 1984 as they waited patiently in the hot sun to cast a secret ballot: their signal of an end to horror.

It is our assistance which helps sustain the resolve of voters in transition states. All international observers will tell you that the cases of El Salvador and Honduras are reflective of a larger pattern. More often than not, it is the result of chaos generated by inexperience.

In May, 1991, Paraguay held municipal elections for the first-time. Many observers approached the mayoral elections with considerable distrust and well-founded reservations as to the intent of the governing authorities. Those suspicions reached a peak on election day as turmoil and disarray ran rampant through the streets of Asuncion, the capital city.

In fact, the confusion throughout the whole Ministry of Elections was such that many observers felt that the elections should be postponed. After repeated visits to the returning office headquarters and also the various candidates' camps, I became convinced that the chaos was not contrived or deliberate on the part of the central election officials, but merely the result of a shortage of skills and the lack of adequate preparation.

While this was not true in all regions of the country, administrative failure meant that the elections were suspended in 20 municipalities. Most of the elements of organizational disaster were evident on election day. Electoral materials did not arrive on time, in some cases did not arrive at all, or in sufficient quantity. Many voters became discouraged as a result, feeling that the overwhelming chaos around them had predetermined failure. Some voters left the line-ups before the balloting commenced.

Mistakes on registration lists led to substantial disenfranchisement. In some regions, ballots did not include all the candidates. In others, extra candidates appeared, further compounding the confusion and apprehension felt by often first-time voters.

By mid-afternoon on voting day, the mighty Colorado Party saw that it was in trouble. An independent candidate appeared headed for victory in Asuncion. Some Colorado officials began to side with those who were suggesting a postponement on a nation-wide basis.

Late in the afternoon, I called on the leader of the OAS delegation with some of my own people. The OAS leader wondered aloud if he should call the President or the Chief Electoral Board to counsel postponement. I began to worry when it appeared some of my friends were in agreement, and cautioned them that they were beginning to step outside the role of the international observer. I emphasized that we were there to observe and report, and intervention was not a part of our mandate. If we were asked by the proper authorities, then it might be appropriate to give an opinion.

In part, my argument stemmed from the fact that the flaws were not a by-product of an absence of political will on the part of the Rodriguez regime. I believed at the time that the democratic will of the people was coming through, in spite of the chaos in parts of the country. This was one case where attempts to broker the process would have been inimical to the will of Paraguayans.

As well, such attempts would have further undermined the credibility of the President, who, like many leaders of democratic transition, was faced with all the difficulties inherent in holding elections for the first-time.

In fact, my personal experiences in Paraguay have led me to believe that President Rodriguez will be regarded by historians as one of the Fathers of Paraguayan democracy. As we will see later, this would not have been a role most analysts, including myself, would have believed possible a few short years before.

SOUTH AFRICA
April, 1994 Elections: The Real Enemy Was Chaos

But the course of human history can be unpredictable. There were many who did not believe that South Africa could carry off the first, multi-party, nonracial elections in its 342 year history. Pessimism mounted worldwide as pre-electoral violence resulted in thousands of deaths in that country. There were valid reasons to believe the situation would worsen. In fact, from the time of Nelson Mandela's release from prison in February, 1990, over 12,000 lives had been lost in wave upon wave of political murders and assassinations.

For these reasons, the international press was filled with dire foreboding. Doomsday predictions swept through editorial columns worldwide in the weeks preceding the April, 1994 elections. There was a very strong possibility that the elections would be cancelled due to anticipated violence. But the long-term observation missions based in the country months prior to the election were concerned as well about the massive logistical problems associated with carrying off an election in conditions where the possibilities of chaos seemed endless.

Canadian involvement was very visible on many levels and all part of the long-term pre-electoral involvement of the international community in this historic process. Years of negotiation had preceded the widely anticipated day when over 19.5 million South Africans would cast their ballots, the vast majority for the first-time. As part of the gigantic international commitment to new political beginnings for South Africa, Canada's well known former Secretary of the Treasury Board, Mr. Al Johnson, advised political parties and major political figures on the workings of government, and Canadian constitutional processes which helped prepare South Africans for the post-electoral period.

A former Commissioner of the Royal Canadian Mounted Police, Mr. Robert Simmons, played a major role in negotiations to reduce violence during the election period. In doing so, the RCMP made a major contribution in South Africa, as the force had in Namibia some years before. Its training programme on human rights had greatly impressed all of the foreign observers monitoring the elections in that country.

Ron Gould's international credibility was such as to ensure his involvement in extensive consultations with all the major participants on many levels. The following examples serve only to highlight a much larger picture. Mr. Gould worked on the development of the South Africa Elections Act. He helped produce a document on the ways of reducing violence during the election, and he supervised both the funding and technical support provided by Canada to the South African Election Commission.

All in all, Canada's contribution to South African democratic development was probably our most substantive and cost effective exercise to date. But of the many measures taken to support the process, the practical logistics initiatives on the ground were those which would determine the successful outcome of the process.

As I have said, some international observers felt that the elections in South Africa were doomed because of the anticipated levels of political violence. Realities were very different, however. Logistics monitors understood that the real enemy of the electoral process would be the chaos induced by, inter alia, the fact that approximately 70 percent of the eligible voters in that country had never voted before.

As one logistics official from Elections Canada put it: "I wasn't afraid of the violence - I was just afraid we might not be able to pull it off."[97]

South Africa is a country compartmentalized between the first and third worlds. The national operations centre for the elections was based in Johannesburg, a modern, first world city like most South African urban centres. But entrance to the black townships meant a journey into some of the most impoverished sectors of the global community.

In past electoral contests in that country, most of the voters were located in first world areas serviced by South Africa's communications, transportation, and social services infrastructure. This greatly facilitated the logistical support of the elections. But in 1994, conditions were much different as polling sites had to be set up in locations like the black townships which did not have adequate transportation, communications, or power.[98]

Previous white regimes in South Africa had had no practical reasons to collect vital statistics with regard to the black inhabitants, in spite of the fact that they made up 80 percent of the population of that country. The very logic of apartheid itself therefore generated an enormous potential for logistical disaster when the voiceless majority finally received the right to cast a secret ballot.

For example, there were no electoral lists outside the established areas. One could vote wherever one wished. As a result, no one could predict how many voters would line up at one particular voting station.

Nonetheless, voters were overwhelmingly patient in the face of numerous shortages of personnel and materials. As one observer put it:

> What I saw from my vantage point inside those polling places was the smile on the face of the countless voters as the ballot was finally, carefully inserted through the slot into the ballot box. All those hours standing in line, unheard of here (in Canada) failed to curb their joy. I saw them dance out of the polling place."[99]

There were 10,000 such stations and each station had 22 officers, all with their own carefully segmented tasks. The Independent Electoral Commission had to recruit more than 200,000 individuals to fill positions at the national, provincial, and sub-provincial districts. We must remember that the complexity of the process was increased by last-minute changes in the Electoral Act as well as the late decision of Inkatha to participate.

The technical problems were nightmarish. To avoid fraud, monitors used UV lamps to test for indelible ink on voters, but the lamps required three day supplies of batteries which often failed to function.

Forty-two provincial warehouses were designed to supply the voting stations in these elections, which, it must be remembered were both provincial and national in scope. Because no station knew exactly how much traffic to expect, there was a tendency to hoard ballots and ballot boxes. So, in some areas, the warehouse supplies gave out. To avoid riots, the South African Army supplied the necessary materials to the polling stations by helicopter in a superb logistical operation.

As the Cassandras wailed on the sidelines, outside elections experts worked tirelessly with the South African government and the army to carry the elections to a successful conclusion.[100] The fact that chaos did not cause a suspension of the elections, or serve as a catalyst of distrust on other levels, was in no small way a tribute to their efforts.

When the Chairman of the South African Elections Commission stated publicly that the elections could not have taken place without the involvement and support of the Canadians, we stood a bit taller and were proud of our country.

South Africa needs our continued support and involvement as it plunges into a vast national reconstruction process. As with so many states undergoing important transitions, the international community has an obligation to continue its support.

PART FIVE
SOWING THE SEEDS OF FREEDOM

I have served on international monitoring teams in many countries in this, the dawn of the gigantic leap to democracy. Even in those states widely regarded as republics of fear, the streets on voting day have always been filled with excitement, great exuberance and heady exhilaration. This has happened in spite of the appalling adversity often faced by first-time voters.

My first service in an international observer mission took me to the Philippines in February, 1986. Because of the deteriorating conditions throughout the archipelago, the tensions were expected to be so great that the results would probably not be accepted by all sides involved in the process. The strategic value of the Philippines to the United States meant an additional powerful pressure in the direction of ensuring post-election stability in that country.

These elections were a watershed for me, because I saw very clearly that the little people is, indeed, a giant. I had grown up with this conviction; in fact it was the engine of much I have tried to do in my life. But the wave of people-power in 1986 which led to the exile of President Ferdinand Marcos proved to be one of the most important examples of human courage of our time. My earlier beliefs were confirmed, renewed and revitalized.

I returned to the country in 1987 to watch a remarkable transition in process as Filipinos engaged in one of the first free and fair elections of their turbulent history.

I have chosen Paraguay as a second example of the strength and courage of pro-democracy forces. This tiny land-locked South American country was synonomous with the over three decade long paternalistic, authoritarian rule of General Alfredo Stroessner. In this lovely country, democracy was a dream yet to be realized. Yet a dramatic breakthrough occurred in the May, 1989 elections, even though many analysts labelled them correctly as "semi-competitive".

In spite of the unequal nature of life in that country, the seeds of freedom had been planted. Subsequently,the incremental transition to multi-partyism and pluralism has been nurtured by Paraguayan civics groups and monitored carefully by long-term observation teams over the last few years. My own experience in observing three elections in Paraguay in 1989, 1991, and 1993, has convinced me that the nurturing process has been vital in the levelling process of democratization now underway in this fascinating, colorful country. Paraguay has become a symbol of hope to all those courageous individuals struggling for human rights and democracy across the planet.

The third transition I will examine in *The Seeds of Freedom* is the dramatic struggle for independence in the former south-west African Territory of Namibia and the watershed November, 1989 Constituent Assembly elections which brought the courageous people of that new country to their rightful place among the community of nations. Since that time, Namibia has become, as one of the world's youngest democracies, a model, shining light in sub-Saharan Africa and an incredible achievement for the Namibian people who made it happen.

But the magnificent presence of the United Nations Transition Assistance Group, a force composed of thousands of military and civilian staff from over 21 countries, provided the psychological assault on discouragement which could so easily have overwhelmed this perilous, conflict-laden process. So too did the presence of thousands of observers from non-governmental organizations and donor states; missions which often fulfilled important long-term observation roles.

I was privileged to observe some of the astonishing events which unfolded in Eastern Europe after the fall of the Berlin Wall in 1989 and coinciding with the dissolution of the USSR in 1991. Two of the most important elections of this chaotic, yet hopeful period took place in Hungary and Bulgaria. I was able to observe developments in both countries and have chosen the October, 1991 elections in Bulgaria as a case for special study. I had two reasons in doing so. First, as a reminder to a too often cynical world, that in spite of the setbacks and the end to many hopeful beginnings in Eastern Europe, Bulgaria remains a bright light in a region marred by tragedy. Second, the chapter is designed as a tribute to President Zhelyu Zhelev, who was appointed an honourary patron of Liberal International in 1994 for his dedication to the emerging process of democratization and human rights both in his own country and throughout the global community at large.

15. The Philippines: The Habit of Democracy

On my arrival in Manila in February, 1986, a week prior to the "snap elections" called by President Marcos, I was overwhelmed by the tension gripping the capital city. The very air was charged with it. Filipinos were fearful, yet quietly hopeful. This was a nation living on the edge of great historic change.

I had much difficulty sleeping in the intervening days. So, I daresay, did many of the international observers who had been flown in to monitor the elections. Several days prior to the event, a number of us returned late from watching a huge rally for Cory Aquino from the roof of the Hotel Manila. It was estimated that close to one million Filipinos had been in attendance.

Many in my own delegation were not fully prepared for the violence and intimidation which, it was widely speculated, would accompany the then imminent elections. We all found ways of dealing with our apprehension throughout that long night.

Restless, I left my hotel room to walk in the park across the street. As I walked, I noticed a monument dedicated to Jose Rizal, the Father of Philippine Independence. The inscription which recorded his immortal words helped me through the ordeal of the election period and I have never forgotten them.

> I wish to show those who deny us
> patriotism,
> that if we know how to die
> for our duty and our convictions,
> What matters death
> if one dies for what one loves -
> for native land
> and adored beings.

The Philippine elections of 1986 were enormously significant because they represented a case of nearly perfect electoral abuse within a theoretically sound electoral system. The elections were so patently unfair that it was difficult to imagine any possible addition to the sheer volume of irregularities. In spite of it all, Filipinos of all walks of life participated in a remarkable democratic transition. They served notice to the world of their newly-found sense of democratic entitlement.

There have been many theories advanced for the decision of President Ferdinand Marcos to hold a quick presidential election in 1986, a decision that finally led to his undoing and subsequent exile. One of the more likely stories concerns a trip made by the head of the US Central Intelligence Agency (CIA), William Casey, to Manila in the fall of 1985. It seemed evident that Casey must have made clear to Marcos the concerns of the United States Government over the deteriorating conditions throughout the archipelago which were contributing to the increasing popularity of the insurgent New Peoples Army.

As we have seen in Chapter 11, in the background lay the considerable American strategic interests represented by the Clark and Subic Bay air and naval bases. There is no doubt that the Reagan administration was facing a classic quandary. The US wanted to provide more military assistance to counter the insurgents, but it didn't want to be accused of propping up the Marcos regime.

Elections would clearly afford the United States government some relief from the dilemma, as well as serving as a means of disarming some of the growing criticism of the corruption and rampant fraud associated with the Marcos regime in that country.[101] While President Marcos was probably not disposed to buckle under to US pressure, he evidently made the decision to capitulate based on the urgent need for increased American credits.

The political history of the Philippines, in which an oligarchic form of government by an elite-dominated Congress was the rule, not the exception, was characterized by electoral abuse. On only two occasions did that situation change: first, as a byproduct of Japanese occupation during the Second World War, and second, as a result of President Marcos' declaration of martial law in 1972.

Ferdinand Marcos had been inaugurated as President of the Philippines in 1965. But his administration had been increasingly beset by student demonstrations and violent guerrilla activities throughout the country. He imposed martial law on Sept 21, 1972, holding that subversive opposition forces had precipitated a crisis for his government. When the respected Benigno Aquino, among many others, criticized Marcos, he was jailed and held in detention for eight years. His assasination by Marcos security forces in 1983 would become the catalyst for the transformation of his courageous widow, Corazon, into a formidable political opponent in the "snap elections."

Under martial law, the president assumed extraordinary powers, which included the suspension of *habeas corpus*, as well as other fundamental rights and freedoms. In 1981, martial law was lifted. Marcos won the presidential elections of that year by a huge margin because the leading opposition parties did not participate in what they viewed to be a deeply flawed political process and one in which all the cards were stacked in favor of the President.

In 1984 elections were held for the Batasang (Parliament). By this point, Marcos was gravely ill and had suffered visible physical and mental deterioration. The kidney transplants which he had tried so desperately to keep from public knowledge had failed and Marcos had to spend extensive periods of time on the dialysis machines installed in the palace. His friends and colleagues began to speculate that he might die at any minute. Nonetheless, the President had no intention of losing the 1984 parliamentary elections which were not meant "to be free, fair orderly and honest. There seemed to be a grand design deliberately planned and executed to ensure the continued dominance of the ruling party in the national assembly."[102]

As we have seen, and as the country crumbled around him, on November 3, 1985, President Marcos announced his intention to hold a snap election. The election laws were approved on December 2, 1985 by the Batasang. That very same day, the Aquino trial ended in the acquittal of the feared Army Chief-of-Staff, General Ver, and 25 other defendants, a verdict which was condemned by Cardinal Sin and which prompted huge protest demonstrations throughout Manila. In the United States, the verdict was decried as a travesty. The following day, Corazon Aquino launched her candidacy for President, all other opposition parties uniting under her banner. She had only two months to prepare for elections which all understood would be fought on one of the most inequitable playing fields in modern history.

The Election Commission, known as COMELEC, was composed of nine members and was appointed by the President. In early January, an advance delegation of NDI-NRIIA observers visited the Philippines in order to review the electoral law. Its summary assessment was that:

> The Code and COMELEC regulations provide a comprehensive framework for the administration of a procedurally correct election. There are numerous provisions designed to protect against fraud and, if fraud occurs, to permit its detection. If problems arise in this area, it will be in the implementation of these procedures by election officials. Further, there are several provisions designed to encourage a fair campaign. However, some of the campaign-related provisions may be unrealistic in the context of this election campaign and, hence, are likely to be ignored.

After evaluating the campaign, the same observer team noted that: "in many cases the spirit of the law was ignored completely". COMELEC was blamed primarily for the simple reason that the massive disenfranchisement of voters (up to 3.5 million) itself implied a well planned, deliberate strategy. The following provides an illustration of the electoral abuse recorded by the NDI-NRIIA observer teams:

a) an atmosphere of intimidation - at some polls, "the Philippine military was running the election to suit itself. ... [in one village]... there were 10 or 12 soldiers armed with M-16 assault rifles who were clearly intimidating people to vote for Mr. Marcos". Political killings were by no means new to the Philippines but the violence seen during the 'snap' election campaign was significantly greater.

b) The problem of flying voters: as a result of fraudulent registration practices, many voters cast their ballots in numerous polling sites. It was impossible to estimate the numbers.

c) One of the safeguards to guard against multiple voting by individuals registered under one name was the use of indelible ink. Outside observers noted that the 'ink was easily wiped off by voters following its application'. Also, at some points the election administrators did not appear to be checking

115

voters fingers prior to handing them ballots. Thus it was possible for an undetermined number of voters to cast more than one ballot on election day, particularly in areas where UNIDO and NAMFREL were not well organized.

d) Vote buying was a common practice although the Marcos party did not always benefit ...'in many cases voters were given monies, acknowledged receipt of the monies, "but claimed to have voted the Aquino-Laurel ticket anyway... in this respect, the voters were following the pastoral letters circulated by the Catholic Church which advised [them]... to vote their conscience" (in this way they could take the money and vote their conscience at the same time).

At a press conference immediately on my return from the Philippines, I demonstrated the means of ensuring that those receiving payments actually voted for Marcos:

> Voters carried high-quality carbon paper into voting booths. Voters put the paper under their ballots, later turning a copy in to the people paying up to 200 pesos ($24 Canadian) a vote. The carbon copy was needed to get the second half of their bribe and guarantee the person voted the right way.[103]

Because the Marcos regime did not want a free and fair election, the spirit of the law was ignored. Massive disenfranchisement, theft of ballot boxes and blatant irregularities in the vote count ensured that the popular will of the people would not be heard.

While many observers concluded that there had to be a predetermined plan in order to engineer so much fraud, the 1986 election did have many elements of the tragicomedy about it. For example, the regime tolerated major international media coverage, and the presence of foreign election observers who freely witnessed the rampant vote buying and large scale intimidation.

It is also important to note that the Marcos regime had permitted the establishment of "citizens arms" to monitor election processes in that country. The Philippines Election Code had rendered accreditation to a group known as "The National Citizens' Movement for Free Elections" (NAMFREL).[104]

NAMFREL had already received much praise for its mobilization of volunteers to monitor the 1984 elections. The great irony in all this was that COMELEC did name NAMFREL as its "citizens' arm" for the 1986 election. Along with its monitoring assignment, NAMFREL organized over 500,000 volunteers to work on election day.

The organization trained poll watchers throughout the Philippines. It was also accused of partisanship and threatened with disaccreditation on several occasions by COMELEC. Nonetheless, that did not happen.

NAMFREL's disagreements with COMELEC over the question of "Operation Super Quick Count" reinforces the image of a vastly inefficient, almost absent-minded regime which perpetrated nearly perfect electoral abuse in spite of itself.

The "Operation Super Quick Count" was largely adopted by COMELEC from NAMFREL's experiments in 1984, at which time the quick count enabled the "citizens' arm" to gather results from the disparate regions of the Philippines far more quickly than COMELEC's count. However, in the "snap election" campaign it was not until February 5 that COMELEC and NAMFREL reached a quick count agreement. NAMFREL protested that procedures involved inhibited its ability to conduct a quick count, but it agreed nonetheless. But, "the late date at which the agreement was reached... 36 hours prior to the election... meant that many local election officials and NAMFREL volunteers were unaware of the new procedures established."[105]

Notwithstanding the delays and mutual recriminations, COMELEC and NAMFREL proceeded with their parallel, but no longer coordinated, quick counts. By Sunday evening, 48 hours after the polls closed, COMELEC had tabulated results from 28.2 percent of the precincts, while NAMFREL had tabulated results from 46.2 per cent. The results reported by COMELEC and NAMFREL, however, differed significantly. According to the COMELEC count, Marcos was leading by 150,000 votes, while NAMFREL reported Aquino leading by 750,000 votes.[106]

At this point the process stopped, largely because the count was causing grave concern to the Marcos machine, not because of the breakdown of the NAMFREL-COMELEC quick count agreement.

Marcos tried to achieve a victory by whatever means possible. Desperation can be the only possible explanation for the self-destructive urge to perpetrate massive visible abuse.

For a whole series of reasons, (not the least of which was US pressure) the regime was content to gamble everything in its efforts to showcase free and fair elections. Instead, it showcased fraud. The very strength of the electoral code made the irregularities and intimidation seem that much more appalling to outsiders. The fact that NAMFREL existed (and was soon to become a model to democratic forces around the world) was an irony. The NAMFREL "Quick Count System", as imitated by COMELEC, proved to be the joker in the deck.

NAMFREL volunteers risked much in February, 1986. They were forced from polling sites at gunpoint. They were subject to harassment, threats, and in some cases, murder. For those who braved Marcos' tanks, for those hundreds of thousands of Filipinos who gathered in the almost "festive" uprising which toppled the dictator, NAMFREL became a symbol of fixed purpose and resolve.

The magnitude of the vote fraud and intimidation in 1986 - the sheer terror perpetrated by armed gunmen in villages throughout the Philippines - has been dramatically recounted by observers.[107]

This is what we saw as we entered the tiny village of Pagalungan, observations which would later be recorded by members of my delegation:

> A faded sign indicated the turn off for Pagalungan, where we had expected to find two precincts voting. It was a modest village, a handful of wicker houses in a narrow jungle clearing with a tiny administration building and two small school buildings. No one was present. No villagers. No polling places. Nothing.
>
> Walking around the empty school building, our guide pointed to the wall and said, "Armalite." His reference was to a series of bullet holes in the wall of the school. It had been sprayed with Armalite M-16 automatic rifle fire. Our driver observed that the rifle fire must have recently occurred since the holes in the masonry had not discoloured. We decided quickly to leave the village. This silent village voted for Marcos."[108]

After leaving Pagalungan, we proceeded further up the mountain to Tagpangi. All the villagers, especially the soldiers were shocked to see us there. The place was like an armed camp. When we asked directions to the polling station, the soldiers waved their rifles with a clear indication that we were to leave.

We ignored the warning, and with some trepidation, crossed a shaky suspended footbridge to the site of the polling station which was located in a local school house. A teenage member of the Marcos militia, fanatically loyal to the President and armed with an automatic M16 assault rifle stood in the middle of the bridge. Mark Braden, then chief counsel to the National Republican Committee, and I walked over to the other side, accompanied by our guide and interpreter, Chino.

The local polling station captain was even more shocked than the soldiers to see us. In his temporary state of confusion, he invited us inside the polling station, where we observed a lot of people registering, but none actually voting. Nevertheless, the final tally was overwhelmingly in favour of Marcos.

When we emerged from the school house, Chino was agitated and obviously very concerned. "What's wrong"?, I asked. "The soldiers, they have disappeared," and he pointed nervously to the other side of the foot bridge. "So?", I said. Chino answered that they could be setting up an ambush for us down the road, then blaming it on the communist rebels, which all of us knew was a common tactic in that country.

"Walk Chino, don't run," I urged, trying to stay calm in what could be shaping up to be a moment of insanity. We all crossed the bridge, climbed into our vehicle and spoke not a word until we could see Cagayan de Oro, a much safer place in the distance.

We went immediately to speak with the leader of the NAMFREL units in the region, Father Dimitrio of Xavier University. I told him the story and asked why he didn't have any of his own people in that part of the mountains. "You went up there?", he asked incredulously. "We couldn't get anyone to go."

When I had left Manila originally to go to Cagayan de Oro in the region of Mindanao, a southern hotbed of communist insurgency, I was given the names of two people who could be helpful to me. One was Aquilino Pimentel, a local assembly-man who later became a minister in President Aquino's government. We visited his home. At the time, he was in Manila meeting with Mrs. Aquino. His wife showed us the usual Filipino hospitality. Suddenly, a young boy of 15 burst into the room. He was crying and obviously terrified. Two weeks previously, armed men had shot and killed his older brother, an opposition supporter. The boy had just been told that he was next on the list. He was pleading for sanctuary until after the election.

The other friend was Father Javier, a Jesuit priest, who was the President of Xavier University, a man with whom I felt an instant comraderie because of my strong connections with another St. Francis Xavier University on the other side of the world.[109]

Father Javier and I travelled down the coast to have lunch at a local restaurant with some others in our delegation, where, to our surprise, there were about 12 people, all of them soldiers out of uniform. They were members of the Reform Movement in the armed forces. Their leader was a mild spoken, but fiercely determined man, by the name of Calub.

Colonel Calub was the leader of the Reform Movement in Mindanao. He had been the target of much speculation during the latter years of the Marcos regime. For their personal safety, he had sent his children out of the country, but his wife preferred to stay behind with her courageous husband. In fact, I heard from others, that if Marcos had won, Calub would have been immediately arrested after the election.

I later met Colonel Calub in the little chapel at Xavier University, the day after the election. Calub and I exchanged observations about the electoral events and said good-bye. The next time I saw him was in Washington where he had been posted as the Philippine military attache under the Aquino regime.

So that chapel had a special significance for me. The evening before the election I had met Father Javier there. He had then celebrated a mass for the future of his nation, for the well-being of my family, and for my personal safety.

I served the mass. Except for the two of us, the chapel was empty. In the quiet of that special place, I became acquainted with the heart and the soul of what made that remarkable nation tick.

I shall never forget the Philippine people; their warm smiles and gentle hearts, on the one hand, and their incredible determination on the other.

I felt very sad when I left the country. It was almost as if I was abandoning them at their most crucial hour. I have vivid memories of women, nuns, men and even the very young, sitting on ballot boxes, guarding the contents with their lives. They formed human chains as they transported the boxes from one place to another. It was almost as though they saw this as their last and only chance to find democracy, to change their lives, if not for themselves, then most certainly, for their children.

It was because of the Philippine people who would not be denied their victory, that a new constitution was adopted within a year. Congressional elections were held in May, 1987. President Corazon Aquino was then at the zenith of her personal popularity. The May elections were controversial.

Opposition forces, led by former Defence Minister Juan Ponce Enrile, claimed that the ruling party had "stolen" the elections. International observers came to very different conclusions. "...the absence of violence and intimidation at the polling sites" was strikingly visible and this fact was attested to by many experienced commentators.[110]

The day after the election, following a meeting with President Aquino, I spoke to a press conference outside Malacanang Palace.

I was asked how I would characterize the differences between the 1986 and 1987 elections. "Like night and day," I responded. Later, I was taken on a tour of the palace and shown the hundreds of pairs of shoes Imelda had left as she fled. It is worth remembering that President Aquino always refused to occupy the palace.

For comparative purposes in 1987, I returned to many of the places I had observed in the tense, turbulent year before. The "silent village" of Pagalungan had returned to noisy electoral festivity in 1987. The automatic rifles were conspicuously mute. Filipinos of all walks of life celebrated the democratic transition. They had journeyed long hours together. They had risked much to secure it.

Violence continues to plague this complex, strikingly beautiful and largely impoverished archipelago. Yet later elections have been conducted with great enthusiasm and with much less fraud than those which marked previous polls. President Ramos now presides over a nation which is burgeoning and open for business. It is a country where economic prospects now look much brighter.

Mrs. Aquino's legacy has been the subject of great debate. One part of that legacy is not debatable. It is clear that under her Presidency democracy had taken residence in a country which many had thought immune to institutions of political pluralism.[111]

16. Paraguay: The Invention of Democracy

Several years later, I was invited to co-chair an observer mission to the May, 1989 elections in Paraguay, a country where, for decades, the figure of General Alfredo Stroessner had become synonymous with the lovely, land-locked South American country he governed. The son of a German immigrant, Stroessner rose in the ranks of the Paraguayan army to become a general. In 1951 he became commander-in-chief of the armed forces. Three years later, he deposed President Federico Chavez. In a subsequent election, in which General Stroessner was the only candidate, he assumed the presidency he would hold until deposed by his long-time, right hand associate, General Rodriguez, in a military coup in February, 1989.

By all standards, his tenure was remarkable; his presidency was the longest period of continuous rule by any one leader in a Latin American country.

We had all been briefed on the deeply authoritarian political culture of this one-party state. Stroessner's 34 year rule was easy to account for, we learned; he was well-known for being ruthless and repressive.[112] But there were many other reasons as well, not the least of which was Stroessner's appeal to the innate yearning of many Paraguayans for order and stability. The country was like a large extended family in which, for example, the indigenous Indian culture was preserved and cherished.

It became home, not only to the notorious Joseph Mengeles of this world, but also to hard working Mennonites from Canada who prospered throughout the decades no matter what the regime.

The tragic cycle of 143 years of war and coups preceding the General's arrival in power was a period in the history of that country which very few members of the extended family would want to see repeated.

The General epitomized the deeply personal character of Paraguayan politics. Under his guidance, the spoils system was institutionalized. It was generally based on smuggling, which in the last decade included the lucrative narcotics trade. Party officials and military officers were the principal beneficiaries of Paraguay's geopolitical significance as an important trans-shipment route for Bolivian cocaine bound for Europe and the United States.[113]

Because of, or despite Stroessner, the Paraguayan "misery index" was surprisingly low by South American standards. While the rich lived in luxury, some of the benefits did trickle down to other segments of society. Partly because of Stroessner's influence there were roads and bridges and large hydro projects with Brazil.

But on February 3rd, 1989, the General was ousted after 34 years in power. Even though he governed a nation of marginal significance which was widely regarded by most outside observers as a "Republic of Fear"[114], there was not the kind of "sponta-neous joy" one might expect in the streets of Ascuncion as he went into exile.

As it was, there was very little understanding of an alternative political path to Stroessnerism. As one analyst pointed out, "Paraguay doesn't have to restore democ-racy... Paraguay has to invent democracy."[115]

As Stroessner's political alter ego, the Colorado Party permeated all aspects of life in the oddly genteel country. Also, it seemed rather unlikely that General Rodriguez, the man who ousted him, would be a likely candidate for further democ-ratization. The two men were related through the marriage of their children. Rodriguez was considered to be the most efficient bricklayer in the construction of Stroessner's repressive system. But, as Stroessner's Second-in-Command, he was not expected to tamper with a political and economic order in which he had made a fortune, both for himself and his fellow Colorado officers and friends.

However, on assuming office, the new President took a course which few would have predicted. Rodriguez set out to expand and enlarge trade ties within the region, and that meant he had to improve his country's poor reputation abroad. Paraguay's notoriety as a human rights violator was well established throughout the global community. There was no doubt that the increasing insistence in Western states regarding the linkage between human rights observances and bilateral trade ties was the cause for the Rodriguez turn-around.

General Stroessner had himself been gravely wounded by the criticism of his regime expressed by successive US administrations. His reaction was always the same. Had he not served as a model champion of containment during the Cold War? Was this insistence on human rights reforms not a slap in the face to a true ally and friend - to all those Paraguayan delegations which had been such supporters of Ameri-can interests in the UN and the OAS?[116]

The real problems began when President Jimmy Carter announced in 1976 that, under his administration, advancement of human rights was to be the soul of Ameri-can foreign policy. But in spite of Mr. Carter's very strong signals, General Stroessner continued to thumb his nose at the super-power, remaining intransigent against all outside pressures for democratization.

The early Reagan years represented a return to the *status quo ante* but in his second term, the human rights issue arose again. The President included Paraguay, along with Chile, Cuba and Nicaragua in a list of Latin America's remaining dictator-ships.[117] In 1987, the United States government withdrew the trade benefits allotted under the generalized system of preferences, because of the Stroessner government's continued refusal to grant even minimal rights to organized labour.

A year later, the US Congress came very close to decertifying Paraguay as a candidate for US aid under the terms of the Anti-Drug Abuse Act of 1986. The impact of these kinds of anticipated sanctions would probably not have been that great in strictly quantitative terms, as Paraguay received only minimal military and economic assistance from the US at the time.

In terms of the impact of strict economic and trade sanctions, Brazilian insistence on a democratic transition in Paraguay could have had a much larger bearing on the regime. But as it was, the moral pressures and global clout of the United States turned out to be the critical and deciding factor. That was the conclusion arrived at by most analysts in the immediate aftermath of the February, 1989 coup, and the subsequent surprise announcement by President Rodriguez that elections would be held on May 1.

The overnight decision led to a remarkable series of events in a country where democracy had yet to be invented. The provisional government had to establish conditions which would facilitate the forthcoming electoral process. The initial steps taken illustrated the total absence of a democratic culture in that country. The government had to re-open several independent media outlets to show some semblance of respect for freedom of speech and opinion. There had to be at least a token realization of the rights of freedom of assembly and association. Political parties with the exception of the Communist party, had to be legalized. Provision had to be made for a period of voter registration.

Raul Morodo, a member of the European Parliament from Spain, commented on the political situation in Paraguay after a visit there in early March, 1989.[118] Following his consultation with a cross-section of Paraguayans, including several well known dissidents, Morodo concluded that what he saw was: "...not a clear transition to democracy, but an initial step towards the liberalisation of the regime."

He pointed out that General Rodriguez "... who is without a democratic history and, according to reports has obscure financial connections (smuggling, drugs) ... needs international legitimisation". The May 1st elections were important to the Colorado Party, he argued, because "... they not only want to win, but their victory will be connected to the electoral participation by opposition forces." This was a telling comment, because Morodo saw clearly that the "democratic forces" in Paraguay really could not win in the political landscape then extant, and that the regime intended to manipulate them into a highly unfair and inequitable process.

Morodo felt that the Colorado Party would secure at least 62 percent of the popular vote and that the opposition had little chance of increasing its electoral support. "Fear", he wrote, "was still a factor which counteracts the dissenting opposition".

Very few observers were fooled by General Rodriguez' attempts to acquire a seal of international approval through the specific means of "democratic" elections. Clearly, the attempts at liberalisation were merely transparent signals indicating that democratization was only surface deep.

However, a liaison group from Canada was more hopeful.[119] Its report praised General Rodriguez, calling him a liberator from the dark Stroessner era. Canadian reports emphasized the positive feelings of the British Ambassador, John Macdonald, who had said that the actions taken by the new President to de-politicize the army were significant and progressive steps in the direction of democratization. As well, the initial reforms on the political/human rights front provided compelling evidence that Rodriguez intended to reform the system for the better.

In April 1989, the International Human Rights Law Group published a report which attempted to determine whether the minimal conditions for a "free and fair election" existed in Paraguay.[124] The report concluded that pre-election conditions fell short of international standards. The exacting analysis summarized the situation this way:

> ...there is insufficient time for newly legalized and formed political parties to campaign to present their views to the people - most parties lack access to TV; insufficient safeguards to ensure no fraudulent voting and to ensure that eligible voters names actually appear on voting lists ... serious questions regarding the impartiality of the electoral institutions that supervise the voter registration... voting and vote counting for the entire electoral process is officially dominated by the Colorado Party, a participant in the upcoming election.

The Law Group concluded that despite the observed deficiencies, there was reason to hold some "cautious optimism" that the May elections would be the first step in the transition to democracy.

Most analysts of the pre-election period tended to take the same view. On arrival in the country, I immersed myself in the great debates then ongoing, and was fortunate enough to do so in the company of the distinguished Eduardo Frei of Chile. He was my co-leader on that mission and I recall, while now thinking of his present success, that Brian Atwood predicted at the time that Frei would one day become President of Chile.

By 1989, my personal interest in election observing was increasing by leaps and bounds. A telephone call from one of my sons, David, himself an adventuresome young man, brought this fact closer to home. He had read in a Toronto newspaper that I was to co-lead a delegation to the presidential election in Paraguay with Frei and former US Congressman Bruce Morrison. I had also been invited to participate in monitoring the elections in Panama one week later.

At first glance, the geography and timing seemed perfect. But the election in Panama was on the same day as my son Bill's graduation from St Francis Xavier University - an event to which we all looked forward with great anticipation. So I missed Panama, but was rewarded, not only by Bill's success, but also by David's exuberant company in Paraguay, a trip he financed himself.

Upon our arrival, we found considerable support among the opposition parties in favour of boycotting the elections, because Rodriguez would not postpone the polling and make major changes in the electoral laws. The system of proportional representation built into the Paraguayan Electoral Law (Article 8), whereby the party which received the most votes would get two thirds of the seats of both Houses of Congress, proved to be particularly offensive.

The provisional government refused all requests to strike Article 8, no matter how vocal the opposition criticism became. It refused the right to the formation of alliances among opposition forces. As criticism mounted with regard to the inequities of the electoral process, opposition demands for postponement were met with a wall of silence.

Some headway was made, however. Under persistent pressures, the Rodriguez government did permit the extension of the period of voter registration, as well as the legal recognition of political parties. The right of the opposition parties to have access to government radio was conceded. Unfortunately, time allocation was blatantly and unfairly contrived to the advantage of the Colorado Party.

Although some progress on the electoral front had been made, the report of the Law Group provided convincing evidence that it was insufficient to meet with international standards. In fact, there were those at the time who felt that the decision to send international monitoring teams to observe the Paraguayan elections, only served to advance the international credibility of Stroessnerism without Stroessner. Others suggested that the presence of observers raised false expectations among opposition forces in an unfair and inequitable electoral contest.

For example, the National Accord, the alliance of opposition parties in Paraguay, did decide to participate even though there was no major change in the Electoral Law, and with the fullest recognition that the whole process was stacked against them.

There were solid reasons, both for their frustration and continuing threats to withdraw from the process. As I have recounted above, observers encouraged the respected Domingo Laino, the leader of the Authentic Radical Liberal Party, to stay in the process. The Colorado Party would, and did, finally win - with 73 percent of the vote - to no-one's surprise. But Laino did win a voice in the Senate and with this, the process of democratization could begin, albeit, very slowly.

It is true that the 1989 event was a classic example of a semi-competitive election, but it was the first, hesitating step in a country where civilian structures were unknown.

There were no guarantees that the movement towards democracy would flourish. That would be dependent on the will of the Paraguayan people, and, the unlikely possibility that the Rodriguez regime would act as an agent of that will. To the surprise of many, further democratisation was in store.

Two years later, Paraguay held its first ever municipal elections. In view of the 1989 experience, observers expected the worst. What they saw in May, 1991, was in many ways remarkable.

The victory of some opposition candidates, particularly that of an independent candidate in the hotly contested mayoralty election in the capital city of Asuncion, vied with the recent history of what was, essentially, a one party state. The municipal elections marked an increased recognition of the right to political participation of individual citizens.

An international delegation organized by the National Democratic Institute put it this way: "Paraguay's local governments are now representative of the country's political spectrum. The newly elected city councils will provide forums to democratic debate and determine public policies that effect Paraguayans daily."

Observers saw a sense of entitlement to genuine people-derived government in all the regions of the country. It was an explosion of consciousness which left very few of us dry-eyed. In fact, many veterans of the 1989 elections would not have believed such a groundswell of conviction to be possible in such a short period of time.

But the evolving citizenry of that country clearly did. In the Presidential elections of 1993, the determination of Paraguayans to support the democratic process remained strong and resolute, in spite of the legacy of suspicion and distrust which continued to haunt the electoral process and embitter the political elites.

Whether all this means the habit of democracy will take up residence in this former republic of fear, remains a question for historians of the future possessed of the gift of hindsight. But for now, the "invention of democracy" chugs along the track, and the engine is the spirit of the Paraguayan people.

17. Namibia: A Marvellous Devotion to Democracy

When our pre-electoral mission arrived in Namibia in June of 1989, on the eve of the November Constituent Assembly elections, I thought of the words of one of the many writers on the subject who clearly had difficulty in understanding the significance of this massive desert-like terrain. The writer concluded that "when the Lord made Namibia, he intended it for obscurity." The tiny population, estimated at the time to be 1.23 million of which 78,000 were white, seemed to validate the judgement. Geopolitics and history, however, had determined otherwise.

Namibia had its origins in the great European rush to carve up the continent of Africa in the 19th century. South West Africa, as it was then known, became Germany's first colony on the continent. It would become a mandate of the League of Nations upon Germany's loss of the First World War. But South Africa, in effect, administered the protectorate. When the Second World War led to the eclipse of the League and its replacement by the United Nations, the South African government challenged the UN's authority on the legal grounds that the mandate had lapsed with the death of the League. Subsequently, the International Court of Justice ruled that the UN had final control over Namibia, and in 1966 the world body itself ruled that South Africa's continuing occupation was illegal.

The extension of the apartheid society of South Africa into occupied Namibia was itself an important issue which led to Pretoria's increasing estrangement from world opinion. As Pretoria continued to divide Namibians along racial lines, it enforced its policies with police and military garrisons. The South West African Peoples Organization (SWAPO), rose up against this oppression and conducted an over two decade long armed struggle against South African forces.

It was clear to all of us, as we assembled in the resource rich, strategic territory that June, that we were on the moving edge of history. Yet we were novices in the rites of passage that Namibians would undergo in the attempt to end over a century of colonial rule. We felt like actors on a vast international stage peopled by a bewildering cast of characters. We were soon to discover that nearly every global conflict was played out on Namibian soil in one act or another.[121]

The complexity of the situation almost defies description. The United Nations quarrel with South Africa over control of Namibia was of long duration. But because of its location, Namibia was also central to larger regional conflicts played out against the backdrop of the Cold War and the subsequent thaw in East-West relations.

The situation in Angola, Namibia's tormented northern neighbor, remained a constant source of concern to the South African government. Angola became a battle ground for indigenous tribal factions after it achieved independence from Portuguese rule in 1974. Some of the factions developed ideological kinships abroad. By the early 1980's, for example, over fifty thousand Cubans were assisting in the defence of the beleaguered ruling party, a Marxist coalition with backing from the USSR.

The reverberations of this conflict shook an already nervous South Africa to the core. SWAPO had bases in Angola and in Zambia. When the UN recognised SWAPO as the authentic voice of the Namibian peoples, the apartheid regime recoiled in a paroxysm of rage.

Nonetheless, the South African government made the important decision to support the implementation of UN Resolution 435,adopted by the Security Council on September 29, 1978, which outlined the steps towards Namibian independence. The reason was simple. The counter insurgency war the apartheid regime had been waging for 20 years had created intolerable economic burdens and had become, in this sense, politically unsustainable. It must be remembered that South Africa was engaged at the time, not only in combatting domestic strife, but in a massive regional struggle against anti-apartheid frontline states.

Over the years, the UN continued its efforts to implement 435, but the major problem in doing so was the linkage of the Territory's independence to the withdrawal of Cuban troops from Angola. Finally, on December 22, 1988, two historic agreements were signed at UN Headquarters after over eight months of back-breaking US backed negotiations. Angola and Cuba signed a bilateral document on the withdrawal of Cuban troops. Then, South Africa approved a tripartite text which implicitly acknowledged the principle of linkage and set out the important elements of the independence process. This meant, in turn, the staged withdrawal of Cubans from Angola, and South Africans from Namibia.

On January 17, 1989, the Security Council passed resolution 629 setting April 1st, 1989 as the beginning of the Namibian independence process and the implementation of Resolution 435. Preparations to deploy the massive United Nations Transition Assistance Group began immediately. With a 4,650 strong military force contributed by 21 countries, a $416.2 million budget and about 2,000 civilian staff, including electoral supervisors and professional police officers, UNTAG was widely acknowledged to be the largest UN force deployed since the Congo operations of the early 1960s.

The UNTAG mission was to oversee the release of political prisoners, repeal discriminatory laws, launch a huge voter registration process, supervise the return of refugees, monitor the ceasefire, and ensure the electoral process in Namibia was free and fair. This was truly a herculean task. By mid-November, the last of the South African troops were scheduled to leave, along with the first contingents of the UNTAG force. Namibia's Independence day was foreseen to be April 1, 1990. The last UNTAG worker would leave the world's youngest democracy on that day.

Mr. Martti Ahtisaari, the Special Representative of the UN Secretary-General in Namibia had no illusions about the huge problems which, at the time of the deployment of the UNTAG forces still lay ahead.

In fact, at the time of our arrival, Ahtisaari was still under heavy fire for what was viewed as the lacklustre UNTAG response to the April 1st SWAPO "violations" of the cease-fire agreement. SWAPO had its own account of the incident, of course. This included a claim of self-defence against attacks by South African forces south of the 16th parallel.

The fast track to independence suffered from early, nearly disastrous problems. Resolution 435 and the complex Settlement Plan which accompanied it had provided for the restriction of South African and SWAPO armed forces to bases, and confirmed that the UN would "monitor the restriction to base of the armed forces of the parties concerned."[122] The Settlement Plan led to great confusion, however. A staged withdrawal of South African troops was foreseen, but it outlined no specific location for these bases. As it was, 15 hundred troops were to remain in Namibia, restricted to two bases until the election results were known.

Further confusion stemmed from the provisions with regard to the peaceful return of SWAPO guerillas through specific entry points, at which time they would participate freely in the independence process. But South Africa rejected any interpretation of the Settlement Plan which recognized the pre-existence of SWAPO bases inside Namibia and remained intransigent on the issue.

On April 1st, SWAPO incursions from bases in Namibia were timed to coincide with the implementation of Resolution 435. These forced the process off track and fuelled the already substantial fears of a nervous South Africa. With this, South Africa became even more committed to iron clad control of the transition process.

The security interests of South Africa dictated that Louis Pienaar, the South African appointed Administrator General of Namibia, had both legislative and executive responsibilities with virtually no constitutional limitations on his powers. Only the government of South Africa could remove him.

My delegation felt the excitement and anticipation, as well as the sense of mistrust and apprehension in the air immediately upon our arrival. We were there at the request of the United Nations. NDI had been asked to assess the pre-electoral process, and perhaps produce some recommendations for changes in the Electoral Law to keep the process on track.

Upon arrival, the delegation split up into groups, and headed off to different regions of the country to monitor feelings with regard to the situation.

I went up to Ovamboland on the Angolan border. In flight, the pilot informed us that we were flying at tree-top level to avoid possible ground-to-air missiles. A little later, a hefty Irishman by the name of Peter Fitzgerald in the UNTAG force asked me how high I estimated we had, in fact, been flying. He thought my estimate of 50 feet was a little exaggerated. "That high?" he asked jokingly.

More surprises awaited. One of my contacts was a Lutheran minister from Finland by the name of Olof Erikson. He felt we should interview one of the headmen of a neighbouring tribal community. We took the back roads at my request. As we navigated the terrain, the minister described the fierce fighting in the area as a result of the then recent April 1 SWAPO incursions from Angola. I asked where the UN soldiers were located. "They don't come here", my friend told me. "They don't yet have the casspirs"; that is, the huge steel reinforced trucks which could withstand the blast of a land mine. But surely there aren't any land mines where we're travelling?" I asked. When he replied in the affirmative, I asked what in the hell we were doing there. "But I know the way," he responded confidently.

The Namibian delegation was one of the most talented I have ever had the good fortune to lead. The Chief Electoral Officer from Barbados, Mr. Dennis Smith, and the Joint Secretary of the Election Commission of Pakistan, Mr. Mohammad Humayun Khan provided us with expert counsel. The Clerk of the Assembly in Botswana, Mr Charles Mokobi, and Masipula Sithole of Zimbabwe, were distinguished and respected members of our team. Frederic Cowan, then Attorney General of the State of Kentucky, was a pillar of strength. Patricia Keefer has always been a reliable and dedicated source of expertise in the many fine missions NDI has organized over the years.

I remember being very impressed by a young Harvard Law professor who was part of the mission at the time. Upon his return to the United States, Christopher Edley, Jr. wrote an article which beautifully encapsulated the feelings of the entire delegation.

He reflected on the "marvellous devotion to democracy" which existed in Namibia, a nation of approximately 600,000 people speaking over 20 languages. For all of us who had travelled the country, that spirit was all-consuming.

Namibia was a violent, unhappy country caught up in a geopolitical nightmare, yet Namibians themselves showed resolution in the struggle towards the democratic transition. These were people who often had never worn shoes, nomadic bushmen, those who could grow sorghum in the dust. This was a nation to whom constitutional values were, in theory, largely unknown. Yet this very evident devotion to democracy existed. All of us who had the privilege to work in Namibia were greatly moved by it.

But, Edley warned, the major threat to the transition was the climate of intimidation, perpetrated by all sides, but most visibly so by the South African trained counter-insurgency force known as "KOEVOET".

While UN Resolution 435 and the complex Settlement Plan which accompanied it had required the dissolution of the force, KOEVOET alumni had, in the meantime simply acquired new uniforms in SWAPOL. (South Western African Police).

UNTAG "represents protection against government abuse ...people believe that UNTAG has come to save us (them)"... Edley mused in citing the commentary of Namibians he interviewed.[123]

Clearly, UNTAG was seen to be all things to all people. Because of that, very few people envied the Special Representative's job. Mr. Ahtisaari's powers to supervise and control the transition process were all vaguely defined. The Special Representative had to ensure that the elections were conducted in a free, fair manner, all the while taking care to ensure that the other provisions of the general UN scheme for Namibia, such as amnesty law and the repeal of discriminatory legislation were respected.

Furthermore, he had to force the process to a halt if he felt Louis Pienaar was attempting to subvert the electoral process. Mr. Ahtisaari, largely because of the complexity of the assignment he had undertaken, as well as the ambiguity surrounding his mandate at large was to become the object of much international criticism. Most of this was entirely unfair and failed to take into account the dimensions of a nearly impossible assignment.

As it was, Mr. Ahtisaari did draw much criticism for his hesitant responses to Mr. Pienaar's draft electoral laws. It was clear that they were unacceptable to the international community. In response to widespread criticism, the Special Representative eventually insisted on substantial changes which were ultimately incorporated in the final election law. But the resultant delay in the official promulgation of the law, until October 13, 25 days before the first day of balloting, threatened the agreed upon timetable and hence the credibility of the process.

But he had other problems to contend with as well. The provisions of UNTAG's mandate were often vague and ill-defined. There was, for example, no reference to police monitoring in the Settlement Plan. As it was, SWAPOL was highly suspicious about the role of the UN Civilian Police (CIVPOL). This led to a situation which approached almost comic proportions at times. When civilian police from some of the 23 countries that were represented complained about the excesses of KOEVOET,[124] SWAPOL had some difficulty in taking them seriously.

Resolution 435 had been drafted in a specific historical context, with terms of reference which changed dramatically as time passed. For example, its authors had foreseen military confrontation to be the major obstacle to the transition process. In fact, the real problem became that of intimidation.

Because of this, Mr. Ahtisaari had to triple the number of CIVPOL police. The UN civilian police were constrained by the limitations of a "monitoring role". It is generally forgotten today that UNTAG had to monitor the border areas as well as confine to base the South African defence force troops in Namibia. CIVPOL had to monitor the actions of SWAPOL and the dreaded counter insurgency faction KOEVOET.

It is true that UNTAG never obtained the complete cooperation of SWAPOL in arresting incidents of intimidation, and the latter continued to be a serious problem throughout the campaign. Critics insisted UNTAG should have been more aggressive in demanding the cooperation of SWAPOL. It must be remembered, however, that UNTAG would not have been able to fulfil its reconciliation mandate, without the cooperation of South Africa and its agent, Louis Pienaar.

Mindful as we were of the difficulties faced by UN officials in Namibia, my delegation was unanimous in its conviction that a very unlevel playing field existed with regard to the unravelling of the electoral process. We felt that the Special Representative would have to exercise his full responsibilities under Resolution 435 to keep the process on track. At the time we presented our report to the Special Representative of the Secretary General (SRSG), we believed that Louis Pienaar had the upper hand.

The report recommended 13 changes to the then highly unsatisfactory Electoral Law,[125] 75 percent of which were accepted. Needless to say, this was an occasion to advance democratic development of which I was most proud. In a phrase, we had the opportunity to level the playing field considerably.

The report, and its virtually complete adoption and implementation, is a good example of the kind of mediator role observer missions often play. It is reproduced here in full, as I delivered it verbally to Mr. Ahtisaari and key members of his team at a meeting at the UNTAG headquarters in Windhoeck:

NATIONAL DEMOCRATIC INSTITUTE FOR INTERNATIONAL AFFAIRS REPORT TO MARTII AHTISAARI, UN SPECIAL REPRESENTATIVE (WINDHOECK, NAMIBIA - JUNE 5, 1989)

As citizens of six countries of the community of nations, we are pleased to present this report to you. It is based on our own personal observations in Namibia over the past seven days.

It is designed to provide you as objective a view as humanly possible of the election procedures currently in place or being contemplated for Namibia's election this November. In the report, we provide some recommendations which we hope will assist you in achieving the free and fair elections that are the foundation of a democratic society.

Although our visit to Namibia has been short, we believe that our observations and recommendations merit your attention. Each member of our delegation has had significant experience in the election process in our own countries.

We found a sense of wonder and awe in the citizens throughout Namibia; being present at the birth of a nation is a rare and special moment in history, and Namibians are universally excited and eager to carry on with the election process.

On the other hand, we found a number of distressing strains in the national fabric that threaten to rip apart and unravel the entire election process. These strains, if not repaired, could cause a nation with great hopes and expectations to be tragically stillborn.

An atmosphere of distrust permeates the political scene. None of the major political parties trust one another; few trust the Administrator General to adequately and impartially administer the elections. Regrettably, I must say, some do not even trust the United Nations Transitional Assistance Group.

A startling lack of communications about proposed election laws and procedures is also evident. Key actors in the process seem at times to be communicating only through rumour. A sense of participation in the process of developing the laws regulating the election is noticeably missing. Uncertainty about the process is rampant.

Finally, and most seriously, an atmosphere of intimidation seems to hang over the country like a great sword. Charges and countercharges of intimidation seem to be uppermost on the political parties agendas. Rumours, as well as actual instances of intimidation, fuel a fire of distrust, suspicion, and anxiety. If unchecked, these rumours and instances of intimidation could be disastrous.

We believe that as the United Nations Special Representative, you must move quickly to assert firm supervision and control of the election process as contemplated by Resolution 435. We believe that virtually every citizen of Namibia desires to see the election take place on schedule and is willing to take steps to ensure free and fair elections. Resolute leadership is necessary to secure that goal.

We are honoured to be able to participate in this small way in a noble endeavour. We hope that our report will be useful to you, the Administrator General and the citizens of Namibia. Our greatest satisfaction will come from the birth in November of a free, peaceful and democratic nation.

Intimidation

The atmosphere of suspicion, mistrust and fear easily leads to intimidation of individual voters to such an extent that some feel they may not cast their ballots freely and with confidence-that their votes will remain secret. Under paragraph 10 of the Settlement Proposal (S/12636) the Special Representative is directed "to take steps to guarantee against the possibility of intimidation or interference with the electoral process from whatever quarter." Immediate steps are essential to carry out that responsibility.

The NDI delegation considered reports and allegations from six different regions of the country it visited, as well as press reports and other information provided by party leaders, community leaders and UNTAG personnel in Windhoek. It is important to note that misconduct was reported or alleged on behalf of at least two of the major political parties.

Some of the allegations and reports included police attendance at political rallies with an unnecessary show of force; individuals threatened with abduction of their children; violence at political rallies; destruction of crops and houses for failure to demonstrate political support; disruption and politicisation of the educational process; and concern that all weapons of demobilized commandoes may not have been returned to authorities.

In addition, NDI delegates have a special concern based upon numerous reports and observations in the northern part of the country. Despite the official disbanding of the counter-insurgency-force, KOEVOET, the units "assimilation" into existing forces has clearly not removed the threat citizens feel. The fear of KOEVOET looms large in the minds of citizens.

In fact, the delegates received reports that KOEVOET members have remained as operating units within SWAPOL. No factor contributes more to the atmosphere of intimidation. Press reports of shootings by police at Onankali this very day underscore our concerns.

Given these widespread allegations and reports, it is not surprising that an atmosphere of intimidation exists that threatens to undermine the guarantee of free and fair elections. We believe the following steps are imperative:

First, remnants of the KOEVOET must be removed from SWAPOL immediately. You, Sir, should insist on this without compromise in order to discharge your responsibilities under the Settlement Proposal. All necessary steps must be taken to ensure that former KOEVOET members, once removed from SWAPOL, do not continue, as civilians, to intimidate and harass those with whom they disagree.

Second, SWAPOL must revise operational procedures to conform with accepted police practices. In particular, the use of casspirs in routine police patrols, and at political rallies, are psychologically intimidating. Moreover, the use of casspirs, especially those with cannon or machine guns, is a violation of the Settlement Proposal: "The police forces would be limited to the carrying of small arms in the normal performance of their duties." (S/12636,para.9) SWAPOL should be absolutely impartial. Its officers should not engage in any political activity whatsoever, and in controlling crowds, should be scrupulously nonpartisan.

Third, the Commission of Inquiry into Intimidation must be assured sufficient investigatory and other resources. It should complete its investigations expeditiously if it is to enjoy public confidence. The Commission should interpret its mandate broadly to investigate patterns or practices of intimidation, rather than limiting its attention to individual complaints.

Fourth, UNTAG officials must take more decisive action to satisfy themselves that all complaints of intimidation receive prompt, fair and thorough attention from SWAPOL, the Commission on intimidation, prosecutors and magistrates. UNTAG police monitors should assert and exercise authority to accompany SWAPOL investigators and review investigative files. If necessary, UNTAG should supplement SWAPOL investigations or undertake investigations on its own, referring the results to prosecutors, or to the Commission on Intimidation, when appropriate. Exercising this authority is essential if you are to discharge your responsibilities under paragraph 10 of the Settlement Proposal.

Media

The mass media will be indispensable in voter education. Because SWABC is, in effect controlled by the government, it has special obligations to be impartial and to educate voters in the mechanics of registration and balloting. Radio is particularly crucial because so many voters are illiterate and population density is so low.

We understand there are, as yet, no comprehensive plans or principles shaping SWABC's role in this all-important election. We make the following recommendations:

First, SWABC should provide an equal amount of time, in comparable time periods, to every registered party.

Second, SWABC should apply the principles of fairness, balance and access in news reporting, commentary, and the sale of advertising time to political parties.

Third, UNTAG should take immediate advantage of the time allotted it by SWABC TV and Radio.

Election Procedures

During the past seven days we studied the electoral process, including the proposed methods of voter registration, election procedures and counting of votes. We paid particular attention to the draft registration law and the planning underway by the AG's office.

We appreciate the enormous challenge facing those responsible for the election, and we commend their intentions and efforts to design a process that will withstand the strictest scrutiny. However, we find the planned mechanisms for registration, voting and the counting of ballots to be unnecessarily complex and time consuming. This creates a perceived risk of manipulation and potential abuse.

The centralized registration and voting system creates possibilities for fraud. The plan for verifying voter identity and counting ballots is cumbersome, unnecessary, and jeopardizes ballot secrecy. The time involved in the process - a minimum of two weeks - will undoubtedly give rise to allegations of tampering. It is also a serious impediment to assuring the peaceful acceptance of the results of the election since it invites charges of fraud and manipulation of the results.

We recommend that the AG establish an Independent Election Commission "to give all political parties and interested persons, without regard to their political views, a full and fair opportunity to organize and participate in the electoral process." (S/12636, para.6)

The members of the Commission should be appointed by the Administrator General, subject to the approval of the Special Representative.

The Commission would be responsible for the administration of all aspects of the election process. This recommendation is consistent with the approach taken by the AG in establishing the Independent Commission of Inquiry into Intimidation.

Election commissions are common throughout the world. They exist primarily to ensure public trust in the system. Their effectiveness depends on their independence. They should be people who do not have a stake in the outcome of the election. For this reason, it is critical that the appointees of the Commission be universally regarded as individuals of unquestioned integrity.
We believe that this simple step will in itself, greatly enhance the likelihood of free and fair elections in Namibia.

Conclusions

Namibians and members of the international community are grateful to the people who come from many areas of the globe as part of the United Nations force to keep the peace and assist in the implementation of Resolution 435.

Most everyone, especially the younger generation in this country, have placed their hopes in 435. All they want is a stable society in which they can get on with their lives.

In the long history of these negotiations there has always been time. What is needed is the combined efforts of all concerned and the human will to succeed. If the United Nations does not succeed this time, we may not have another Namibia to save in the future.[126]

When I presented our recommendations to the Special Representative, I felt his resolve to act in accord with our conclusions strengthen. Later, I spoke with Mr. Ahtisaari's top aide, Cedric Thornberry, and asked him how he thought the meeting went. "You had a lot of people on our side cheering you on", he said. I then asked him how he thought we'd do in our meetings with Louis Pienaar the next day. "He'll pee on you from great heights", he responded.

Fortunately, that was not to be. The Administrator General was direct and, of course, very much the spokesman for South African security interests. He was extremely sensitive about our commentary with regard to the presence of KOEVOET in the region. Pienaar praised the force as the salvation of the country, calling its members heros who had courageously resisted the incursions from Angola.

He was also somewhat critical of my remarks concerning the control exercised by the government of South Africa over the broadcasting system (SWABC) in Namibia. He continued to insist on its fundamental independence, but gradually became more receptive, as we pointed out to him that radio was the most important means of educating people about democracy, particularly in the remote areas. Therefore, we pressed, the political parties had to be assured equal time in order to curtail mounting international criticism of the obvious control exercised by his government over SWABC.

This had become a fundamental embarrassment for South Africa and it was clear that Pienaar had to back down over the further pressures created by our delegation report. All in all, while the meeting was difficult, it was enormously constructive and was conducted in an atmosphere of mutual respect. The acceptance of the bulk of the recommendations was proof enough that the long hours had paid off for all of us.

The successful conclusion of the process in November was ultimately a triumph for UNTAG and was a personal triumph for Martii Ahtisaari. His resolution in the face of enormous pressure led to free and fair elections for Namibia, and in increased credibility for the United Nations itself. But we must remember that none of this could have been possible without the eventual, if grudging, cooperation of Louis Pienaar.

Despite the overwhelming challenges presented by the Namibian transition, the UN accomplished a great deal. It can be argued that Namibia proved to be a catalyst to a more activist, multifunctional role for UN civilian peacekeeping and monitoring efforts. The day to day negotiations between a complex series of actors, for the UN had installed operations paralleling many of the functions of the domestic government itself, led to free and fair elections. Considering Namibia's tragic history this was a remarkable outcome.

UNTAG's presence gave people confidence that the process would work. The international team repatriated 42,000 Namibians from 46 countries. UNTAG provided administrative assistance at all levels, and demanded an internationally acceptable Electoral Law. It monitored every step in the final balloting and counting phases of the Namibian elections.

In fact, the very thought of the UN and Resolution 435 contributed to the "sense of entitlement" and the clear-eyed resolution held by Namibians. Resolution 435 became an infectious and symbolic number in that country. There were 435 parties, and 435 townhall meetings, and 435 sports events, and 435 dances.

And then there was the story of the little girl who, when asked what she wanted to be, responded gravely, "a nurse". She was 14 years of age and had never gone to school. When asked how she intended to get to where she wanted without an education, her face filled with delight and confidence as she recited the magic numbers, "4-3-5." Enforcing 435 was difficult - but its significance was almost supernatural.

The presence of the blue berets and many non-governmental organizations, such as our own, helped broker the democratic process in that country.[131] But in the final analysis, however, it was the "wonderful devotion to democracy" in the hearts and minds of Namibians which made the process work.

The Republic of Namibia has gone on to a marked period of stability under one of the most liberal constitutions anywhere. The governing SWAPO has busily courted international investors and abandoned its doctrinaire socialist past. An unvengeful black government now woos Afrikaners with a policy of national reconciliation. With the election of a new, free government in South Africa, the expectations are for a further continuation of pluralist democracy in a country which stands as a beacon of hope for pro-democracy forces across the continent. For those of us who served in Namibia, this was one process that really worked.

18. Bulgaria: A Bright Light in a Dark Place

There are always special times in history when empires come to an end. A revolutionary spirit builds in the hearts and minds of all those who awaken to a springtime of hope. The contagion which gathered strength in 1989 amongst ordinary Czechs and Russians and Bulgarians and Romanians drew potency from the drama played out in Tiananmen Square, in the Peoples Republic of China - a place where compliance to the system was widely viewed as mechanical. The shock waves of a million Chinese demonstrating in the wake of the oppression, demanding something better than the system they knew, had a cumulative impact in Eastern Europe.

In 1989 the Berlin Wall came down, but that was only a symbol of the feeling throughout the Eastern Bloc that democracy was an idea worth coming out in the streets for. And they did, in the hundreds of thousands. It was clear the Soviet Empire, never a natural entity and held together by Soviet military might and an ideology which contained the seeds of its own destruction, was on the eve of thunderous disintegration. The year 1989 will always have a special aura in history because it coincided with the remarkable possibilities for change and transformation carried within the human spirit. In 1789, something similar happened. So too in 1848-49. So too in 1917-19 and 1968.[127]

As in most revolutionary periods, the floodlamps of transition usually focus on a few courageous individuals. It is clear that the last General-Secretary of the Comunist Party of the Union of Soviet Socialist Republics, Mikhail Gorbachev, was one of these. He understood that Soviet control in Europe would have to end and that the USSR had "overstretched" itself militarily and financially. It was clear that the Marxist-Leninist system would need drastic revolutionary change from within, because like most imperial systems in history, it was dying of suffocation.

Its high priests and party apparatchiks had learned nothing and forgotten nothing. Many, indeed, could not understand the hatred and contempt in which they were held. In *Darkness at Noon*, Arthur Koestler described the almost pathetic lack of understanding of the mass disaffection from the totalitarian systems the apparatchiks represented. "All our principles were right, but our results were wrong...our will was hard and pure, we should have been loved by the people. But they hate us. Why are we so odious and detested?"

The groundswell of reform which swept across Eastern Europe in the aftermath of the dismantling of the Berlin Wall had dramatic implications for the Balkans as well. After four decades of totalitarian rule, Bulgaria was rife with thoughts of reform. The Communist Party, or the Bulgarian Socialist Party (BSP), as it was called, had developed a Euro-Socialist orientation and was receptive to Gorbachev's new thinking. Bulgaria had the equivalent of a Western middle class and the Party had developed a successful industrial base. A substantial proportion of the population had access to higher education. Bulgaria had become a part of the Soviet empire which was richer and more developed than the imperial power itself.

Nonetheless, in the late 1980s, there was a great upsurge in political activity and a number of opposition groups began to emerge. Anti-government demonstrations increased in both size and volatility and on November 10, 1989, long-time party chief Todor Zhivkov was removed from office. Only a few days later, a mass demonstration of over 100,000 protestors in Sophia tipped the scales. It had become clear that the movement towards democratic reform could not be resisted. Yet, when the BSP called for elections to be held in June, 1990, most Bulgarians were justifiably suspicious. In a country where brutal intimidation had been the rule, not the exception, the idea of holding free, fair elections seemed a pipe dream at best.

The election campaign was of short duration, and this had its greatest impact on the fledgling opposition parties. In December, 1989, the co-ordinating organization known as the Union of Democratic Forces (UDF) - which embraced several dissident and independent groups - was formed, with the widely respected Dr. Zhelyu Zhelev as Chairman.

Dr. Zhelev was best known for his philosophical works and treatises which in the earlier years directly attacked Leninist principles and led to his expulsion from Sophia University in 1974. One of his major works was entitled "The Fascism" which was a philosophical disavowal of totalitarian states, such as Nazi Germany and fascist Italy. But the reader could easily see the implications of the book for the communist regime then in control of Bulgaria. The regime confiscated it from bookstores and libraries; its publishers were fired and subjected to political persecution.

As Chairman of the UDF and leader of the opposition, Dr. Zhelev took an active part in the round table discussions with the ruling BSP which led to the campaign for the June, 1990 parliamentary elections. As the campaign got under way, it became clear that the Central Election Commission (CEC) faced enormous challenges. The CEC had to put in place a complete electoral infrastructure with all the attendant strains, one of the most challenging of which was the implementation of a massive voter education campaign. Registries had to be compiled, ballots had to be printed, and electoral officials had to be trained.

As the campaign got under way, observers in the country reported that there appeared to be fair treatment of the opposition parties. They pointed to the fact that newsprint space was allocated to the opposition press, and television time was made available for the major contestants. The major parties were represented fairly at most of the 13,000 polling sites throughout the country.

However, the United Democratic Forces (UDF) complained bitterly that it was not represented on election commissions in about 800 rural sites, singling them out to the attention of international observers. Most of them were in the countryside where the BSP clearly conducted a more "traditional" campaign, which included substantial intimidation. The habits of rural Bulgarians were not to be easily transformed; most had only a nominal acquaintance with the idea that a vote was a fundamental right, and that the act of casting a ballot was secret.

On election day, the Bulgarian Socialist Party won 211 seats in the Grand National Assembly, while the UDF took 144 seats. The BSP's success was attributed to the strength of its local organizations in the rural areas and also to the opposition's lack of political experience.

Due to the nature of the electoral system, the BSP received 53 percent of the seats in the Grand National Assembly. Because it failed to gain the two-thirds majority of seats in the legislature necessary to secure support for the approval of constitutional and economic reforms, the BSP invited the UDF to join a coalition government.

The UDF, which had been persuaded to accept the validity of the results largely due to the quick counts held by international observers, refused to do this. They pointed bitterly to the fact that the campaign had suffered from many irregularities, although technically the balloting and counting processes were fairly conducted.

In their view, a level playing field had not existed during the June elections. The UDF pointed to huge levels of intimidation; clearly the most deceptive force in the BSP arsenal. But the level of intimidation, which often lurks just below the surface in authoritarian states, was difficult to calculate in the Bulgarian campaign. As one observer pointed out: "...overall, the ability to assess intimidation proved complex. ...given its modern history, it is difficult to measure its effect in votes... we can only say it was a factor."[128] To the frustrated opposition, the big question remained: by how much was the opposition vote minimalised as a result of the all - pervasive impact of fear during the election campaign?

The UDF tended to dominate in the cities and enjoyed commanding support from professionals and the young. UDF supporters found it difficult to accept that the communist party could govern Bulgaria with a new face. The extreme disappointment of educated, urban Bulgarians stemmed from what they saw to be an unfair victory of the old commissars.[129]

In the aftermath of the elections, the political situation deteriorated. The majority party did not have the power to really control the country. The UDF remained suspicious and distrustful of the BSP. This problem was exacerbated by incipient factionalism as the UDF began a substantial drift into internal turmoil. This was a problem which even the popular Zhelyu Zhelev, elected President of Bulgaria on August 1, 1990, could do little to resolve.

At the same time, the "minorities" question in that country was brought to center stage by the success of the Movement for Rights and Freedoms (MRF),which represented Bulgaria's Muslim minority. It had elected 23 candidates to the Grand National Assembly from areas dominated by ethnic Turks, a legacy inherited from 500 years of Ottoman rule.

The Bulgarian political culture has an evident anti-Turkish edge. Campaigns of forced assimilation and the appeal to anti-Moslem sentiments by successive communist regimes were common in that country. Ethnic Turks were sometimes forced to take Bulgarian names. In 1989, 350,000 Turks were expelled from Bulgaria; subsequently the socialist controlled Parliament disallowed the teaching of Turkish in the schools.

The country faced a bitter year after the June elections. The economy lurched from disaster to disaster. Western governments imposed a moratorium on assistance as a result of Bulgaria's suspension of payments on its $11 billion debt. Furthermore, Bulgaria was gravely affected by the collapse of COMECON, the trade bloc comprised of the dominant USSR and its east European satellites, a factor which caused an upheaval in trade relations throughout the eastern bloc.

As part of its program of reform to create a market economy, the newly-elected Government abolished price-controls in early February, 1991 in fulfillment of conditions set by the International Monetary Fund. (Bulgaria had joined the IMF in September, 1990) As a result, there were sharp increases in the prices of many goods and services and this exacerbated public resentment over already widespread food and fuel shortages.

Clearly, President Zhelev lacked the resources to launch an effective attack on stagnation. He knew the transition to democracy required strong leadership, but no consensus existed within the Grand Assembly. It was in such a political climate that Bulgarians faced the October 13 elections of 1991 held under a brand new, yet bitterly contested constitution. In these, the UDF won a narrow victory over the BSP. The UDF won a total of 110 seats in the legislature, the BSP 106 seats, while the MRF became the third largest political force, securing 24 seats.

But the internal divisions within the Union of Democratic Forces ensured that narrow victory would not last. Propelled by popular discontent over lingering instability and falling living standards, the Bulgarian Socialist Party won a clear majority in the elections of December, 1994. But in spite of the return of the socialists to government, a pluralist political culture has clearly emerged in this unique Balkan State. Bulgarians have shown great determination in their commitment to the democratic transition which has held throughout the September, 1995 elections. As one analyst put it, "Bulgaria is a bright light in a very dark place...it has demonstrated a consistent commitment to maintaining democracy. It is an island of democratic stability in the Balkans".[130]

I have attended many press conferences in the wake of controversial election processes. I recall well the dialogue between journalists and international observers which ensued at such a conference after the October, 1991 elections in Bulgaria. "When will you no longer consider it necessary to interfere?", one of the reporters asked. I responded: "...when we are no longer invited".

I emphasized that the 75 visitors from 23 countries were present at the invitation of the Bulgarian government, the Commission on Elections, the Bulgarian Association for Free Elections and Civil Rights (BAFECR) and the opposition parties.

> We are not intruders. We are serious people interested in the cause of human rights and the promotion of freedom and democracy. No one has yet found the perfect electoral system, but the evolving democracies seem to be paying more attention to fair election laws than many of the developed countries. It may be that in the future, Bulgarians will be in a position to teach new lessons about fairer electoral laws to others around the world.

It may well be that Bulgarians, along with Guatemalans and Paraguayans and Hungarians and Cameroonians, may one day be visited from afar - as the United States of America was in 1835, when Alexis de Tocqueville wrote his classic account, "Democracy in America".

Tocqueville idealized the American democratic experiment while chastising his fellow Europeans for their political backwardness. Even with hindsight, and some knowledge of the darker dimensions of the American historical experience, it is worth reflecting on Tocqueville's well known conception of a model citizenry:

> I can conceive of a society in which all men would feel an equal love and respect for the laws of which they consider themselves the authors... with every individual in the possession of rights which he is sure to retain, a kind of manly confidence and reciprocal courtesy would arise between all classes, removed alike from pride and servility. The people, well acquainted with their now true interests, would understand that, in order to profit from the advantages of the State, it is necessary to satisfy its requirements...

For many citizens of the Western liberal democracies, such words seem poignantly childlike. They remind us of a time and a frontier with which we have only a vague and uncertain acquaintance. Our collective memory is jogged somewhat by the reminder of what we could have been. We are citizens - we inherit civic cultures - yet we are daily reminded that our struggle for democracy has been a most imperfect one. Most election observers will tell you that time and frontier of which so many of us have only a bleary recollection - the frontier that Tocqueville saw - is evolving in a host of countries across the globe.

PART SIX
FAILED ELECTIONS

Failed elections, as with failed countries, are never popular stories. The Haitian election of 1987 was one of the more tragic examples of how hope can degenerate rapidly into a terrifying battlefield. A brutal military regime presided over this aborted process, which proved to be a source of enormous frustration to the donor countries, such as Canada, which had spent many months providing assistance to the Haitian regime.

But there are many different categories of failed elections. In some cases, authoritarian governments have tried cynically to "swap" show case democracy for credits and foreign aid. The result has been that observer missions in those countries have sometimes been criticized for legitimizing processes held in patently repressive and unfree political environments.

It has been my experience, with regard to this whole problem of legitimization, that the opposite has happened. Observer reports have generally been a highly successful means of exerting influence on the global community, not to speak of a convincing rebuff to show case democrats. I believe it can be solidly argued that, in the end, such staged elections did not secure the anticipated seal of approval because of the presence of observers. In fact, it has been the reports of observer missions which allow us to better understand the reasons behind a number of "failed" elections in our time. They have also been important as a means of influencing governments to reconsider their bilateral commitments, a powerful signal, which we will look at in an analysis of the October, 1992, elections in Cameroon.

Observers must deal with the difficult question of how much unfairness is necessary before an election is characterized as not permitting the popular will of the people to be expressed. My own experience has shown that there is sometimes a fine line between the flawed and the failed.

Most of the time, however, it is immediately obvious when the political will to conduct free, fair elections is absent in a transition state. Even first-time observers are usually struck by the atmosphere of fear and intimidation which is so obvious in such countries.

That was the way I felt when my plane set down in Cameroon. And that was the way observers to the Romanian elections of May, 1990 felt. As one of them pointed out: "the real question was not whether the elections were fair and free, but whether they were meaningful".

We must remember that there is always a certain amount of risk involved when election observers operate in patently repressive and unfree political environments. Still, the many observer teams I have worked with over the years have published very candid reports from the heat of often frightening, electoral battlefields.

In this section of the *Seeds of Freedom*, I will look at the Haitian, Cameroonian and Romanian elections. Observer reports illustrated to the Western democracies the full extent of the inequities in these countries. But the response of too many governments has been haphazard, this reluctance to act which will not escape the attention of dictators across the globe.

Elections are the most important vehicle through which people express their political will, and are a peaceful means of transferring power. When they fail, the larger security of the international community is threatened. It is for this central reason that our collective efforts to foster defence - of democracy mechanisms are so vital to the continuing process of peace and stability in our time.

19. Haiti: The Best Laid Plans Of Mice And Men

The recent, propitious developments in Haiti have put an end, we hope forever, to the vicious series of struggles over the transfer of power in that unhappy country. United Nations military and civilian peace-keepers are presently launching a massive effort to rebuild this tragic "failed country". Canada, the United States, and the United Nations have shared the costs of the mission.

The renewal of the mandate after November 30, 1996, will depend upon a request from President Rene Preval, democratically elected on December 17, 1995 in the cleanest balloting in Haitian history. It is widely expected that the request will be made and that the world body will extend the mandate. Without the UN presence, it is feared that the population of Haiti could return to the years of the dreaded Tonton Macoutes - lawless goon squads of armed civilians who tortured, destroyed and killed indiscriminately.

Haiti is a country which was built on courage and belief in liberty, and received its independence from France after a bloody war which left tens of thousands dead. But sadly, Haiti has never in its history found freedom.

In this respect, the famous words of Toussaint Louverture, the ascetic hero of Haitian liberation, who did not himself live to see the independence of the first black Republic in history in 1804, remain still a dream for most Haitians. Kidnapped and imprisoned in the French Alps by the French in 1802, Toussaint died, but the vision he had inspired in his people remained. "In overthrowing me, you have cut down in Saint Dominigue only the trunk of the tree of liberty, it will spring up again from the roots, for they are many and they are deep."

But the roots, though deep, remained covered in violence and blood over the decades.

After winning a rigged election in 1957, Francois Duvalier, known as Papa Doc, institutionalized the system of terror and coercion used to perpetuate his rule, and which was often associated with the brutality of the Tonton Macoutes. Upon his death in 1971, the title of President for Life went to his son Jean-Claude, who continued his father's pattern of intimidation and gross violations of human rights.

It is estimated that the Duvalier regime slaughtered over 50,000 people. Duvalierism drove a million Haitians into exile and left a grim legacy of poverty, murder, and voodoo. But on February 7, 1986, Haitians celebrated what they thought to be a victory as Baby Doc and his closest supporters were overthrown in a military coup. They subsequently fled into exile as the National Council of Government (CNG), a civilian-military junta headed by Lt. Gen. Henry Namphy took control of Haiti.

The new regime announced its intention to hold elections in November, 1987. This generated much optimism in the international community that Haiti might emerge from decades of hopelessness and despair.

The Canadian government, along with others in the international community, saw the military-led democratization process as a window of opportunity and began a novel assistance programme to democratic development in that country.[131]

Canada did so in response to a letter dated September 19, 1986, from the Haitian military authorities.

The project proved to be extremely ambitious for the officials at Elections Canada who, upon receipt of the Haitian note, immediately established an assistance team made up of elections experts and constitutional authorities, many from universities in Quebec. They defined the Canadian initiative this way: "le rôle canadien en la matière peut être comparé à celui d'un ingénieur-conseil travaillant dans le cadre d'orientations générales définies par l'architecte en chef qui est le Gouvernement d'Haïti."[132] (Canada's role can be compared to that of a consulting engineer working within the framework of general guidelines defined by the head architect, which in this case is the government of Haiti.)

With funding from the Canadian International Development Agency, Elections Canada provided ballot boxes, calculators, ballot papers, voting screens - even lanterns - for the innovative Haitian exercise. Canadian officials trained their Haitian counterparts in election procedures and helped create an Electoral Law. No one could understand why the Haitian Junta decided to abort the process by rampant violence directed at largely defenceless voters.

Richard Balasko reported what he saw on election day. He was Executive Assistant to the Chief Electoral Officer of Canada when he was asked to observe the November 29th, 1987 Haitian Election, as part of the official Canadian mission to that country. The first few paragraphs recorded a deceptive calm. He noticed a general sense of orderliness on the part of the electoral officials.

He noted also the warm reception with which the Canadians were received by voters waiting patiently in line to cast their ballots. After viewing two or three polls ("...all in one location and only in what was thought to be a relatively safe and middle to upper class area of the city") he admitted to being "favourably .impressed... I found organisation, purpose, and quite proper administration of the polls."[133] The rest reads like a John Le Carré novel.

> On entering the third poll, Mr. Cote and I were first checked for weapons (as were all persons). The third poll operated basically the same way as the first two. Immediately after exiting from our inspection of the third poll, however, and just after Mr. Cote had entered his vehicle and

as I was just about to enter my vehicle, automatic weapons fire opened at very close range directly above and behind us. I quickly jumped into the back seat of my vehicle and laid as flat as I could across the back seat. Both our vehicles took off at high speed, but the gunfire continued behind us, and it seemed to me also at our side. As we took evasive action and turned down one street the gunfire faded but then quickly resumed and again seemed close to us. All about us, people scurried for cover. The Embassy officials and drivers deserve commendation for acting so professionally in getting us out as quickly, directly, and safely as possible.

...Shaken by our experience, it was more than apparent to us that the observation of polling places was not safe in this area of Petionville which earlier had been estimated to be one of the safest in Port-au-Prince. After stopping briefly for a quick consultation, Pierre F. Cote and I determined to abort our plans to continue that morning to observe at other polls.

Our situation at the poll was a very close call. Embassy staff say that it couldn't have been closer. I could not erase from my mind the image of people lining up in an orderly way to vote nor the enthusiasm in the faces of the people and the election officials that we encountered. I had concern for the safety of all those people and for their aspirations, and I marvelled at the faith and hope of those also in the countryside, for example, those persons we met at Cabaret who only a day or two before were so enthusiastic and so encouraged by our presence. By about 10:00 a.m., radio reports announced that the election had been cancelled by the C.E.P. By 10:30 a.m. the gunfire was no longer audible to us. There were, however, reports of fourteen people killed, and of polling stations burned to the ground.

This sunny election Sunday was a day on which Haitians hoped to break the three decade long cycle of Duvalierist tyranny. Instead, "Bloody Sunday", as it became known, was a day of horror. Elizabeth Abbott, historian and journalist, described what happened at one of the polling stations in a school yard in Port-au-Prince.

At about 8 a.m. the Macoutes poured into the school yard. "We're vigilantes here to protect you," one shouted, then suddenly sprayed the milling throng with machine-gun bullets. Scores of men and women fell into bloody heaps on the ground, dead or dying. Macoutes without guns hacked at wounded victims, who pleaded for their lives, severing hands still clutching precious electoral slips, cleaving limbs from torsos... [134]

For days after, the country was in a state of shock. Haitians grieved for their dead. The international community reacted in disgust to General Namphy's betrayal and treachery. A *New York Times* editorial stated:

When Sunday's election in Haiti was voided, it shattered hopes for democracy and denied Haitians their first chance in thirty years to elect a President. The culprits are General Henri Namphy's junta and the murderous Macoute thugs whose rampages gave the junta the pretext it needed to call off the vote.[135]

The rage swirling around Western capitals was a direct reaction to what many saw to be the cruel and vicious joke perpetrated in the 18 months prior to the election. Many onlookers believed that the Junta was serious about the democratic transition as their repeated requests for electoral assistance implied. I was shocked and horrified by the events of "Bloody Sunday" - the more so because I had urged a very good friend, Senator Gildas Molgat, to be part of the NDI observer delegation to the November elections. As Senator Molgat speaks fluent French and understands the political system extremely well, his presence was a decided plus.

I met with him shortly before his departure to brief him on some of the modalities of international observing. I was light-hearted and optimistic, believing, as so many did, that the democratic transition was on track in Haiti.

Before I left his office, I turned to him and said: "if you don't make it back, will you leave me that old red bomb you drive around Ottawa? and as a bonus, you could leave me your wine cellar too."

A few days later, I heard that Senator Molgat was holed up in a hotel in Port-au-Prince as all hell had broken out in the capital. I tried to make contact with him though External Affairs and was told the next day that a US government charter had evacuated the observers.

The massacre of voters that took place on election day was denounced by governments across the globe. The OAS Permanent Council took note of the deplorable acts of violence and disorder in Haiti, and stated that all necessary measures would have to be adopted for the Haitian people to express their will through free and fair elections without any form of pressure or interference.

Needless to say, my carefree conversation with Senator Molgat on his departure for Haiti was forgotten, as the full tragedy of the situation impacted on the world.

Senator Molgat is now Speaker of the Senate of Canada.

20. Romania: A Failed Revolution

The stories of the brutal world controlled by Nicolae Ceausescu and his wife Elena had begun to surface in the West several years before the starving, angry mobs in Romania revolted against the control of the dictator in December, 1989. This was the worst dictatorship in Europe. From the time Ceausescu became First Secretary of Romania's Communist Party in 1965, he had built up a regime in which, it was said, one-third of the population were informers. Romania had the dubious distinction of having the largest number of secret police within the entire Soviet bloc.

The one-time fervent communist, who had been imprisoned for years because of his beliefs as a young man, had become a parody of a dictator and his rule distinguishable only as a personality cult; indeed one of the most most vicious and depraved in history.

Yet the Ceausescus were courted by the West because for a time his independent policies made him a useful ally within the Warsaw Pact. It was well known that Ceausescu had been generally a thorn in the side of the Soviet Union. He supported the independent "tilts" of Marshall Tito in Yugoslavia, and gave support to the reformist thrust in Czechoslovakia, backing the Prague Spring of 1968 and condemning the hard line response and invasion of that country by the USSR which followed in its wake.

His visits to the White House were a subject of some chagrin to Moscow. Ceausescu was able to win the Most Favoured Nation trade status and economic benefits unavailable to other Bloc countries. Romania's links with China and Israel were substantial, in spite of the fact that the USSR had severed theirs. For these reasons, Western politicians who should have known better, regularly honored and cultivated the friendship of a man whose sheer ruthlessness drove Romanians into starvation and despair. As a result of the Ceausescus, an entire nation was imprisoned.

A journalist who was in Romania in the months prior to the bloody revolution of December, 1989, put it this way:

> As long as the Securitate controlled every place of work and every street and housing estate in the country, Ceausescu's could do what he wanted. He would consider pulling down the villages, or reducing living standards to African or Central American levels, or repaying the entire national debt in an absurdly short space of time, because he was immune to opposition. If he looked after the Securitate he was safe; the Securitate were his murderers, reckless in what they did in spite of the world. [136]

In 1982, Ceausescu decided to pay off the large foreign debt which his government's mismanaged industrial ventures had largely produced. He ordered the export of much of the country's agricultural and industrial production. This was the final abomination. Romanians starved. They had no fuel or energy or medicine. Eggs became a form of currency, changing hands many times before they were eaten. Western visitors were unnerved by the sight of the suffering. During the horror, Ceausescus' two English bred Labrador dogs, presents from the Queen, continued, to be fed the finest lean steak and to be chauffered in their own limousines.

Revolution, as in 1789, was only a matter of time. When Mikhail Gorbachev became General Secretary of the Soviet Communist Party in March, 1985, Ceausescu's usefulness to the West became a thing of the past. There was no further reason, as Gorbachev himself began to advocate reform within the empire, to support and fete a leader previously thought of in the West as a Trojan horse within the Warsaw Pact.[137]

His regime collapsed after he ordered his security forces to fire on anti-government demonstrators on December 17, 1989. As the demonstrations spread, the Romanian army defected to the demonstrators. Ceaususcu and his wife fled the capital, but were taken into custody only a few days later. On December 15, the couple were tried and convicted of mass murder and a host of other crimes. They were shot by a firing squad.

Because no dissent had been tolerated in the country for decades, opposition groups had not developed in the totalitarian fiefdom of Elena, Nicu and Nicolae Ceausescu. One must analyze the Romanian "revolution" against this backdrop. While there is much debate over the precise order and ranking of the key actors in the events of December, 1989, it has been widely assumed in the West that Ion Iliescu and other career party members joined with disaffected elements of the Romanian army to oust Ceausescu.

The National Salvation Front Council surfaced to become a transitional government. Its members included party apparatchiks such as Iliescu and others, like Doina Cornea, Romania's chief dissident in the final years of Ceausescu.

The Front enjoyed substantial popularity in the weeks following the December Revolution, but doubts about its stated commitment to a democratic transition became evident by late January, 1990. Iliescu backtracked on earlier commitments to disband the Front's "Stewardship" and remain neutral in the elections scheduled for April, 1990. The Front's decision to field candidates infuriated newly formed opposition groups who began to question its commitment to democracy.[138]

It became clear to many that the so called "peoples' revolution" had become the vehicle for the authoritarian stranglehold of the old establishment. The idea of a "betrayed revolution" circulated, and by early February several former dissidents resigned from the Front. From this time on, and until the May elections, the Front leadership showed a disturbing lack of any real affection for pluralism and the workings of democracy. This was shown as Iliescu and his colleagues criticized other political forces for "divisiveness" and "misunderstanding of the revolution", as well as "their refusal to find a place in the new order for the collective good."

Although there were repeated attempts by the leadership to define pluralism, they were done so "in an organic fashion in which various political elements would discuss the execution of policies but not their formulation".[139]

When we reflect on the fact that the "enemy of communism was often formed in the likeness of the system he was fighting" we cannot help but observe that in Romania, whether as a friend or enemy of the prevailing system, the ideological legacy of Marxist-Leninism reigned supreme. The carefully bred slave of communism did not die in the "revolution" of December 22.

In the months leading up to the elections, students and opposition groups tried to influence the Front by means of street demonstrations. These were quickly broken up by elements of the police and armed workers who had been mobilized to deal with "counter-revolutionary" elements. Confrontation after bloody confrontation followed. The elections were then postponed for a month until May, presumably to allow the fledgling parties more time to organize.

In fact, this provided only a superficial veneer to a genuinely farcical campaign where the effective use of intimidation (the campaign showed unmistakeable similarities with the tactics of the Communists during the 1944-47 period in Romania's history) visibly revealed the heritage of the Front's leadership. The conclusions of the joint NRIIA - NDI mission that did make the decision to observe the May 20 elections told the story.

1. Given Romania's long experience of brutal communist dictatorship, the May elections represent an historic opening and a necessary first step toward the achievement of a democratic political system. Nonetheless, there were very significant flaws that affected the overall fairness of the electoral process and that underscore the need for major structural reforms in the Romanian political environment.

2. The Front had considerable advantages during the electoral campaign, including control of newspapers, campaign funds, printing facilities, vehicles, telephone lines, and other supplies and resources basic to a political campaign. Moreover, the Front used its position as the dominant party in the interim government to exploit these advantages rather than to level the playing field of the campaign, and its general attitude was not conducive to the promotion of a free and open campaign. Consequently, despite its large margin of victory, the democratic credentials of the Front have not been established with these elections.

3. The human rights environment of the campaign was poor. Opposition candidates' and parties' exercise of their basic rights of expression and assembly was frequently met with intimidation and harassment, including serious beatings and physical destruction, often instigated by Front supporters. The Front-dominated government failed to condemn and discourage acts of violence.

4. The opposition was weak and fragmented not only because of the intimidation and harassment, but because of the inherent difficulties in simultaneously reconstituting parties from nothing and conducting a national campaign in the space of five months.

5. The balloting process was not marked by systematic fraud, although there were many procedural problems in the administration of the election, and a number of the irregularities benefitted the Front. Given the large margin of victory, it appears that irregularities did not affect the outcome of the elections. Nonetheless, to avoid the recurrence of such irregularities in future elections, the delegation recommends the adoption of several administrative reforms to promote greater confidence in the process.

6. Finally, the Romanian electorate, particularly in rural areas, faced the election uninformed and without a real understanding of choice and the concept of a multi-party, secret ballot. There is an urgent need to undertake education programmes designed to ensure that voters in future elections are better informed about the process and the choices they may exercise.

It was clear that the National Salvation Front used its position of dominance to control access to the media and to those resources essential to a political campaign. It instigated considerable harassment of opposition parties which enjoyed no basic rights either of free expression or of free assembly. These were actions which the executed dictator, himself, would have thoroughly approved of. The biggest portrait of Ion Iliescu, the president-elect after the May elections, hung outside Bucharest University. "But the president-elect was not alone in the photograph. Next to him was the all too familiar face of Nicolae Ceausescu. The caption read: "Preteni" (friends). The day after the election the portrait mysteriously disappeared."[140]

The observer report made it patently clear that the government really had no legitimate claim to office, or the subsequent benefits of commercial ties. The presence of observers was therefore not a means of legitimising a showcase election. Instead, this became the principal source of information to the outside world that a revolution had been betrayed.

Nonetheless, in the June 1996 municipal elections in that country, the popular expression "what goes around, comes around", seemed highly applicable. President Iliescu's government reaped the full measure of its unpopularity with Romanian voters, as it lost most big towns throughout the country, including Bucharest. There, the Democratic Convention opposition candidate defeated former tennis star Ilie Nastase in a dramatic upset.

It is clear that young, urban Romanians want a better future for themselves and their families. This is a revolution of aspirations within the hearts and minds of a new generation who have caught a glimpse of the possible. It seemed doubtful that, as autumn parliamentary elections appeared on the horizon, the old guard would be able to stop the inexorable democratic clock from ticking beyond a time of betrayal, and into a new dawn.

21. Cameroon: Designed to Fail

The absence of political will to conduct a free and fair election is blatantly obvious upon arrival in some transition states. That absence was immediately apparent the moment I arrived in Cameroon. I had been asked to co-chair the NDI observer delegation to the October, 1992 presidential elections in that country along with former Attorney General Jim Tierney of the American state of Maine.

NDI's Ned McMahon greeted me and briefed me on the situation. The Cameroon government was then charging that there had been no formal invitation sent to Washington for an NDI mission to Cameroon, and that therefore there was no proper accreditation for our delegation. I knew there was no substance to the government's claim as NDI had received a letter of invitation from the Cameroon Ambassador to the United States.

Ned finally arranged a meeting with the Minister of Territorial Administration who was responsible for elections in that country. I recall being seated with some members of my delegation in the waiting room. When the Minister appeared, we were commanded to "All rise."

That command set the tone for the ensuing conversation. I told him that if we did not receive the necessary accreditation, I would pull the entire delegation out on the first plane available, and tell the international community why.

I knew at the time that the Cameroonian government had ordered a cease and desist command to all their embassies around the world to prevent any more foreign observers from being granted visas. In fact, four of the members of my delegation, then recently arrived, had just been deported from the country.

The minister repeated the general government line that an invitation to observe had not been extended. I was able to produce the letter attesting that it had, in fact, been made. As it turned out, the Minister had the letters of accreditation ready. I wondered at the time at their intentions. Was the pressure designed to frighten us? Was it to test our resolve?

That feeling increased in intensity as Ned and I began our rounds of the capital. On election day I decided to visit the Presidential polling station where the President was to vote. This was located in a school house not far from the extravagantly ostentatious Presidential residence. Ned suggested that the Cameroonian authorities might not appreciate any observers near the President's voting station.

The place was surrounded by military, including sharpshooters on the rooftops, but the atmosphere was festive. A large crowd waited to see the President come and vote. As we got out of our van, the dancing and singing stopped. Ned is 6 feet 6 inches tall. He felt, and perhaps justifiably at the time, that if one of us was going to be shot, it would be him.

There was dead silence as we walked through the line of soldiers and headed towards the school house which housed the voting station. When I turned to McMahon and asked if he was as uncomfortable as I was, he responded: "Oh yeah, let's get out of here". But we both knew we had to make the point. We showed the soldiers our papers, did a cursory round of the station, and tried to walk casually back to our van.

Later in the day I went back to the same station with Jim Tierney. Both of us felt that it was important to give the necessary signal - that we were not intimidated, and that our election report would hold the government fully accountable for the already substantial signs of cheating and fraud noted by our delegation.

After completing our report, the US ambassador faxed a copy to Washington and attached the following comment: "The NDI delegation hit a home run."

We concluded that the full weight of responsibility for the "failed" election had to be assumed by the Government of Cameroon and President Paul Biya.

I will briefly summarize the evidence supporting our conclusions. In the first place, the election was scheduled hastily by President Biya, before the adoption of an election code. Once enacted, the code provided for a 30-day campaign period, an impossibility, given the date already set for the election.

The election system provided civil administration officials responsible to President Biya, including the minister of territorial administration, senior divisional officers, and divisional officers, with excessive discretion in matters of voter registration and ballot tabulation. Many officials abused this latitude to further the political interests of the incumbent President.

The tabulation of votes was conducted under the authority of the minister of territorial administration, whose partisan support for President Biya was unmistakable. This was in violation of the electoral code originally decided to prohibit political party representatives from obtaining tally sheets of election results at the polling sites. While this decision was ultimately reversed, the electoral code did not provide an opportunity for party representatives to monitor the transfer of tally sheets to the divisional supervisory commissions.

The National Commission for the Final Counting of Votes, which was appointed only days before the election, failed to inspire public confidence in the integrity of the tabulation process. The composition of the Commission did not represent ethnic, regional or political balance.

The early election date, and the failure to reopen the registration process, needlessly restricted voter registration. The early election in effect disenfranchised the many Cameroonians who had boycotted the March 1 legislative elections.

Little control was exercised over the distribution of voter registration cards, thus creating an opportunity for multiple and underage voting. Handfuls of cards were repeatedly offered to the observers as proof of a lively marker in voter card trafficking.

We all witnessed the distribution of these cards by opposition parties as well as by supporters of President Biya.

Voter registries were generally not published before election day, which meant that parties or voters could not review the lists to ensure their accuracy. In several instances, officials refused to allow individuals to vote whose names appeared on the voter roll, and whose voter cards had been stamped during the March legislative elections, which demonstrated that the same individuals had been permitted to vote at that time.

Biased news coverage and the partisan use of the government controlled television and radio in favour of the incumbent president marred the election campaign. For example, the television news broadcast on October 7 provided the government and its campaign 142 minutes of coverage, while only 12 minutes were allotted to the opposition.

On election day, rules regarding voter eligibility were not uniformly applied. Throughout the country, the names of eligible voters were improperly crossed off the register.

Polling sites were arbitrarily moved in some areas - including Yaounde, Maroua, Douala, Garoua and Ebolowa - before election day; this created confusion and reduced voter turnout in specific regions.

Political party poll watchers were prevented from entering polling sites and, in one case, were barred from entering the entire territory surrounding the town by Rey Bouba in Mayo-Rey Division, which was controlled by a traditional leader who supported President Biya.

Fictitious polling places (i.e., polling places that did not exist on the official list distributed before the election) reported overwhelming vote totals in favour of President Biya, contrasting dramatically with the results from other polling sites in the same area. In Foumbot in the Noun Division in the West Province, for example, 10 polling places that did not appear on the official list of polling places were reportedly cited in a compilation of results forwarded by the senior divisional officer to the divisional supervisory commission. The results from these polling places generally provided overwhelming, and similar, vote totals in favour of President Biya, while the remainder of the area voted largely in favour of another candidate.

Statistically anomalous results were reported from several polling sites. One particularly egregious example involved a cluster of polling sites from the Mvila Division in the Ebolowa area that reported a 100 percent turnout of 5,856 voters and 100 percent support for President Biya. Similar, although slightly less extreme examples, were recorded in neighbouring polling places.

Without authorization in the electoral code, the Ministry of Territorial Administration released unofficial partial results well before the final counts had been tabulated. The release included subjective analysis as to why President Biya would emerge the final victor.

The authorities failed to publish polling-site-by-polling-site results that precluded the possibility of a credible, independent review of the overall election results.

I might add to this already overwhelming list of abuses the fact that the Chief Justice of the Supreme Court of Cameroon himself listed them as he announced the official results. So too did the Minister of Justice in an interview with a Cameroonian newspaper shortly after the election.[141]

The October 1992 elections were seen throughout the international community as an important indicator of the progress of African democratisation. In response to our report, the United States reduced its aid to Cameroon. Canada cut its bilateral aid programme by approximately 50 percent - a direct signal to other showcase democrats that the government intended to make conscience its guide in determining aid levels.

Germany also seriously reviewed its bilateral commitments to the West African nation. On a multilateral level, the IMF and the World Bank sent similar signals. I believe this kind of action takes us in the right direction. But it must be applied fairly, squarely and across the board.

In the aftermath of the NDI report on Cameroon, a five-person delegation was despatched by the government in an effort to challenge some of our observations. They visited Bonn, Paris, London, Washington, and Ottawa. It is my understanding, that while officials in all capitals listened attentively, the central thrust of our message prevailed - that there was much, much room for improvement before one could clearly accept that democracy was alive and well in one of Central Africa's most promising nations.

Despite the pessimism I felt when I left Cameroon, I believe that more positive signs are now in evidence. In 1989, Cameroon applied for membership in both the

Commonwealth of Nations, and La Francophonie. The latter organization accepted Cameroon almost immediately.

But the Commonwealth was much more hesitant. In the first of a three-step process, its Secretary General, Chief Anyaokw, visited Cameroon in 1994. Then followed meetings with a more technical delegation. In the third and final step, a four member "Eminent Persons" mission, including Canada's Speaker of the Senate, Gildas Molgat, visited Cameroon in the summer of 1995.

The mission was to apprise itself of the steps taken by the Cameroon government in establishing a democratic system consistent with the Harare Declaration. A report was subsequently filed with the Commonwealth Secretary General, suggesting that significant progress had been made, with assurance from President Biya that local elections would be held by the end of October, and that new constitutional proposals would be presented to Parliament before the end of the year. Cameroon was officially admitted to full membership in the Commonwealth of nations on November 1, 1995.

Local elections were eventually held. The opposition won in a number of important cities, but we have been told that officially directed manipulation of the electoral process in Yaounde, ensured the capital city remained under the control of the ruling party.

Now it has been my experience, that whenever African voters have been given the chance to choose those who will govern them in free and fair elections, they have opted for honest leadership. While there is no doubt that ethnic and tribal loyalties have been a real problem on that continent, voters have recognized leaders who transcend narrow provincial ambitions.

We need only think of the trans-ethnic and cross cultural backing for Moshood Abiola in Nigeria, a tragic figure, who won fairly in the widely observed 1993 elections in that country, only to find the will of the people cynically violated when the military annulled them.

When General Babangida annulled Nigeria's election results of June, 1993, he called upon the Western powers to exercise patience and understanding.

> Most nations that are now established democracies went through very difficult and rocky roads...and brought great suffering to their people. Some of these nations executed their kings and queens...many took centuries even to arrive at universal adult suffrage, which is the assumed basis of our present democratic experiment.[142]

In fact, General Babangida's remarks were nothing but a shabby evasion of the realities in Nigeria. First, his annulment of the "fairest" election in Nigeria's history was nothing but a travesty. Second, he trampled upon the very evident "aptitude" for democracy shown by the people themselves - and widely commented upon in the international press.

With this action, the magnificent country of Nigeria, blessed with rich farmland, enormous oil reserves and 100 million industrious citizens, fell back under the control of a brutal tyranny. When General Sani Abacha forced Babangida to step aside, the vicious nature of Nigeria's most recent tyrant was revealed to a shocked and horrified world.

On November 10, 1995, Ken SaroWiwa, a gifted poet and novelist, as well as a courageous environmental and human rights activist, was arrested, along with eight others on trumped up charges. They were tried in a kangaroo court, they were murdered in a grisly state execution, and their corpses were carried off in garbage bags for secret burial. The Commonwealth suspended Nigeria and gave Abacha a two year deadline to restore his country to civilian rule. The European Union hit Nigeria with an arms embargo.

Yet Abacha continues to snub his nose at the world, saying he will ignore the two year deadline. The general is betting that the political will to do more than talk is absent. He would have good reason to believe this. Too often in the recent past, despots on the continent have staged elections, called the bluff of the Western powers, and been met with only half empty threats.

But times have changed dramatically with the advent of President Nelson Mandela at the helm of a new, free South Africa. In the long-term, a solution to the Nigerian tragedy may come from Africans themselves. The presence of Nelson Mandela heralds change and inspiration for the many courageous Africans involved in the quest for fully democratic and accountable governments across the continent.[143]

PART SEVEN
CONCLUSION

A Glimpse of the Possible

When I first began observing elections a decade ago, the idea of electoral assistance to democratic development was still relatively new. I believed from the outset that democracy was not a process which simply unfolded according to the dictates of history. My upbringing and education in a mining community in Cape Breton had a lot to do with this conviction. I understood the unwritten codes of the coal culture and something of the vagaries of a resource-based economy at a young age. I learned from the outset that liberty from powerlessness meant that ordinary men and women had to become masters in their own houses.

I never lost my belief in the collective power of little people and I always knew about the giant lying just below the surface. I understood that if you give them ideas, the giant would emerge and blow the roof off. In many ways, it was these beliefs which were the engine of almost everything I have tried to do in my life.

Throughout my public life in Canada, I have been privileged to play a small part in the creation of a political culture of respect for people. Later, at Liberal International, we tried to do the same thing on a global scale. Most of us were pragmatic idealists who believed that taking the road less travelled would make the world a better place.

Long before I served on my first observer mission in the Philippines, I believed that the process of democratization not only could be, but had to be assisted from outside. The experience of the 1986 elections in the Philippines both confirmed and sharpened my thoughts on the world. I was able to observe the tumultuous, courageous, and joyful commitment of Filipinos to the democratic process and I saw that together they were, indeed, a giant. I also saw that the little people of that country, while they were the catalyst to the demise of the Marcos regime, needed all the support they could get from their friends.

In all the elections I have observed since that time, I have understood that courage and commitment can never be enough, particularly in countries where fear and intimidation are marshalled against pro-democracy forces.

Elections are defining moments in the lives of men and women in transition states, because they are the means of advancing and securing the value-systems which anchor the pluralist institutions so critical to the successful consolidation of democracy. First-time elections embolden people to believe that the dream is possible. They are the important first steps in the long journey towards a new law on earth.

The global community cannot afford to let those defining moments slip away. I believe that peace and democratic development are two sides of the same coin. There is therefore an urgency to the flow of international support, both to the long-term observation process and to the consolidation of democracy which comes in its wake.

The citizens of the mature democracies cannot forget their special responsibilities to the newcomers in this regard. We can't "love them and leave them". And we must remember as well that we are all part of the same process. The success or failure of our models will drastically influence the consolidation process in key states around the world. The renewal and revitalization of the Western democratic systems is, in this sense, integrally linked with the success or failure of the new democracies.

The engine of successful democratic consolidation is fired by the development of real civilians and the growth of civic cultures. A citizenry exists when people believe that law supercedes power. Citizens are people who feel they can resolve problems through bureaucratic channels and civic institutions rather than bribes or violent actions. Citizens feel empowered to take action because they feel a government derives legitimacy from them.[144]

Civic culture exists for a whole series of reasons in countries like Canada, Costa Rica, Uruguay, and Chile. In the case of the latter, a civic consciousness did endure the often brutal authoritarianism of General Pinochet's regime. Perhaps that is because Chileans did have a lengthy historical acquaintance with democracy prior to Pinochet. Nonetheless, a sense of civic culture did survive even in the dark years after Pinochet.[145]

In fact, its all pervasive spirit had much to do with the extraordinary series of events leading up to the 1988 Plebiscite. The longevity of the historic Chilean sense of democratic tradition was symbolized in March, 1990, as Augusto Pinochet unwillingly, yet peacefully, passed the Presidential sash to Paticio Aylwin.

In August, 1995, I was invited to participate in a programme aimed at promoting efforts to enhance the effectiveness, responsiveness and accountability of political parties in the Americas. It was to be held in Marbella, Chile. Present were the key party leaders and representatives of selected civic groups from Latin America.

I came away, newly impressed by the desire of leaders and very influential spokespersons to take more serious steps in encouraging the modernization and democratization of the political party system in that hemisphere.

The Conference was organized by the National Democratic Institute, which is the best organization of its kind in the world. NDI assistance to free and fair elections, as well as democratic development in the long-term, has taken many forms. In some cases, direct operational grants have been disbursed to struggling pro-democracy groups around the world. In others, NDI experts have organized seminars on themes such as political party development, party reform and civic organizations.[146] But I would like to focus on its training programmes in political pluralism and civilian structures.

I have already made reference to the wonderful work done by the Centre for Democratic Studies in Paraguay.[147] The CED was not only closely involved in the process of civic education on a general level, but it was also a key player in pressuring for reforms in the electoral law prior to the 1989 elections. As well, it undertook the arduous task of preparing Paraguayans for the 1991 municipal elections, the first in that country's history.

The BAFECR in Bulgaria is another inspirational model for civic education efforts in the future. Like NAMFREL in the Philippines, BAFECR has distinguished itself in election monitoring efforts, as well as the dissemination of information on democratic systems. BAFECR was able to recruit and train over 10,000 volunteers to serve at polling sites throughout the country in the 1990 and 1991 elections. The parallel vote tabulation was a means of convincing the public that the elections were free and fair.

The GERDDES, based in Benin, provides us with yet another example. This is a civic organization which has operated in more than 15 West African countries.[148]

NDI has also facilitated linkages between the members of civic education institutes and its many monitoring missions. A good example of this was shown in the activities of the Etica y Transparenci (Ethics and Transparency ET) nonpartisan monitoring group which which so effectively and enthusiastically contributed to the successful October, 1996 elections and the strengthening of democracy in Nicaragua. ET has managed to maintain a diverse political base, with 18 member civic and academic organizations and a board of directors that could be considered the most broad-based leadership of a Nicaraguan civic group in the country's history.

Its thousands of voluteers observed the controversial voter registration process in Nicaragua's northern and central municipalities. The group monitored nearly 90 percent of the polling sites in the country. It was ET which concluded that the irregularities observed in the election, including logistical and administrative problems, were not of sufficient magnitude to invalidate the polling process or the integrity of the outcome. The group also conducted a quick count of the presidential results which mirrored the voting tendencies reported by Nicaragua's Supreme Electoral Council (CSE). But most importantly, ET will continue to monitor the ongoing political process after the international observers have left the country.

The Nicaraguan experience shows the great importance of linkages between civics groups in transition states. I think back to my second Philipine mission in 1987. On this occasion, Filippinos really felt they didn't need any outside help, as they had already taught the world some classic lessons about bringing democracy peacefully to a country that for years had been torn by greed and oppression. We shifted terminology to meet with new realities. In 1986, we had been monitoring the process. In 1987, we were "learning by observing."

At this time, NDI felt it was an excellent opportunity to assemble representatives from transition states where the struggle for democracy was ongoing. The morning following the election, the delegates held a debriefing session. They felt it was important, not only to review their findings, but also to evaluate the whole experience to determine whether all the time and travel had been worthwhile.

I might add that all of them were resolute and hopeful about the possibilities of implementing some of what they had learned in their own home countries.

In particular, I recall the time that Victor Baez, a Paraguayan trade union president announced upon arrival that the 60 hour flight from Asuncion to Manila was "all a waste of time." (all this had been complicated by late planning, missed connections etc.) By the time of the debriefing, he had made a 180 degree turn. He went back to his own country with new determination that what Filippinos had accomplished could be repeated by Paraguayans.[149]

I paid my respects to the gentleman in question while observing, in three subsequent missions, the invention of democracy in a country where no one believed this to be possible.

This is in no way a blind imitation of Western models. Rather, the citizens of evolving democracies are interested in adapting the democratic process to the specific needs and conditions of their own countries.

For example, the Secretary of BAFECR reported in December 1990 on "what we could take from the American political system....as blind imitation would be unwise...we should take the positive grain from a system absolutely differing from our own and try to create a variant most suitable for Bulgaria."[150]

The idea of the "positive grain" struck me at the time. Democracy, we must remember is a delicate flower. It assumes many hybrid shapes in as many different countries. But there is, of course, a special seed from which all the others take their essence. Call it a positive grain. It is the conviction that ordinary people have the right to participate in the construction of a fair polity. All of our assistance to democratic development tends to nurture that conviction.

In my opinion, it is the evolving citizenry of the transition states who are now paying more attention to fair election laws than many of us of the Western liberal democracies who have only a vague understanding of what the struggle really means.

In Namibia, for example, I counted on the wisdom and experience of Mr. Mohammed Khan, Joint Secretary of the Election Commission in Pakistan. A man of formidable intellect and conviction, he had lived the difficult process of democratisation in his own country. His service in Namibia showed me that he was probably in a better position than most of us to advise upon fair electoral legislation.

A genuine international amity has developed through shared experiences in observer delegations.[151] While on a mission for NDI on the eve of the October, 1993 elections in Pakistan, I had the good fortune to meet up in Islamabad with Mr. Khan. Needless to say, our personal conversations in Islamabad helped to refute many of the misunderstandings regarding the NDI mission in that country at the time. In part, it is these kinds of ties which have helped keep elections on track in countries where fear and distrust threaten to usurp the process.

I have already referred to the lengthy association with democratic practices and the strong spirit of civic culture which endured in the collective memory of Chileans, surviving in spite of the longevity of the Pinochet regime. President Eduardo Frei personifies the commitment of Chileans to restore and deepen civic institutions in a country many outside commentators had felt would be marred for decades as a result of the long years of authoritarianism. He and I had co-chaired the international observer team which monitored the 1989 Paraguayan elections. I had therefore been privileged to witness the strength of his commitment to the democratic process at first-hand.

The meaningful collegiality and bonds of trust which had developed as a result of our work in Paraguay served in good stead as I was invited by the President to meet with him after the Marbella conference in Chile. I travelled over 1,000 kilometers south of Santiago to Puerto Mont, where Frei had assembled his cabinet for meetings in lieu of the severe and unseasonable climactic conditions which threatened local farmers with disaster.

My travelling companion proved to be yet another colleague made from shared experiences in election monitoring - this time from the Bulgarian mission. I had the pleasure of the company of Genaro Arriagada-Herrera, the Minister and Secretary General of the Presidency of Chile, as we flew south.

I met Eduardo Frei again in Puerto Vars. The President invited me to sit with him on the stage for the official opening of a new housing development for one of the poorest areas of the region. At the ribbon cutting ceremony which followed, the President snipped a piece of the ribbon bearing the Chilean flag colours, passed it to a young lady, and asked her to pin it to the lapel of my jacket. The symbolism of the gesture greatly moved me. We had been colleagues in a country where democracy had yet to be invented. Now he was President of a country where many thought democracy had been forgotten. It had not been. The great democratic heart of the country, now restored and revitalized, beat very visibly as I watched hundreds of proud Chileans sing their National Anthem in the driving rain.

And it is a compassionate heart. While listening to the President's powerful speech, the Minister of the Interior, Carlos Figueroa, leaned into my ear and whispered: "Now Senator, you are seeing the other side of Chile. We are spending the greatest percentage of our budget on social programmes - where it is needed most."

In fact, I was told that the government of Chile is now spending 70 percent of its budget on the welfare of people, a far cry from the policies of the past. As the bridges of the North American Free Trade Agreement (NAFTA) open across the hemisphere, and the debate over the harmonization of values ensues, it has become clear that the Chilean example will ensure that process remains on an upwards course. This is an enormously important signal to my own fellow citizens, intent on entering into a significant new phase of open trade relations with the southern hemisphere.

For this to occur, linkages based on trust and understanding must develop on many levels. The ribbon attached to my lapel was a visible symbol of the bonding formed from the on-going struggle for human rights and freedom. It meant membership in a complex web of global linkages and associations which will serve as an infrastructure of ideas for the global community yet to come.

It meant also the shared understanding that democracy is a goal, not a starting point. The continuing challenge facing all democracies, no matter what the state of their development, is how to build political cultures of fairness and equity and respect for people. That is as true for Canadians as it is for Chileans. We must never forget that trust and belief in one another are the moral ingredients in the never-ending process of pluralist engineering and re-vitalization. Trust is the vital social cement, and without that powerful material, no democratic foundation can withstand the test of time.

In my own country, that important social capital has been noticeably in short supply as of late. Canadians must work hard to restore that sense of belief in one another. Trust is the anchor of all we have done together in the past. Belief is the beacon of all we will do together in the future. We have played, and must continue to play a unique and important role in the world community. We must stand united because we have promises to keep.

I thought of those promises during a visit to Quebec city last winter, my first in several years. I felt a need to visit there since the October, 1995 referendum. At that time Canadians nearly lost one of the most vital parts of our nation.

During my stay, I wondered how I could convince more of my fellow Canadians to visit that beautiful city which symbolizes all the drama and passion of our past - the city which sits as guardian over the great St. Lawrence river, gateway to a continent.

For many tourists, Quebec City is renowned for the battle sites of the Plains of Abraham. But for those who understand the city, the real story is about a compact between peoples of very different ethnic backgrounds and ancestral experiences. It is a story about a compact conceived by Canadians who were determined to leave the world a better place than they had found it.

I took my own walk in the snow along the Plains of Abraham. A little plaque caught my eye. I wiped the snow away, to better read the caption. Surprised to see the words "O Canada", I read on:

> This glorious National Anthem, verse by Sir Adolphe Routhier, music by Calixa La Vallée, was first sung at the First Congress Catholique Canadiens-Français, on the Fête of Saint-Jean Baptiste, 24th June, 1880.

As I read and re-read the lines, I was moved by the near loss of this vast and remarkable province, three times the size of France. I realized that this was in fact the homeland of many of those committed patriots who helped to engineer, through the beauty of our National Anthem, a country of compassion and justice - a country destined to become one of the most fortunate on the face of the earth.

I wondered what it would take to have that great event of 116 years ago repeated. I wondered how we could regain that simple trust, that same belief, that same confidence in one another which prompted our ancestors so long ago to lift their voices together in a moving tribute to our home and native land.

I thought of the belief and conviction on the faces of the hundreds of Chileans I had watched in August, 1995 as they proudly sang their National Anthem in the mud and the rain. We have much to learn from their courageous struggle. Like our Canadian ancestors of long ago, Chileans of today are moved by ideas larger than themselves. And like the Canadians of 1996, they have promises to keep.

They must work hard to restore and deepen the spirit of civic culture in their own country. Canadians must do the same. We must remember that freedom is not a gift bestowed, but a reward hard won.

We must remember that the seeds of freedom are not harvested in nations which are careless of tolerance and human rights. They are not harvested in nations where trust and belief are scorned and marginalized. Democratic leaders of the more mature democracies must take particular care to remember these basic truths. They must remain the kind of people who sail against the wind; who believe, in the words of Matthew Arnold, that life is not only a having and a getting, but it is a being and a becoming. So too, is the struggle for democracy.

My own experience has taught me that every man and woman who plants and nurtures the seeds of freedom across the world has one thing in common. No matter what their nationality or status in life, they believe that all persons and all nations owe it to themselves to seek the full realization of the potentiality that exists within them.

I believe that the great Cameroonian poet, Bernard Foulon, singled out the common thread linking so many of the leaders of democratic transitions in the developing world. On a flight from Rome to Yaounde, I read these beautiful words, words that leaders of the more mature democracies might take care to reflect upon:

> No thinker-scholar worthy of the name will be tempted to degenerate into a rabble rousing demagogue; into a perverted genius seeking to pull down where others strive to build; for thought, normally, does not develop in the crowd, in the marketplace, nor on the soap box, nor in perverse scheming and intrigue. It germinates and grows in seclusion, in research and meditation, in a mind not only fertile but steeped in intellectual honesty.

But such intellectual honesty must be paralleled by the conviction and courage of little people, for it is ultimately their marvellous devotion to democracy that makes change happen. As it is, they have caught a glimpse of the possible, and for this reason, their lives are changed forever.

Endnotes

1   A new law on earth is taken from Hannah Arendt, *Origins of Totalitarianism* (New York: Harcourt, Brace, 1973), p.ix, "Human dignity needs a new guarantee which can be found only in a new principle, in a new law on earth."

2   When my own boys were old enough to understand that I played at St. F.X. they were always interested in learning how big their "great one" was. It was a carefully guarded father's secret. That is, until Dr. Packy McFarland, now Athletic Director at the university produced a record of every football, basketball and hockey game in which St. F.X. ever participated. When the book arrived at our home in Sydney, the kids got to it first, eager to check my record. It was simple: 1948-49 - Al Graham - one goal - three assists. Someone confided to them later that was the year the goaltender had four assists.

3   But Saturday night was party night in Antigonish, particularly after a home game. The phone rang at home and I heard a stern voice say: "Alasdair, this is Bishop MacDonald. I was at the game this afternoon and heard you describing Geno running up and down the field while he was still sitting on the bench." I was speechless. The Bishop then exhorted me to remember the St. F.X. motto-Quaecumque Sunt Vera. (Whatsoever Things Are True.)

4   John Diefenbaker's state funeral in August, 1979 was an unparalleled event in Canadian history. I was asked to represent the Liberal Party on the train which, he had instructed, would take his mortal remains from Ottawa to Saskatoon for burial. This was to be a three-day journey. When we stopped at Sudbury at midnight on August 19, several hundred people gathered at the station. Joel Aldred, DFC, a long-time Diefenbaker friend spontaneously took on the chore of chairing the arrival. In his deepest, sonorous broadcasting voice, Aldred spoke meaningfully of the Chief to all assembled. He recalled the ecumenical service that had been held in Ottawa and pointed out that this was, indeed, an ecumenical train - "Witness the presence of the President of the Liberal Party of Canada, Senator Al Graham." - and much to my surprise, he added: "whom I now invite to speak." Buoyed up by Tory hospitality, I surprised myself at the quality of my eulogy to the fallen Chief. As soon as we were back on the train, I sought out the company of the country's best known journalist - Charles Lynch. "Charlie", I asked, "did I make a fool of myself?" "No," he said, "it was great. I didn't know you loved the old gentleman so much."

5   NRIIA is now known as IRI, the International Republican Institute.

6   John Simpson, *The Darkness Crumbles* (Hutchison, 1992). Phrase adapted from the title of this cogent, moving history of the period.

7   The idea of "defining moments" appears in James N. Rosenau and W. Michael Fagen, "Domestic Elections as International Events", in Carl Kaysen, Robert A. Pastor, and Laura W. Reed, *Collective Responses to Regional Problems* (American Academy of Arts and Sciences, 1994).

8   Ibid note 7 p. 35.

9   See, for example, David W. Gilles, "Commerce over Conscience: Export promotion in Canada's aid programme" *International Journal* XLIV (Winter 1988-89)at p.102 and T.A. Keenleyside - Nora Serkasevich, "Canada's Aid and Human Rights Observance: Measuring the Relationship", *International Journal* XLV (Winter, 1989-90) p.138.

10   *Independence and Internationalism* or the Hockin Report. The Special Joint Committee of both Houses of Parliament on Canada's International Relations, (Ottawa: Queen's Printer, June 1986) p.99.

11   A statement made in his 1986 report by the administrator of the Canadian Code of Conduct for Canadian Companies operating in South Africa.

12   See David Gillies' 1988 interview with Dr. William C. Winegard, then Chairman of the House of Commons Standing Committee on External Affairs and International Trade, as reprinted in *Human Rights, Development and Foreign Policy: Canadian Perspectives*, edited by Irving Brecher (Institute for Research on Public Policy, 1989), p.396.

13   Robert Miller, "The International Centre for Human Rights and Democratic Development: Notes on its Mission", in *Human Rights Development...*, p.378.

14   Government Response to the Recommendations of the Special Joint Parliamentary Committee Reviewing Canadian Foreign Policy, Ottawa, February, 1995, p. 65.

15   See Robert Pastor, "Forward to the beginning: widening the scope for global collective action", *The International Journal*, Autumn, 1993 p. 641.

16   Richard J. Bloomfield, "Making the Western World Safe for Democracy? - The OAS Defense-of-Democracy Regime", in *Collective Responses...* supra note 7 p. 16.

17   Ibid. p.20. As the author points out, the non-intervention principle is still very much alive as Article 18 of the OAS Charter illustrates: "No state or group of states has the right to intervene, directly or indirectly, for any reason whatsoever, in the internal or external affairs of any other state." See quote from the Charter.

18   *Document of the Moscow Meeting of the Conference on the Human Dimensions of the CSCE*, Oct. 3, 1991 p. 2.

19   Andrei Kozyrev, "Russia: A Chance for Survival," *Foreign Affairs*, vol.71, no.2, Spring 1992 p. 13.

20   Quoted in Gidon Gottlieb, *Nation against State*, (Council on Foreign Relations Press, 1993) pps. 20-21.

21   Larry Garber, *Comment*, in *Collective Responses to Regional Problems* p. 70.

22   Boutros Boutros-Ghali, *An Agenda for Peace* p. 9.

23   Micheal Ignatieff, *Blood and Belonging: Journeys into the new Nationalism*, (London: Chatto & Windus, 1993) p.186.

24   See G. John Ikenberry's article entitled "The Myth of Post-Cold War Chaos", in *Foreign Affairs*(May/June 1996), p.90.

25   James N. Rosenau, *Turbulence in World Politics; A Theory of Change and Continuity* (Princeton:University Press, 1990.)

26   Lester M. Salamon, "The Global Associational Revolution: The Rise of the Third Sector on the World Scene," *Occasional Paper No.15*, (Baltimore:Institute for Policy Studies, April, 1993), p. 1.

27   Doh Chull Shin, "On the Third Wave of Democratization", in *World Politics* 47 (October, 1994), p.151.

28   Larry Diamond, "The Globalization of Democracy: Trends, Types, Causes, and Prospects", in Robert Slater et al, *Global Transformation and the Third World* (Boulder, Colo., Lynn Rienner, 1992).

29   Some authors take the view, and very justifiably, that such categorization really distorts the meaning of the word. For example, Juan J.Linz and Alfred Stepan make the point that no regime should be called a democracy unless its rulers govern democratically. "In sum, when we talk about the consolidation of democracy, we are not dealing with liberalized nondemocratic regimes, or with pseudo-democracies or with hybrid democracies where some democratic institutions coexist with nondemocratic institutions outside the control of the democratic state. Only democracies can become consolidated democracies." In "Toward Consolidated Democracies", *Journal of Democracy*, Vol.7, No.2, April, 1996 p. 15.

30   Samuel P. Huntington, "Democracy for the Long Haul", *Journal of Democracy*, Vol.7, No.2, April,1996, pp.9-10.

31   Linz & Stepan supra note 29 p. 15.

32   Michael Chege, "Between Africa's Extremes", *Journal of Democracy*, Vol.6,No 1, December,1994, pp.50-51.

33   As an example of this kind of thinking, see Brian Beedham's "A Better Way to Vote", *The Economist* (Sept. 11-17, 1993) p.S5.

34   Charles S. Maier, "Democracy and its Discontents", *Current*, December 1994 pp. 25-32.

35   Huntington supra note 30 p. 11.

36   Ibid, p. 10-11.

37   Headline from Thomas Friedman's article entitled "This time it's Russia's Turn to take a Great Leap Forward", as reprinted in the *Globe and Mail*, Monday, July 15, 1996.

38   The Chris Gueffroy case, I was to learn later, was significant because the East German border guard who shot him was convicted in a Berlin court and was sentenced to three and a half years in jail for manslaughter. This case was the first of its kind in which former East Germans were convicted by the courts of unified Germany for actions that had been legal under East German law. Defense attorneys had argued that the defendants were only following the laws of East Germany when they shot at Gueffroy. But Trial Judge Theodor Seidel compared the shooting to the crimes of German Nazis in World War II and said it was "against the essence of human rights. The legal maxim that 'whoever flees will be shot to death' deserves no obedience."

39   What comes first, democracy or development, is a question which preoccupies growth economists. The whole subject enjoys a resurgence of academic interest in our time. Surjit Bhalla's well known article entitled "Democracy or discipline: Which works best?" is an example of this kind of analysis. I read it in the *Globe and Mail*, September 24, 1994 at D4, - a reprint from *the Economist*. He argued that freedom is conducive to long-term growth. His findings revealed that economic, as well as civil and political freedoms and a regard for individual rights account for the fact that nearly all of the world's richest countries are free and nearly all of the poorest countries are not.

40   Christopher Cramer, "Rebuilding South Africa", in *Current History*, May, 1994 p. 209.

41   Mandela's article entitled "South Africa's Future Foreign Policy" appeared in *Foreign Affairs*, Vol.72, No.5, November/December 1993 pp. 86-97.

42   Andre Brink, "A Democratic Dawn: Election Day in South Africa", in *Harper's*, August, 1994 p. 70.

43 Fadzai Gwaradzimba, "SADCC and the future of South African Regionalism", in *Issue: A Journal of Opinion*, Vol XX/1-2 1993.

44 Ibid p. 55.

45 See Robin Broad and John Cavanaugh's compelling treatment of the impact of globalization entitled "Don't Neglect the Impoverished South", *Foreign Policy*, Winter 1995-96, at p.29.

46 Ibid p.26.

47 Maria Sol Martin Reig, "The Mexican Presidential Elections of the 21st of August, 1994", presented at the 1994 Annual Meeting of CALACS, the llth of November, 1994, Ottawa, Canada.

48 Edward Broadbent, "A Free Election but not Fair", the *Toronto Star*, August 26,1994.

49 "Zedillo offers Mexico the chance of Change and Continuity", the *Manchester Guardian*, September 11, 1994.

50 *New York Times*, February 24, 1995.

51 James A. Shear, "Bosnia's Post-Dayton Traumas", *Foreign Policy*, No. 104, Fall 1996, p.91.

52 *The Guardian Weekly*, September 15, 1996.

53 Rosenau & Fagen supra note 7 at p. 63.

54 Rosenau & Fagen supra note 7 at p.31.

55 Larry Garber supra note 7 p. 69.

56 *The New Republic*, Jan. 20th, 1986, p.8.

57 Robert A. Pastor, "Elections, Monitoring", draft manuscript, p.2; scheduled for publication in *Encyclopedia of Democracy* (Congressional Quarterly Books, forthcoming).

58 See Sadia Touval's article in *Foreign Affairs*, September/October, 1994, pp. 44-57. He asks interested parties to stop dumping on the United Nations for tasks it can't perform and makes the important point that intractable disputes are best mediated by states, with the UN lending support.

59 Robert A. Pastor, "Nicaragua's Choice: The Making of a Free Election," *Journal of Democracy*, Vol. 1 (Summer, 1990), p. 18,21.

60 The superb efforts of the Supreme Electoral Council of Nicaragua with regard to voter education must be noted. The idea of a secret ballot was promoted and advertised across the country in voting guides.

61 Pastor supra note 59 p. 650.

62 Larry Garber, "A New Era of Peacemaking: United Nations and Election Monitoring", pp. 8-9.

63 Ibid p. 9.

64 See the arrival statement of President Carter, Chairman of the Freely-Elected Heads of Government, in Managua, February 23, 1990, in appendices. Note his expression to the fact that "Sunday is your day."

65 "Healing Nicaragua", *The Toronto Star*, 24 October 1996, A28.

66 Richard W. Soudriette, "Ballots not Bullets" (A Perspective on International Election Assistance), presented at the Second Annual Trilateral Conference on Electoral Systems, Ottawa, Canada, May, 1995, p.12.

67 "Its interesting to see, for the first-time, a police force and a Supreme Court led by people who are competent and committed to the rule of law", observed Enrique ter Horst, The UN's chief in El Salvador recently. Quoted in "Blind at Last", *the Economist*, August 13-19, 1994 p. 42.

68 *New York Times*, Sunday, October 20, 1991.

69 Steven R. Ratner, "The United Nations in Cambodia: A Model for Resolution of Internal Conflicts?" in *Enforcing Restraint, Collective Intervention in Internal Conflicts*. ed. by Lori Fisler Damrosch (Council on Foreign Relations Press, 1994), p.258.

70 Barbara Shenstone, "Supervising Elections in the Killing Fields", *bout de papier* (Fall/Winter,1993), p.18.

71 Ibid p.21.

72 Garber, "Comment", p. 70.

73 Ibid p. 70.

74 Manuel Antonio Garreton, "Redemocratization in Chile", *Journal of Democracy*, pp.146-158, Volume 6, Number 1, January 1995, p.148.

75 Franck, "The Emerging Rights to Democratic Governance," pp. 50-51.

76 Larry Garber, *Guidelines for International Election Observing* (Washington D.C: International Human Rights Law Group, 1984) p.13.

77 Expression widely ascribed to Maurice Bishop, former Prime Minister of Grenada.

78 See Francisco Goldman's description of the "pomp and terror in a dark country", "Guatemalan death masque", *Harpers*, Jan. 1986 at pp.56-60.

79 Marilyn Anne Zak, "Assisting Elections in the Third World",*Washington Quarterly*, Fall Issue, 1987.

80 Louis Lavoie, *Democratic Elections in the Kingdom of the Mayas*, January 1986.

81 As cited in *The New Republic*, June 30, 1986 pp. 13-17.

82 Cited in *The New York Times* special article on the elections, Wednesday, January 10,1996 p. 5.

83 Sterling Seagrave, *The Marcos Dynasty*, (Harper & Row Publishers, New York, 1988), pp. 403-404.

84 A sworn affidavit of one of the COMELEC project managers, Mr. Pedro Baraoidan, can be found in appendices.

85 As quoted in *The Globe and Mail*, February 10, 1986.

86 Stefan Mair, "International election observation: one form of democratisation assistance", *Inter Nationes* (Research Institute for International Politics and Security) April/July, 1994, p.19.

87 In all of the missions I have participated in, I have been quick to stress that our delegation is not sent to interfere in the electoral process and that we are there at the invitation of the government in question. See, for example, my Pre-Election Statement in Paraguay on the eve of the 1993 elections in appendices.

88 Robert A. Pastor, "Nicaragua's Choice: The Making of a Free Election," *Journal of Democracy*, Vol. l(Summer, 1990), p.18.

89 Election observer check-lists are vital sources of information but the relative simplicity of the documents belies the complexity of the process. See appendices for an example of the kind of form used by observers.

90 Adebayo Adedeji, "An Alternative for Africa", *Journal of Democracy*, October, 1994, p. 127.

91 Michael Chege, "Between Africa's Extremes", *Journal of Democracy*, January, 1995, Vol.6, No.1, p.49.

92 Ibid.

93 The Foreign Ministers of Latin America and Caribbean countries proposed the establishment of an advisory body to dispense technical advice in the promotion of elections in that Hemisphere. The Centre for Electoral Promotion and Assistance (CAPEL) was founded in 1983 in San Jose, Costa Rica.

94 Observing the Honduran Election, p.3, Nov. 24, 1985.

95 For a highly sympathetic, yet compelling look at the advances made in that country, see Oscar Santamaria's "Investing in El Salvador", in *North/South - Magazine of the Americas*, July/August 1994.

96 Marilyn Zak, p. 182.

97 In conversation with Luc Dumont, Chief of Accessibility and Analysis, Elections Canada.

98 Thomas Bayer, "IFES works with IEC to ensure elections for all", in *Elections Today, News from IFES*, Vol 4, No.4.

99 Dana DeBeauvoir, "Foot Soldier for Democracy", in *Elections Today, News from IFES*, Vol.4,No.4.

100 We cannot underestimate the truly monumental efforts made in the area of voter education by many organizations prior to election day. Civic education institutes are vital in emerging democracies. See appendices for examples of the fine work they do.

101 *ASEAN Forecast*, December 1985

102 NDI, *NRIIA Report*, Annex XIII.

103 *Globe and Mail*, Monday, February 10, 1986.

104 See examples of some of NAMFREL's magnificent work in educating Filipinos on the essentials of the electoral process, including, of course, the importance of the secret ballot, appendices.

105 "A Path to Democratic Renewal", *A Report on the February 7 Presidential Election in the Philippines*, by the NDI-NRIIA International Observer Delegation p.58.

106 Ibid p. 59.

107 Some of my own conclusions were published in the Globe and Mail, February 10, 1986. See appendices.

108 E. Mark Braden and Elaine K. Shocas, "The Day Before   Democracy", *Barrister Magazine* (Summer, 1986).

109 I have always treasured my correspondence with the highly respected Father Javier.

110 Larry Garber, Elaine Shocas, *The New Republic*, September 14 and 21, 1987, p.6.

111 In her Independence Day Message, President Aquino made it very clear that although "one law now channels the unswerving loyalty of all Filippinos to democracy and its ways", that this "is just the beginning of a long journey."

112 *New York Times*, Feb. 2, 1989.

113 Riordan Roett, "Paraguay After Stroessner" *Foreign Affairs*, Spring 1989, pp.124-142.

114 *New York Times Magazine*, Sept. 23, 1984.

115 In the *Miami Herald*, February 20, 1989

116 Riordon Roett, pp. 131-132.

117 *New York Times*, April 2, 1989.

118 *Liberal International Report*, Madrid, March 12, 1989.

119 External Affairs, Canada, LSR/Jones, Liaison Visit to Paraguay, March 7-8, 1989.

120 *First Steps After Stroessner, An Analysis of the Upcoming Paraguayan Elections*, Washington, D.C. April 1989.

121 It was also a place which fascinated people across the globe. The dialogue in my own country reflected the international interest. I recieved a note addressed to me from another former President of the Liberal Party of Canada, Iona V. Campagnola. In it, she wrote of a conversation she had with then Senator Lorna Marsden, now President of Sir Wilfred Laurier University, a woman of tremendous international sensitivity - with whom I was privileged to serve for many years in Liberal International.

122 See United Nations Security Council Resolution 435 in appendicies.

123 Christopher Edley, "Can Democracy Take Root In Namibia?", *Legal Times*, June 26, 1989.

124 Remarks from an interview with Chief Superintendent Larry Proke who served in Namibia as the Contingent Commander, RCMP, and was then seconded to UNTAG where he was appointed Chief of Staff to the Civilian Police, Ottawa, July 10, 1991.

125 As reported in the *Namibian*, June 9, 1989. There were many critics of the Law who argued that the U.N. and Ahtisaari had eleven years since his appointment to ensure the drafting of an internationally acceptable Law, along with regulations providing for essential civic education in Namibia.

126 An account of our report entitled "Distressing Strains in the National Fabric" was printed in the *Namibian*, June 9, 1989, and appears in the appendicies.

127 Many of us treasured the memories. Frederic Cowan called the experience "...one of the most rewarding...in my professional life." See appendices for the Cowan note.

128 See John Simpson's wonderful account of the events of 1989 in *the Darkness Crumbles*.

129 The June 1990 Elections in Bulgaria, NDI/NRIIA international Delegation Report, see p. 46 for examples of more subtle forms of intimidation.

130 John D. Bell, "Post Communist Bulgaria", *Current History*, December 1990, pp.417-420.

131 Luan Troxel, "Bulgaria: Stable Ground in the Balkans?" *Current History*, November 1993, p. 386.

132 A substantial number of Haitians in Canada were opposed to the government's decision to give aid to the Haitian junta. The process of democratisation was seen as a cynical ploy to improve Haiti's access to international loans and credits.

133 Louis Lavoie, Rémi Deshaies, Louis Massicotte, Mission de Faisabilité, October 1986

134 *Report on the Canadian Mission to observe the 29 November 1987 Haitian Election.*

135 Elizabeth Abbott, *Haiti: The Duvaliers and Their Legacy*, McGraw-Hill Book Company, 1988, p.3.

136 Ibid p.5.

137 John Simpson, p.279.

138 Ibid at p.222.

139 Trond Gilberg, "Romania: Will History Repeat Itself?", *Current History*, (December, 1990), pp. 410-411.

140 Ibid p.411.

141 Anna Husarska, "Ceausesus's Ghosts", *The New Republic*, June 11, 1990, p.13.

142 See *NDI Executive Summary*, the October 1992, Election in Cameroon. See also NDI invitation in appendicies.

143 *Economist*, Sept. 4th, 1993.

144 Michael Chege, *Current History*, May, 1994.

145 See Tina Rosenberg's fine article, "Beyond Elections," in *Foreign Policy*, Fall 1991, pp.72-91.

146 Rosenberg: "Chileans always took pride in the tradition of afternoon tea and habeas corpus; the country, they said, had a lawyer's soul... the legalistic, democratic Chilean political culture survived the general's best attempts to eradicate it." Ibid at p.76.

147 A sample of the kind of work they do in training election monitors and observing elections is seen in a memo from Ned McMahon, dated 18.9.92 and is included in the appendices.

148 Examples of the CED contribution to voter education appear in appendices.

149 Larry Garber,"Observers at Polling Places must include those without a Stake," *Christian Science Monitor*, May 13, 1992.

150 From the *Svoboden Narod Daily*.

151 This can be seen, in its simplest form, in the exchanges of the participants which took place during the Namibian mission. I first met the present President of Albania on a mission to observe the Bulgarian elections of 1991. Doctor Sali Berisha wrote me shortly after and, as seen above, we were able to continue a most valuable association in later years.

The International Legend Lester B. Pearson and the
Young Candidate in Antigonish 1958

Ottawa - Election Night - May 22, 1979
Prime Minister Trudeau concedes defeat in the 1979 election with
the author, then Party President, in the backgound.

Ottawa - Election Night - February 18, 1980
"Welcome to the 1980s" - Pierre Trudeau
Nine months later on the same stage in Ottawa, Trudeau and
Graham celebrate the return of the Liberal Party to government.

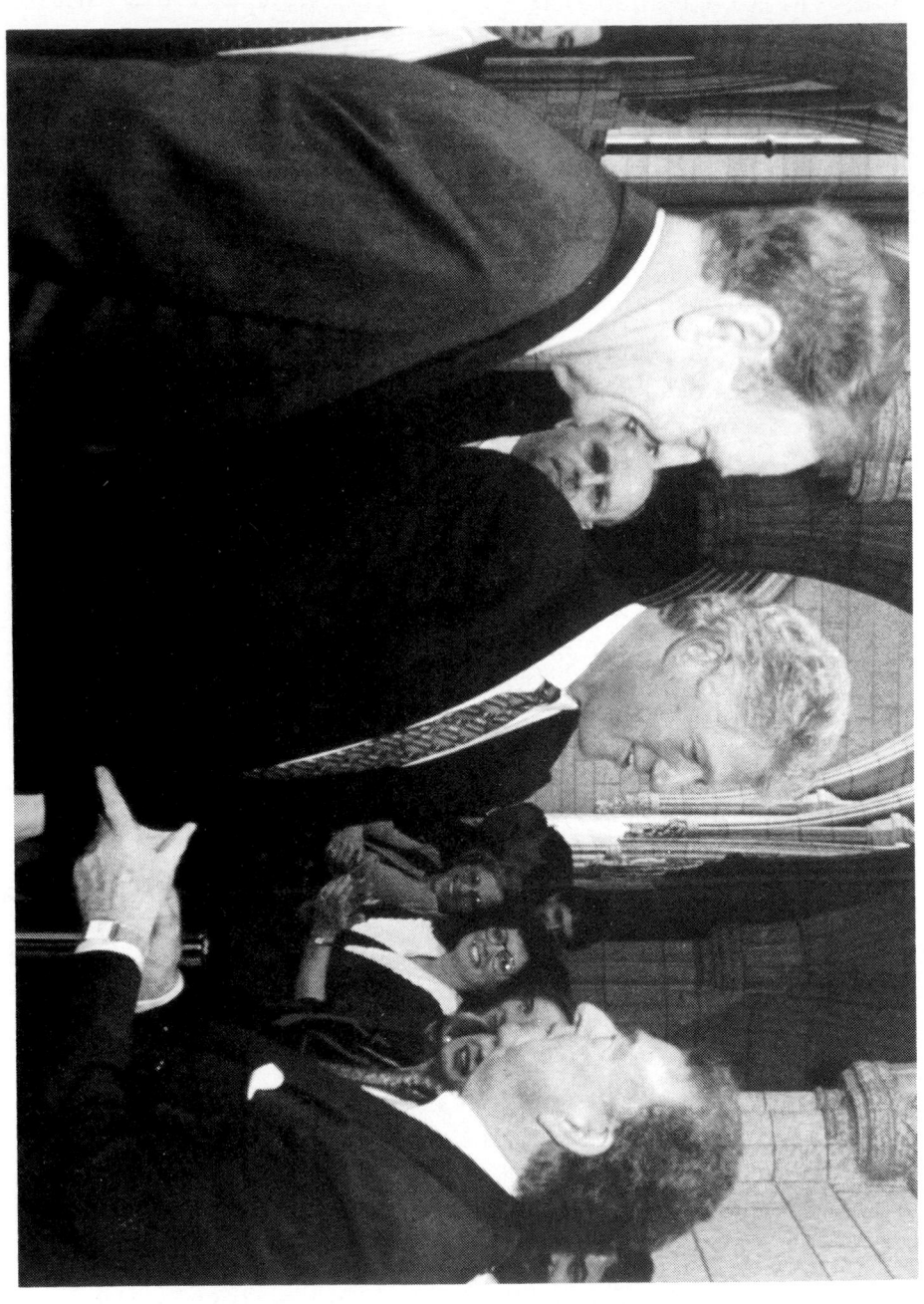

US President Bill Clinton visits Ottawa
23 February 1995

With Violetto Chomorro the
night before she was elected
President of Nicaragua

With President Carter the
night before the election in
Nicaragua

)elegation leader Al Graham introduces May 1987 observer/study
group to President Corazon Aquino. NDI Executive Vice
President Ken Wollack is seated at Aquino's left

With Juan Carlos Wasmosy,
New President of Paraguay.

At polling station wih
President Eduardo Frei of Chile

1984 with Shimon Peres, the day he was sworn in as Prime Minister of
Israel, and Italian Senator Giovanni Malagodi President of
Liberal International

With Tribe Leaders in Ovamboland

Peacekeepers on the Namibia-Angola Border

With hockey legend Maurice "the rocket" Richard, at a benefit hockey game for the Children's Hospital of Eastern Ontario

The author with his sons and three future stars following the 1994 Annual Graham-Joseph Boxing Day hockey game at Centre 200 in Sydney, Nova Scotia. l. to r. Bill, David, the Author, Alasdair, Jack and Danny. In front l. to r. Jack's children Hannah and John, and Danny's son Andrew

With President Zhelev of Bulgaria

Cape Breton's Mira River connects with the Danube at Budapest

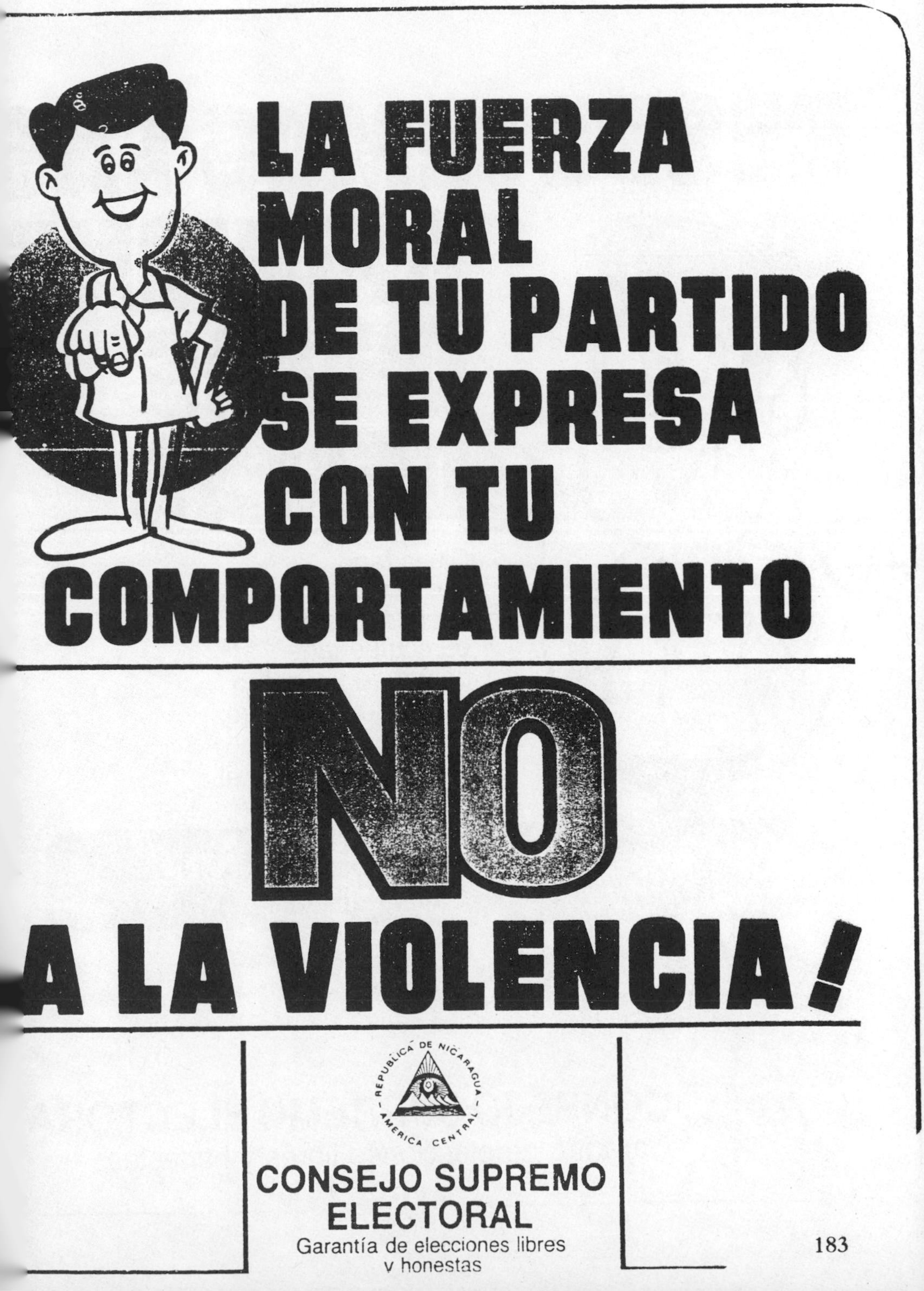

**LA FUERZA
MORAL
DE TU PARTIDO
SE EXPRESA
CON TU
COMPORTAMIENTO**

**NO
A LA VIOLENCIA!**

**CONSEJO SUPREMO
ELECTORAL**
Garantía de elecciones libres
y honestas

RESPETEMOS LAS OPINIONE DE LOS DEMAS

Ciudadano,
Vos tenés
el deber moral
de comportarte
dentro de un marco
de cultura y madurez
durante
la campaña electoral.

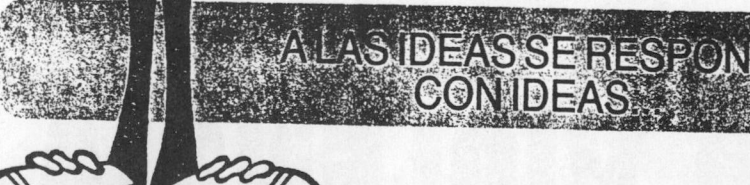

A LAS IDEAS SE RESPONDE CON IDEAS.

CONSEJO SUPREMO ELECTORA
Garantía de elecciones libres y honestas

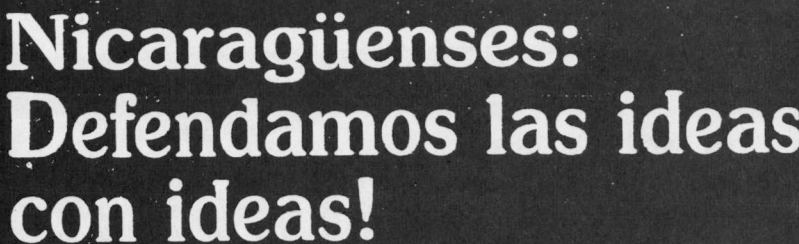

Nicaragüenses: Defendamos las ideas con ideas!

Es responsabilidad de todos que las elecciones de 1990 sean libres y honestas

RESPETEMOS LAS OPINIONES DE LOS DEMAS

REPUBLICA DE NICARAGUA · AMERICA CENTRAL

consejo supremo electoral

Garantía de Elecciones libres y honestas

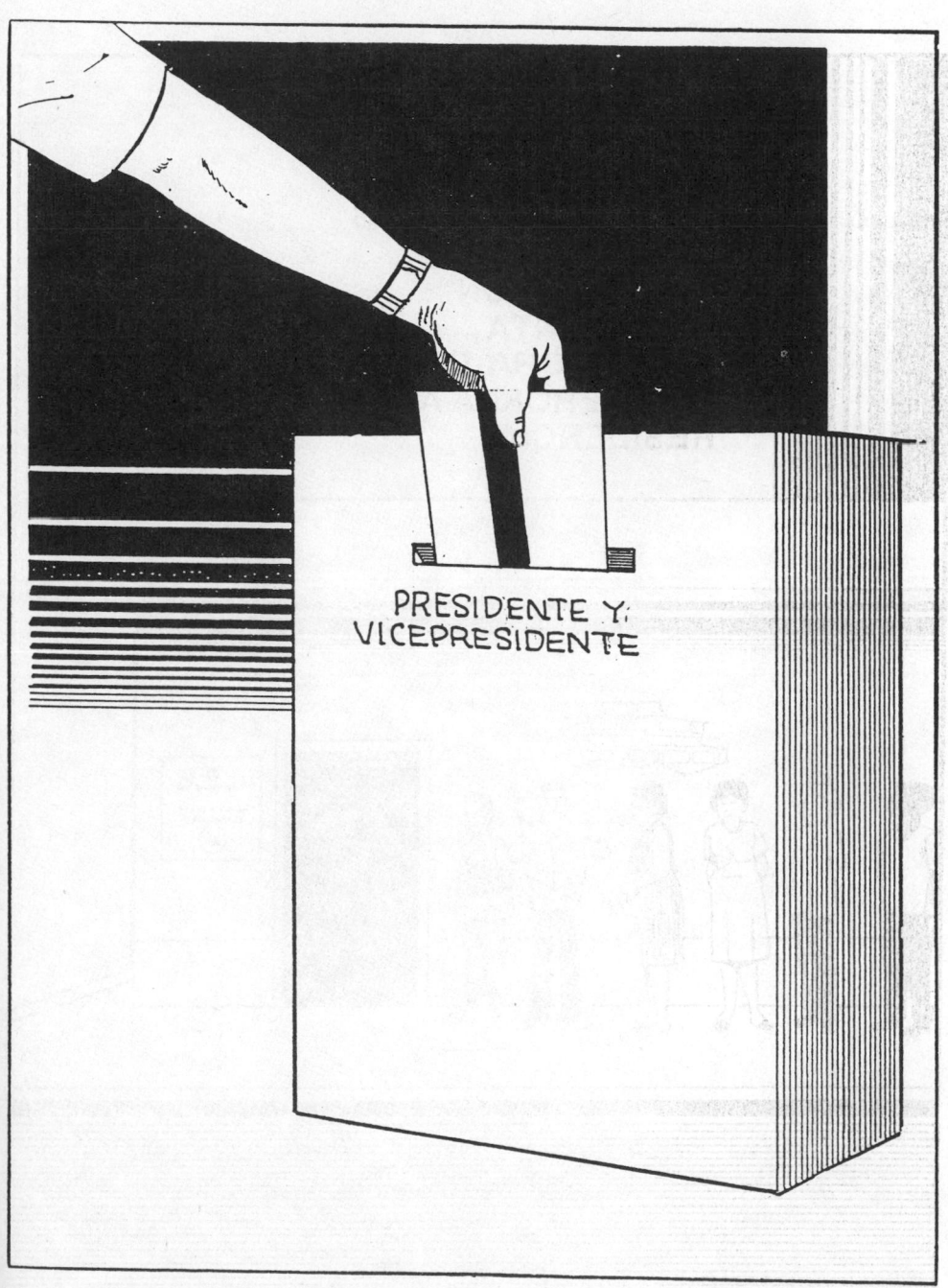

EN OCTUBRE RECIEN
PASADO
TODOS LOS
CIUDADANOS APTOS
PARA VOTAR SE
INSCRIBIERON
EN LA JUNTA
RECEPTORA DE VOTOS
MAS CERCANA A SU
RESIDENCIA.

Recuerda que el

25

de Febrero

Todos los ciudadanos inscritos debemos ejercer nuestro derecho al voto secreto en la misma junta en la que nos inscribimos.

Las Votaciones
daran inicio a las

7:00 a.m.

**Entrá detrás del recinto secreto
y marca con una**

**cada boleta electoral en la
casilla de tu preferencia.**

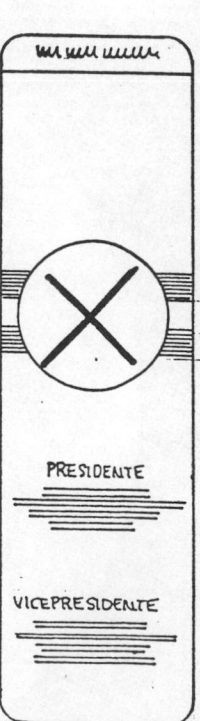

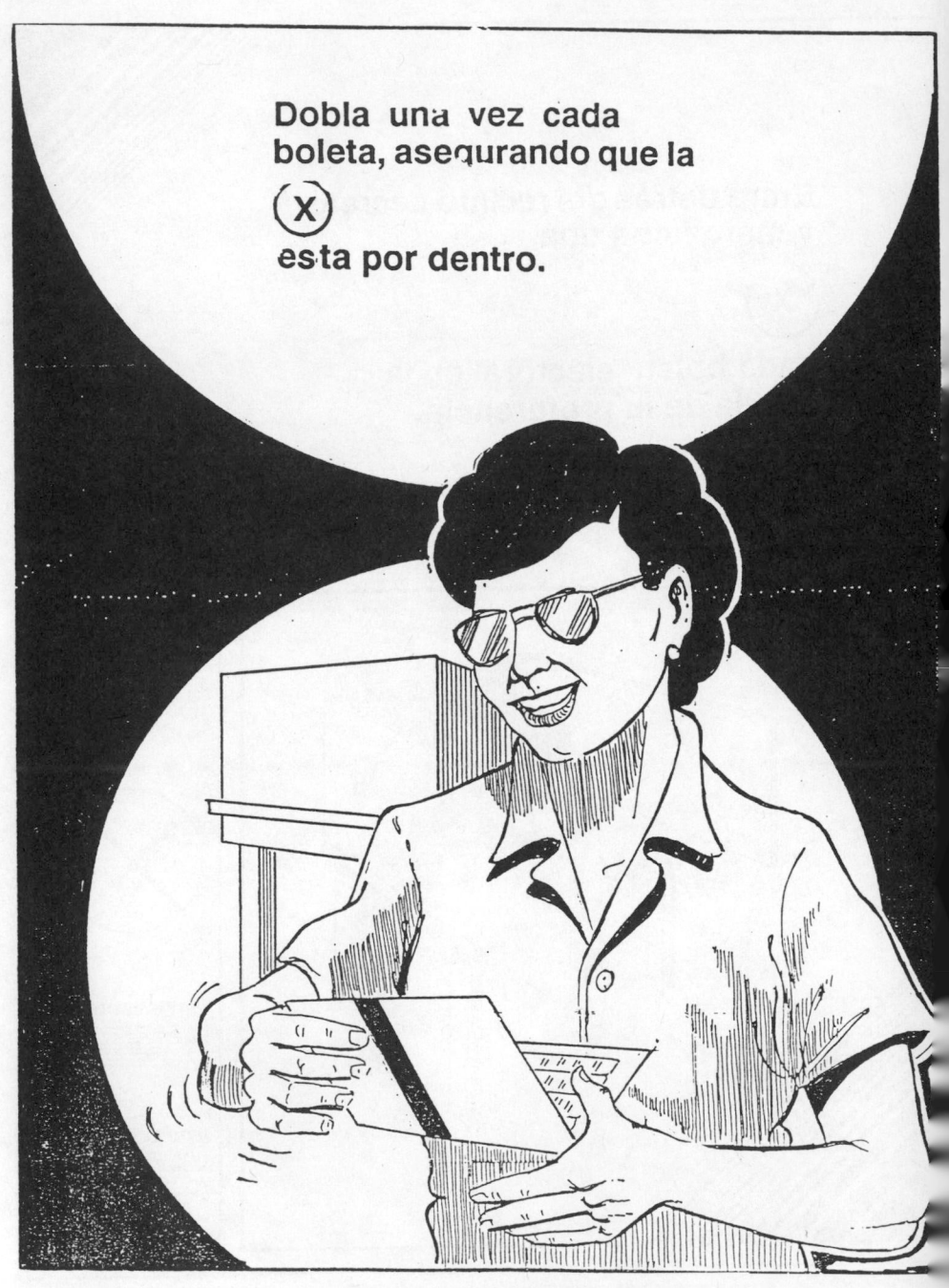

Deposita cada boleta en su urna correspondiente. Cada urna llevará una leyenda y distintivos colores.

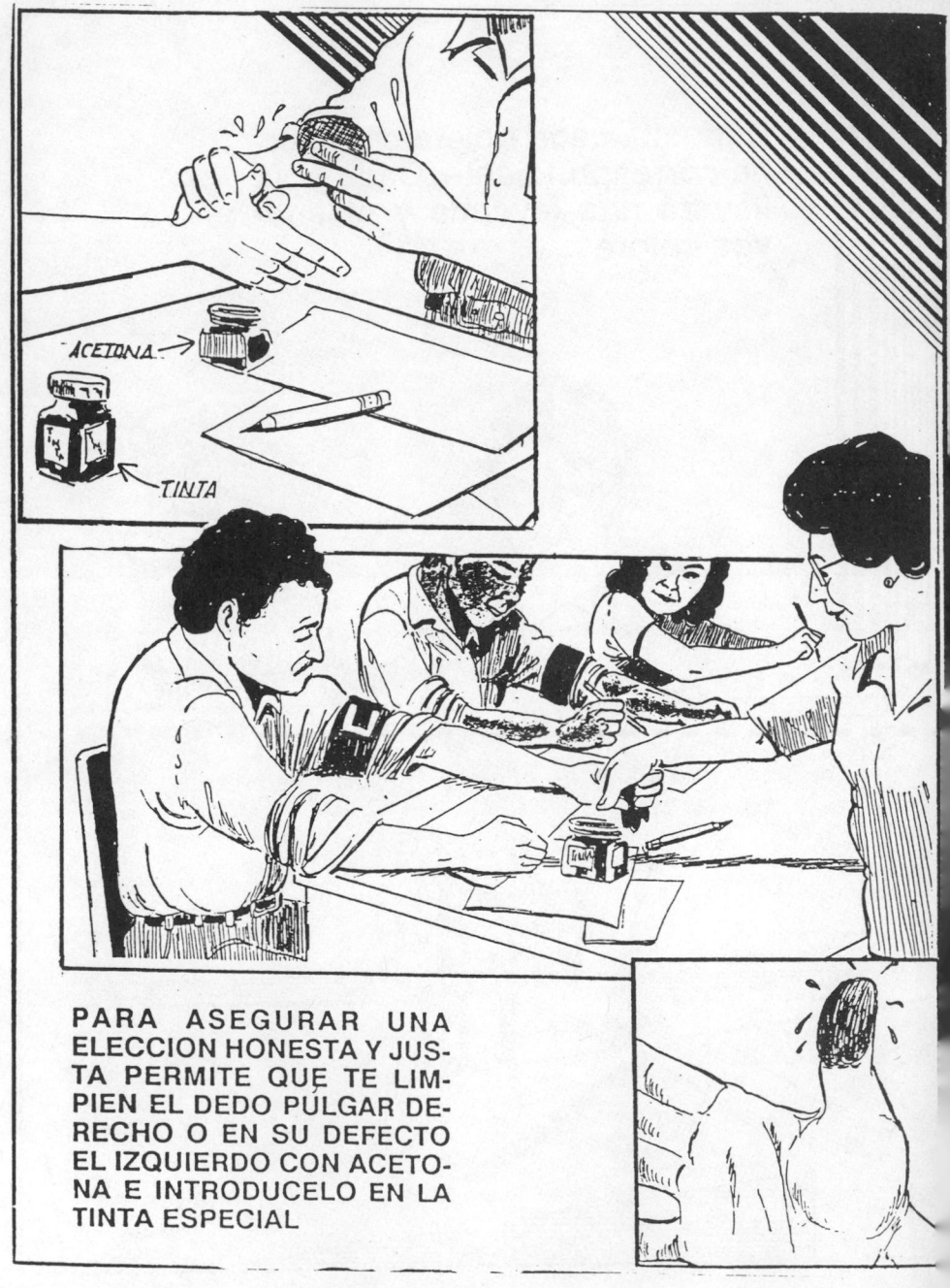

PARA ASEGURAR UNA
ELECCION HONESTA Y JUS-
TA PERMITE QUE TE LIM-
PIEN EL DEDO PULGAR DE-
RECHO O EN SU DEFECTO
EL IZQUIERDO CON ACETO-
NA E INTRODUCELO EN LA
TINTA ESPECIAL

Appendix B

English translation/original in Spanish

ARRIVAL STATEMENT OF
Hon. Jimmy Carter, Chairman
Council of Freely-Elected Heads of Government
Managua, February 23, 1990
DELEGATION TO OBSERVE THE NICARAGUAN ELECTIONS

Thank you, Prime Minister George Price, for making that statement on behalf of all of us who are members of the Council of Freely-Elected Heads of Government and the rest of our delegation.

Our delegation is international and bipartisan with twelve members of Congress from both parties in the United States, and leaders from the two major parties of Venezuela and Costa Rica.

We come here at the invitation of the Nicaraguan government, the opposition, and the Supreme Electoral Council, and we arrive with profound respect and appreciation for Nicaragua's sovereign right to decide its own future. We have come to support the people of this courageous country who want to vote and build a democracy.

We expect Sunday to be a festive day, and hope that everyone will vote and be confident that your vote will b secret and that your vote will count. We are here to make sure of that.

Tomorrow and Sunday, our delegation will work with the OAS and UN and travel to every region of the country. We will monitor every step of the process and do parallel tabulations of the vote to guarantee that the final results reflect the will of the people.

This is an historic moment for the people of this nation - an opportunity to choose your leaders and heal this divided land. After Sunday, regardless of who wins, we hope that all of you will treat each other with tolerance and respect.

Sunday is your day. We will observe, but only Nicaraguans can vote. Choose well, and we will work to ensure that the results reflect you decisions and are respected.

To the people of Nicaragua, I want to say thank you for your hospitality and for giving me the opportunity to work with all of you - all ten parties - who have worked to build a new democratic Nicaragua. And finally, let me thank you for your patience in listening to me speak Spanish.

Appendix C

Council of Freely-Elected
Heads of Government
Carter Center of
Emory University
One Copenhill
Atlanta, Georgia 30307
404)420-5175

National Democratic Instit.
for International Affairs
1717 Massachusetts Ave. N.W.
Suite 503
Washington, D.C. 20036
(202) 328-3136
(202) 939-3166 (fax)

Pre-Election Statement

INTERNATIONAL DELEGATION TO NATIONAL ELECTIONS IN
PARAGUAY

May 7, 1993

Asuncion, Paraguay

I am Al Graham, a senator in the Parliament of Canada. I am pleased to once again co-lead an international observer delegation to elections in Paraguay. The other leaders of this delegation, former U.S. President Jimmy Carter and former Costa Rican President Rodrigo Carazo Odia, will arrive on Saturday.

This delegation is being organized by the National Democratic Institute for International Affairs (NDI), a democratic development institute in Washington, D.C. that conducts nonpartisan programs around the world, and the Council of Freely Elected Heads of Government, an informal group of 21 former and current heads of government from throughout the hemisphere, based at the Carter Center of Emory University in Atlanta, Georgia. NDI has organized election observer delegations in more than 20 countries in Europe, Africa, Asia and Latin America, and the Council has observed the electoral process in eight countries in the Americas, four with NDI.

My colleagues on this delegation include former heads of state, legislators, leaders of political parties, election experts and civic leaders. The 31 delegates are nationals from Argentina, Brazil, Canada, Chile, Costa Rica, Guyana, Honduras, France, Malawi, Mexico, Panama, Peru, Russia, South Africa and the United States.

As many Paraguayans have noted, these elections are significant because they provide the first opportunity for a transition from one elected government to another in the country's history. A successful electoral precess will represent an important step toward the consolidation of Paraguay's young democracy.

The delegation is not here to interfere in the internal affairs of Paraguay. We are here to demonstrate international support for the democratic precess at the invitation of Paraguayans and to report our impressions to the international community.

As observers, we have taken no position regarding the outcome of the elections. The members of our delegation are here because they have demonstrated in their careers a strong commitment to democracy. We expect to learn a great deal to take home to our respective countries.

Paraguayans from across the political spectrum have welcomed this attention and have expressed appreciation that this and other international observer delegations will be present for the elections. The Paraguayan government itself has encouraged our presence here, and the Central Electoral Board has provided us with credentials.

NDI, which organized observer delegations to the 1989 and 1991 elections, has supported civic education programs in Paraguay during the past four years and recently organized workshops to train local officials. NDI also has provided assistance to SAKA, the consortium of nongovernmental organizations, to conduct a quick count for the election, which will permit an accurate projection of the presidential election results hours after the polls close. NDI also sponsored a visit b two Panamanian experts in voter registration to help the political parties review the registration lists. The experts concluded that although the lists were flawed, the irregularities would not prevent the holding of a legitimate electoral process.

In March, NDI sent a five-person international team to study the electoral process. This week, the institute published a report base on the team's findings and the observations and research conducted by NDI Program Officer Steve Griner, who has been in Paraguay for six weeks. (Copies of the report are available.)

Yesterday and today, the delegation is meeting with a broad spectrum of political leaders, candidates, military officials, civic leaders and members of the Central Electoral Board and Central Electoral Tribunal. Tomorrow, the delegation will divide into six reams and disperse throughout the country. While in the interior, the delegates will meet with candidates and local election officials. On Sunday, the teams will observe the balloting and counting.

The delegation will regroup in Asuncion on Monday to exchange impressions. We expect to report our views to the international community on Monday or Tuesday.

While concerns have been raised regarding the electoral process, we are confident that the active monitoring of the process by Paraguayans, supported by us and other international groups, will guarantee the detection of any significant attempt to manipulate the election.

We have been told repeatedly by Paraguayans that fairly conducted elections are in the interest of all Paraguayans. We are grateful for the opportunity to contribute to this laudable goal.

Appendix D

ELECTION OBSERVATION CHECKLIST

I. General

    A. How many voting tables are at the polling site?
    B. At what time did the polling site open?
    C. Were all the election officials present?
    D. Which parties are represented by pollwatchers?
    E. Were the required electoral materials present?
    F. Identify any sources of intimidation.

II. Polling Process

    A. Were voters identified in accordance with the law?
    B. Was the ballot secret?
    C. Was the voter marked in indelible ink?
    D. Was the polling process challenged in any way?
        1. Who make the challenges?
        2. How were the challenges handled?
    E. How long did it take to process each voter?
    F.   AdditionalComments:

III. Counting Process

    A. What time did the polling site close?
    B. Who was present at the closing?
    C. Was the process in accordance with prescribed procedures?
    D. Were there any challenges to the counting process?
        1. Who made the challenges?
        2. How were they handled?
    E. At what time was the counting completed?
    F. Did the party pollwatchers receive certified copies of the results?

IV. Other Comments

Appendix E

NAMFREL
GUIDELINES FOR VOLUNTEERS

NAMFREL National Office, 8th Floor, RFM Building, Pioneer St., Mandaluyong, Metro Manila Tel.: 77-24-72 ● 77-24-74 ● 77-24-81 Series 1987

Statement of Position

(To be read in meetings to orient and train volunteers or use as guidelines for those speaking in forums on behalf of NAMFR

IN ANTICIPATION OF THE COMING ELECTIONS, the call is once again being raised: "NAMFREL needs volunteers. NAMF
needs you!"

While, many of us will take up the call and readily volunteer as before, there will be people on the other hand who will ask
questions: "Is NAMFREL still relevant? Isn't NAMFREL partisan?

These are good questions.

And if we are to continue to attract the support of our people, then we must provide crystal clear answers to calm their minds
these gut issues. We must once again and, if it need be in the future, over and over again, explain what our cause is and why ou
also their cause.

AND SO, WHAT IS OUR CAUSE?

First and foremost, NAMFREL is people. We are an aggrupation of the poor and the rich, the young and the old. Christians and
Christians; businessmen, religious, government employees, laborers, farmers and all who are bound by the common conviction
popular democracy works. We believe that all have equal votes and, when the occasion arises to make our choices known, we bel
that the choice of the majority should rule, and this choice should be arrived at freely and honestly.

This is why advocates of armed struggle will never espouse the cause of NAMFREL. Although we may share with them common
rations of progress and a better life for our people, yet we do not agree that the man holding the gun rules. The same goes for thos
the other end of the ideological spectrum who will impose the rule of force on an unwilling populace.

This is why the man who cheats and manipulates the results of election and makes a mockery of the popular will can never take up
cause of NAMFREL. This man has nothing in common with us. We will never allow ourselves and our children to live in an atmosp
and condition which he controls with fraud and in which one must cheat in order to succeed. After all, the root of the word "v
means" to speak solemnly" and whoever interferes with our right to vote is in effect degrading the solemn voice of the people.

This is also why the defeatist, the negativist, and the free loaders will find the cause of NAMFREL unattractive. In the 1984 anc
1986 elections, in the face of hardships, threats and uncertainties, NAMFREL offered hope that the people could undertake ch.
without the use of violence. NAMFREL kept the faith burning in people's hearts that they could make the difference against all c

And finally, this is why the grafter will continue to be monitored and condemned by NAMFREL. Although he may have secure
office and position through an honest election or through a legitimate appointment, yet he prostitutes his mandate and service fo
benefit of a favored few and at the expense of the people.

We have heard this before and yet it is worth repeating. "We the sovereign Filipino people, imploring the aid of Almighty (
resolve, "to build a just and humane society and establish a Government that shall embody our ideals and aspirations, promot
common good, conserve and develop our patrimony, secure to ourselves and our posterity the blessings of independence and d
cracy under the rule of law and a regime of truth, justice, freedom, love, equality, and peace . . ."

And in another article: "Sovereignty resides in the people and all government authority emanates from them . . ."

ND NOW WE ASK THE QUESTION. "IS NAMFREL STILL RELEVANT?"

his question is usually asked by people who feel that with the present government, the need for protecting the ballot is no longer felt d urgent. This is just as if to say that now that Mrs. Aquino is in power NAMFREL has ceased to be relevant.

is is a gross error. It is not correct to equate the existence of NAMFREL with the elevation of Mrs. Aquino to power. If this uation were true, then NAMFREL richly deserves to die!

AMFREL exists for the people and not for any individual, whether in enforcing honest elections or in securing honesty in govern- nt. In a democracy as young as ours, the protection of the people's rights must be a continuing exercise and every facet of our mocratic institutions must be built on painstakingly, bit by bit, time over time, and trial after trial.

this coming elections, about 130 candidates are running for senators and about 1000 candidates are expected to run for congress- n. There are precincts whose number of voters is about 200 but there are much more where there may be more than 400 voters a precinct. Each voter is supposed to fill up 25 names of candidates in the ballot. There are only less than 6,000 employees in the MELEC and only three (3) members of the Board of Elections Inspectors in each precinct. All voting must be squeezed in the scribed voting hours of about 8 to 10 hours.

ere is definitely a need for NAMFREL.

ong many other functions, NAMFREL is committed to provide the following services:

1. Provide and sponsor forums for voters to meet candidates in their respective communities as well as for candidates to ventilate their platform and other election issues. The time is dawning -- and NAMFREL has a distinct role to make this come about – for people in the cities as well as in far-flung barrios to vote on the basis of issues and platforms and not simply on the basis of how popular a candidate's name sounds or how easy it is to spell and write on the ballot.

   NAMFREL in the past fought to ensure that our elections are clean, honest and orderly. Now, NAMFREL must also ensure that the people are given the opportunity to vote intelligently.

2. Assist voters in the polling places and provide service to the BEI in whatever way required to facilitate traffic, location of voters' names, delivery and accomplishment of election forms and documents, counting of ballots and accomplishment of precinct tally sheets, delivery of ballot boxes and election returns to municipal and city halls.

3. Promote citizen's vigilance, conduct poll watching activities and institute safeguards in the entire electoral process to ensure fair play among competing candidates and enforce pertinent election laws.

4. Participate in the canvassing of election returns in all municipalities and districts.

5. Conduct an Operation Quick Count that aims to bring about the results in less than one week as COMELEC proceeds to officially canvass election results.

uch a demanding task as this, who says that NAMFREL has no more relevance?

e wish to ensure the permanence of our democratic institutions and harvest its fruits and blessings, then we must invest time and rt and be willing to continually incur sacrifices.

like a father who passes on the inheritance of a lifetime work to his son, we too will ask our children, as we leave behind the ocratic heritage we have worked for, to carry on and build on it.

AMFREL TRULY NON-PARTISAN?

e people say that NAMFREL is partisan because its leaders who were supposed to be non-partisan during the snap elections have pted appointive positions in the present government. Others say that they have been used by NAMFREL leaders to advance their onal ambitions.

issue about former NAMFREL officials accepting appointive positions in government works on the underlying assumption that e leaders betrayed the cause of NAMFREL by accepting government work. And another assumption is that they are not qualified ssume the positions and have indeed taken them to enrich themselves in office.

spirit and cause of NAMFREL — that which keeps it alive — is love of country, self-sacrifice and unswerving commitment to ect the will and welfare of the people.

y accepting these government positions, these leaders threw this spirit to the winds, then they have truly betrayed the cause of FREL and we, who have worked with them, have truly something to be sorry for.

But if, by accepting these positions, they continue to uphold and carry on this cause, then we who are left behind have great reaso[n] to rejoice. For, from our ranks arose true and committed national leaders to serve the people through direct involvement in gover[n]ment affairs. We should also rejoice for the reason that while private citizens fight for their rights and honesty in government from t[he] outside, we now have a greater number of people fighting for the same objectives within the structures of government.

The second assumption about qualifications is easier evaluated now on the basis of the performance of these leaders. How do [we] assess the performance and dedication to duty of the following individuals: Jose Concepcion, Ting Jayme, Winnie Monso[n,] Joey Cuisia, Ed Espiritu, Dante Santos, Benjie Lozare and others? Do you think they accepted their appointive positions becau[se] they wanted to enrich themselves in office? We leave it to your judgement to answer these questions.

But, assuming these leaders and other volunteers did betray the cause and spirit of NAMFREL and did in fact commit an error [in] accepting their appointive positions, can we now, therefore, say that NAMFREL is partisan?

These leaders are not NAMFREL and NAMFREL is not these leaders. NAMFREL is more than 500,000 volunteers during the sn[ap] elections and the millions more who sympathized and supported its cause. We do not say that a religion is evil because of sinners in [its] rank and file. Neither can we say that NAMFREL is partisan because some of its rank and file erred on the issue of partisanship.

The most effective guarantee that NAMFREL is non-partisan is the volunteers themselves. NAMFREL is open to all Filipinos, irr[es]pective of their personal choice, provided that they abide by the cause of NAMFREL. Any volunteer, whether in rank or in fi[eld] who plays partisan politics in his work will soon be exposed because of the single-minded dedication and number of NAMFR[EL] volunteers. As we guard the electoral process against the fraud and dishonesty, we also guard ourselves.

This is why no NAMFREL leader can effectively and for long carry out a partisan scheme. It is foolish to believe that anyone [or] groups of men can manipulate NAMFREL without being uncovered because of the sheer number of volunteers and the comp[lex] series of activities that need to be manipulated to accomplish a hidden agenda. If any of you doubts this, you should try it som[e] time.

But this is not to say that we can relax our guard on this issue.

We must institute a program of action to promote and perpetuate non-partisanship in our local chapter organizations. It may [be] necessary to hold ceremonies in which volunteers will take a pledge of non-partisanship and commitment to NAMFREL's objecti[ves.]

Basic to this program is a clear-cut definition of what partisanship means. Then, a consensus must be arrived at and resolved by [the] leaders and members of each local NAMFREL chapter how this definition applies to specific situations and activities involv[ing] NAMFREL volunteers. Such resolution and consensus should bind all NAMFREL volunteers and include sanctions against those w[ho] violate the norm.

There is no better place to begin the definition of partisanship than the Election Code:

"The term 'election campaign' or 'partisan political   activity' refers to an act designed to promote the election or defeat of a pa[rti]cular candidate or candidates to a public office which shall include:

   (1)   Forming organizations, associations, clubs, committees or other groups of persons.

   (2)   Ho'ding political caucuses, conferences, meetings, rallies, parades, or other similar assemblies.

   (3)   Making speeches, announcements, commentaries, or holding interviews.

   (4)   Publishing or distributing campaign literature materials.

   (5)   Directly or indirectly soliciting votes, pledges, or support for or against a candidate."

                    (COMELEC Resolution 1835, March 4, 1987 -- Section 3)

ALL NAMFREL volunteers are forbidden to undertake any of the above activities.

But in the more positive way, all NAMFREL volunteers must be non-partisan, in that they must, without fear or favor, protect [and] strengthen the process of a free, orderly and honest election, irrespective of who the candidates are and who among them will w[in.]

And so, the call is once again being raised: "NAMFREL needs volunteers. NAMFREL needs YOU!

This call is not given to everyone. Only to those who believe in the spirit and cause of NAMFREL and who are willing to abide [by] them.

ARE YOU ONE OF THEM?

Al Graham

"HONESTY IN ELECTIONS, HONESTY IN GOVERNMENT."

"IT IS BETTER TO LIGHT A CANDLE THAN TO CURSE THE DARKNESS"

"ALL IT TAKES FOR EVIL TO TRIUMPH IS FOR GOOD MEN TO DO NOTHING"

"DEMOCRACY IS BASED ON THE CONVICTION THAT THERE ARE EXTRAORDINARY
POSSIBILITIES IN ORDINARY PEOPLE"

ONE LITTLE CANDLE

It is better to light
just on little candle
than to stumble in the dark
Better far that you light
just one little candle,
All you need is a tiny spark.
If we'd all say a prayer
that the world would be free.
the wonderful dawn
of a new day we'd see:
And if everyone lit
just one little candle,
what a bright world
this would be.

SEND US FOOLS, LORD

O God! Send us fools,
those who commit themselves totally,
those who forget themselves,
those who love in more than words,
those who truly give their lives
and until the end.

Give us fools, proud and fiery,
men capable of making the leap to insecurity,
to the surprises and uncertainties of
poverty.

Give us fools,
who accept to be diluted among the
masses,
without pretensions of erecting their own
pedestals,
without using their superiority for their
own advantage.

Give us fools, fools of the present day,
in love with a simple life,
efficient servants of the people,
lovers of peace, pure of heart,
resolved never to betray,
ready to accept any task,
to help anywhere, free and obedient,
spontaneous and tenacious,
sweet and strong.

Give us fools, Lord, give us fools!

Members of the National Council

National Chairman – Christian S. Monsod
Co-Chairman – Bishop Antonio Y. Fortich DD
Vice-Chairman – Jose Y. Feria

Committees

Sec.-General – Gregorio J. Atienza,
Alfredo Sanggalang
Finance – Cesar A. Buenaventura
DQC – Augusto C. Lagman
Organizations & Treasurer – Teresa F. Nieva
Legal – Ricardo L. Romulo

Regional Chairmen

NCR – Luis & Patricia Sison; I – Reynaldo C.
Bautista; II – Bishop Ramon B. Villena; III – Msgr.
Jose R. de la Cruz; IV – Victor G. Puyat; V –
Damaso G. Magbual; VI – Bro. Rolando R. Dizon
SC; VII – Marie Y. Aboitiz, VIII – Msgr. Antonio
R. Petilla; IX – Bishop Antonio R. Tobias; X – Fr.
Frank R. Demetrio; XI – Fr. Emeterio J. Barcelon;
XII – Ricardo P. Guevarra

Sectoral Representatives

Efren P. Aranzamendez – Pres., Confederation of
Filipino Workers; Bro. Tito A. Caluag, "NAMFREL
Marines"; Fortune B. Cruz – Pres., Phil. Institute of
Certified Public Accountants; Imelda K. Dayrit –
Former Pres., Catholic Women's League; Brig. Gen.
Manuel T. Flores (ret.) – Chairman, New AFP Anti-
Graft Board; Eduardo F. Hernandez – Former Pres.,
Philippine Bar Association; Felicisimo O. Joson –
Treas., Federation of Free Workers; Domingo Lee,
Pres., Federation of Filipino-Chinese Chamber of
Commerce; Estefania Aldaba Lim – Former Vice-
Chairman, UNESCO; Xavier P. Loinaz – President,
Bank of the Phil. Islands; Francis N. Pangilinan –
Pres., Univ. of the Phils. Student Council; Rev. Cirilo
A. Rigos – Protestant Community; Teresa E. Roxas
– Pres., Cultural Center of the Phils., Sis. Luz
Emmanuel Soriano – Sec., Catholic Educators
Association of the Phils., Jesus T. Tambunting –

Vice Pres., Management Association of the
Philippines; Msgr. Francisco G. Tantoco – Asst.
National Chaplain, Knights of Columbus; Ruben L.
Tiangco – Pres., Confederation of Government
Employees Organizations; Lugum L. Uka – Sec.,
Muslim Association of the Phils.; Henrietta T. de
Villa – Pres., Council of the Laity of the Philippines;
Presbitero J. Velasco, Jr. – Pres., Integrated Bar of
the Philippines

Operations

Administration – Cherry S. Flores; Regional Field
Directors – Sis. Annie B. Abion, ACT, Eddie M.
Nuque; Legal Counsel – Reynaldo G. Geronimo;
Public Information – Aurelio O. Angeles; Education
– Ricardo L. Gonzales; Special Action Teams – Jose
A. Bernas; Youth Coordinator – Ino M. Manalo

WANTED 500,000 BRAVE FILIPINOS

15 years old and above. Willing to donate time and energy to a lifetime cause --- the preservation of democracy. Ready to sacrifice for love of country.

If you believe that democracy comes through hard work and continuing vigilance

If you believe that the work of each Filipino goes beyond elections

If you believe that a clean honest government can only come from the united effort of its citizenry

If you believe that a clean honest government can bring about a better life for you and your children

Then join NAMFREL. Now.
Because now more than ever the country needs you.

Democracy demands honesty --- in elections, in government.

NAMFREL

National Citizens Movement for Free Elections and Honest Government
National Office 8th Floor RFM Bldg., Pioneer Street, Mandaluyong, Metro Manila
772472 772477 772481

YOUTH NEEDED URGENTLY

To serve and lead our country, our people.
To dedicate heart, mind and spirit to the cause
of honest elections, honest government.

We worked hard for a new beginning at the risk of
our lives.
We must work even harder, together, to build our
future.
It is our right, and our responsibility.

Together, the youth are strong — and productive.
Together, we can make democracy work in our
country.

Join NAMFREL — a cause greater than that of any
candidate or party.

Democracy demands honesty --- in elections, in government.

NAMFREL

National Citizens Movement for Free Elections and Honest Government
National Headquarters 8th Floor RFM Bldg. Pioneer St. Mandaluyong, Metro Manila
772472 772474 772481 TO VOLUNTEER, call National Headquarters or contact
your local NAMFREL chapter.

The Seeds of Freedom

YOUR VOTE IS A RIGHT

USE IT RIGHT.

CHOOSE RIGHT.

There are many reasons for choosing which candidates to vote for.

1. Vote for the candidates who give you money.
2. Vote for the candidates whose names are popular or easy to spell.
3. Vote for the candidates because your parents, friends or local leaders say so.
4. Vote for the candidates with the best posturing or image-building campaign.

OR

5. Vote for the candidates who can help bring about a better life for our people, for our country.

It is not easy to look beyond appearances and promises. Find out who they really are and what they stand for. Vote intelligently. For your sake. And the sake of your children.

Watch for the NAMFREL Candidates Forum in your community.

Democracy demands honesty --- In elections, in government.

 **NAMFREL**

National Citizens Movement for Free Elections and Honest Government
National Headquarters 8th Floor RFM Bldg. Pioneer St. Mandaluyong, Metro Manila
To volunteer, call National Headquarters or contact your local NAMFREL chapter
772474 772481 772472

Appendix F

Canadian lists abuses in Philippine vote

BY BRYAN JOHNSON
The Globe and Mail
MANILA

The Philippine presidential election has featured intimidation and vote-buying "beyond my imagination" the lone Canadian among international observers said yesterday.

Liberal Senator Alasdair Graham of Nova Scotia insisted there was "just no question at all that widespread intimidation took place. We ran into examples of it ourselves." He cited a long list of abuses he had witnessed on the southern island of Mindanao, and expressed deep skepticism about the slow-paced vote count.

"Now, it looks like they" - the ruling KBL party of President Ferdinand Marcos - "are just trying to decide how many votes they need to win," he said.

The criticism was echoed by the 44-member observer delegation as a whole last night, when they submitted their preliminary findings at a press conference.

"The fact that the Comelec total is different from NAMFREL's tells me that there is something very wrong," said a chairman of the group, John Hume, a British MP from Northern Ireland.

"I would suggest that if there were two conflicting results, it would be very obvious that someone was cheating."

Since the polls closed on Friday, the Government's Commission on Elections (Comelec) has been criticizing and threatening its accredited citizens' arm, NAMFREL. Their agreement to provide a joint "quick count" collapsed when NANFREL showed opposition candidate Corazon Aquino to be leading the race - and refused to slow its count or bring its numbers into line with the Government's figure. Last night, Comelec showed Mr. Marcos in the lead, with 5,846,875 votes to Mrs. Aquino's 5,395,860. NAMFREL shows the opposition challenger well ahead, with 5,286,485 to the Presidents's 4,521,070.

The independent citizens' watch-dog group has been savaged in the Marcos-controlled press and particularly on Government-owned Maharlika television. There were strong indications that Mr. Marcos will halt NAMFREL's count today, turning the decision over to the National Assembly where he holds a large majority.

But the US-financed observer team left no doubt of its high regard for NAMFREL.

"The vast majority of NAMFREL volunteers in the regions we have covered have acted in a non-partisan, professional manner," the group's written report said. "Many have risked a great deal to preserve the integrity of the electoral preocess."

Mr. Graham noted that only the media in the Philippines appear to doubt the citizen group's impartiality.

"Personally, I didn't hear any actual voter complain about NAMFREL," he said. "All the complaints are coming from the newspapers, television and Government party."

The observers, chiefly parliamentarians from 19 countries, also supported NAMFREL's contention that its observers were harassed, intimidated and forced away from many polling stations on election day.

Mr. Hume reported visiting a large Manila precinct called Tajeras, with 25,000 eligible voters, where "we saw clear evidence that pollwatchers from both NAMFREL and the opposition were removed. Obviously, that is a very serious matter."

The international team said it could not tell yet whether election malpractices were "enough to distort the final result," but reported a wide range of major abuses. Vote-buying, intimidation attempts, ballot-box snatching, election returns that had been tampered with and the disenfranchisement of thousands of voters left off registration lists were all witnessed by the observers.

Appendix G

Resolution 435 (1978)
of 29 September 1978

The Security Council,

Recalling its resolution 385 (1976) of 30 January 1976 and 431 (1978) and 432 (1978) of 27 July 1978.

Having considered the report of the Secretary-General submitted pursuant to paragraph 2 of resolution 431 (1987) and his explanatory statement made in the Security Council on 29 September 1978 (S/12869),

Taking note of the relevant communications from the Government of South Africa to the Secretary-General,

Taking note also of the letter dated 8 September 1978 from the President of the South West Africa People's Organization to the Secretary-General,

Reaffirming the legal responsibility of the United Nations over Namibia,

1. *Approves* the report of the Secretary-General on the implementation of the proposal for a settlement of the Namibian situation and his explanatory statement;

2. *Reiterates* that its objective is the withdrawal of South Africa's illegal administration from Namibia and the transfer of power to the people of Namibia with the assistance of the United Nations in accordance with Security Council resolution 385 (1976);

3. *Decides* to establish under its authority a United Nations Transition Assistance Group in accordance with the above-mentioned report of the Secretary-General for a period of up to 12 months in order to assist his Special Representative to carry out the mandate conferred upon him by the Security Council in paragraph 1 of its resolution 431 (1978), namely, to ensure the early independence of Namibia through free elections under the supervision and control of the United Nations;

4. *Welcomes* the preparedness of the South West Africa People's Organization to co-operate in the implementation of the Secretary-General's report, including its expressed readiness to sign and observe the ceasefire provisions as manifested in the letter from its President of 8 September 1978;

5. *Calls upon* South Africa forthwith to co-operate with the Secretary-General in the implementation of the present resolution;

6. *Declares* that all unilateral measures taken by the illegal administration in Namibia in relation to the electoral process, including unilateral registration of voters, or transfer of power, in contravention of resolutions 385 (1976), 431 (1978) and the present resolution, are null and void;

7. *Requests* the Secretary-General to report to the Security Council not later than 23 October 1978 on the implementation of the present resolution.

Adopted at the 2087th meeting by 12 votes to none, with 2 abstentions (Czechoslovakia, Union of Soviet Socialist Republics).

The Seeds of Freedom

MAY 23 '89 18:17   P.02

News Release

National Democratic Institute
For International Affairs

1717 Massachusetts Avenue, N.W.
Suite 605
Washington, D.C. 20036
(202) 328-3136
Telex 5106015068 NDIIA
Fax (202) 328-3144

FOR IMMEDIATE RELEASE   FOR FURTHER INFORMATION, CONTACT:
                               Larry Garber   328-3136

INTERNATIONAL DELEGATION TO MONITOR
NAMIBIAN ELECTORAL PROCESS

WASHINGTON, DC, MAY 24, 1989 The National Democratic
Institute for International Affairs announced today the first of
three missions to observe the election process in Namibia.
Heading the seven member international delegation is Senator
Alasdair Graham of Canada. The delegation will arrive in
Windhoek, Namibia on May 29 for a seven day fact-finding
mission.

The purpose of the mission is to demonstrate international
support for a free and fair election process as Namibia prepares
itself for independence. On November 1, 1989, Namibians are
scheduled to elect a constituent assembly that will draft a
constitution.

In addition to Senator Graham, the delegation includes
election officials and experts from Barbados, Botswana,
Pakistan, the United States, West Germany and Zimbabwe. The
delegate from the United States is Attorney General Fred Cowan
of Kentucky, a leading proponent of clean elections in his own
state after his office brought charges of election fraud in
1987. Serving as advisor to the delegation is Harvard Law
School Professor Christopher Edley, who served as issues
director to the Dukakis/Bentsen campaign.

-more-

Under the terms of U.N. Resolution 435, the elections and campaign will be administered by the South African government and overseen by a special United Nations peacekeeping force.

The NDI delegation will review the legal framework and dministrative procedures being set in place by the South frican government. They will identify problem areas and report heir findings and recommendations to U.N. Special Represent- tive Martti Ahtisaari before departing Namibia on June 5.

The delegation will meet with government and U.N. officials esponsible for the elections, political party leaders, and epresentatives of other organizations involved in the nplementation of U.N. Resolution 435.

Senator Graham led the NDI-sponsored international observer elegations to the May 1, 1989 Paraguay election and to the May 11 87 Philippine legislative elections.

Chaired by former Vice President Walter F. Mondale, NDI nducts nonpartisan political development programs overseas. I received bipartisan acclaim for organizing international server delegations to the May 1989 Panamanian elections, the tober 1988 presidential plebiscite in Chile and the 1986 nap" presidential election in the Philippines. It has also nducted a series of programs in nearly 30 countries, including jentina, Barbados, Brazil, Haiti, Nicaragua, Northern Ireland, iegal, South Korea, Taiwan, and Uruguay.

Senator Graham was also a member of the observer team which iitored the "Snap" Presidential Election in the Philippines in 1986.

Appendix I

a South   **Vol.1 No.47**   **50c (GST Inc.)**

day June 9 1989

DEMOCRATS REPORT: 'Distressing strains in national fabric'

"DISTRESSING strains in the national fabric" threaten the Namibian election process, according to a report presented this week to UN Special Representative Martti Ahtisaari.

The report, prepared by an international delegation organised by the United States-based National Democratic Institute for International Affairs (NDI), urged Mr Ahtisaari to "move quickly to assert firm supervision and control of the election process as contemplated by Resolution 435".

The delegation's most serious concerns involved an "atmosphere of intimidation" that could undermine a free and fair electoral process, and the "startling lack of communication" about the proposed election laws and procedures.

The delegation was led by Senator Alasdair Graham of Canada, and included election officials and experts from Barbados, Botswana, Pakistan, the United States and Zimbabwe. Altogether, the members of the delegation have studied and observed elections in some 40 countries. Its report was based on a seven-day fact-finding mission to Namibia, which ended on Tuesday. Chaired by former US Vice President Walter Mondale, NDI conducts nonpartisan democratic development programmes around the world.

The delegation's report forwarded to Mr Ahtisaari's this week stated that a number of distressing strains in the national fabric had been found "that threaten to rip apart and unravel the entire election process".

"These strains, if not repaired, could cause a nation with great hopes and expectations to be tragically stillborn," said the report.

It added: "An atmosphere of distrust permeates the political scene. None of the major political parties trust one another; few trust the Administrator General to adequately and impartially administer the elections; some do not trust UNTAG."

Referring to the lack of communication, the report pointed out that key factors in the process "seem at times to be communicating only through rumour and innuendo".

"A sense of participation in the process of developing the laws regulating the election is noticeably missing. Uncertainty about the process is rampant."

Describing the atmosphere of intimidation as hanging over the country "like a great sword", the NDI report stated: "Charges and countercharges of intimidation seem to be uppermost on the political parties' agendas. Rumours, as well as actual instances of intimidation, fuel a fire of distrust, suspicion and anxiety."

The report urged Mr Ahtisaari to move quickly to assert firm supervision and control of the election process.

The NDI delegation considered reports and allegations from six different regions of the country it visited, as well as from press reports and other information provided by party leaders, community leaders and UNTAG personnel in Windhoek.

"Some of the allegations and reports included police attendance at political rallies with an unnecessary show of force; individuals threatened with abduction of their children; violence at political rallies; destruction of crops and houses for failure to demonstrate political support; disruption and politicization of the educational process; and concern that all weapons of demobilised commandos may not have been returned to authorities," it said.

In addition, the NDI delegates expressed a "special concern" regarding the role being played by the police Koevoet unit.

"Despite the official disbanding of (Koevoet), the units' 'assimilation' into existing forces has clearly not removed the threat citizens feel," the report said.

"The fear of Koevoet looms large in the minds of citizens. In fact, the delegates received reports that Koevoet members have remained as operating units within SWAPOL. No factor contributes more to the atmosphere of intimidation."

The delegation said it believed several steps were imperative.

"First, remnants of Koevoet must be removed from SWAPOL immediately. The Special Representative should insist on this, without compromise, in order to discharge his responsibilities under the Settlement Proposal," the delegates said. "All necessary steps must be taken to ensure that former Koevoet members, once removed from SWAPOL, do not continue, as civilians, to intimidate and harass those with whom they disagree."

"Second, SWAPOL must revise operational procedures to conform with accepted police practices. In particular, the use of Casspirs in routine police patrols, and at political rallies, is psychologically intimidating."

Moreover, it added, "the use of Casspirs, especially those with cannon or machine guns, is a violation of the Settlement Proposal: 'The police forces would be limited to the carrying of small arms in the normal performance of their duties' (S/12636 para 9)."

"Third, the Commission of Enquiry into Intimidation must be assured sufficient investigatory and other resources. It must complete its investigations expeditiously if it is to enjoy public confidence."

"Fourth, UNTAG officials must take more decisive action to satisfy themselves that all complaints of intimidation receive prompt, fair and thorough attention from SWAPOL, the Commission on Intimidation, prosecutors and magistrates. UNTAG police monitors should assert authority to accompany SWAPOL investigators and review investigative files."

Recommendations made by the delegation in this regard were: "A decentralised system of voting, registering and counting is necessary to keep an accurate check on the process ... we propose that every person should register and vote in the district in which he or she resides.

"The 23 districts should be subdivided for the purposes of compiling accurate registration rolls and for voting.

"As monitors, UNTAG personnel should certify every registration form.

"Ballots should be counted in district election centres, which will provide more timely results and, if properly designed, reduce risks to ballot security.

"All registered political parties be permitted to designate agents to observe voting inside the polling stations. Their roll is to observe, not to interfere in the voting process or in any way violate ballot secrecy."

ROLE OF MEDIA

The NDI report also points out that the media will be indispensible in voter education.

"Because the SWABC is in effect controlled by the government, it has special obligations to be impartial and to educate voters in the mechanics of registration and balloting.

"We understand there are as yet no comprehensive plans or principles shaping the SWABC's role in this all-important election."

The report made the following recommendations:

1) SWABC should provide an equal amount of time, in comparable time periods, to every registered party.

2) SWABC should apply the principles of fairness, balance and access in news reporting, commentary, and the sale of advertising time to political parties.

3) UNTAG should take immediate advantage of the time alloted to it by the SWABC TV and radio.

ELECTION PROCEDURES

After studying the draft law on registration and the planning underway by the Administrator-General's office, the NDI delegation found the envisaged "mechanisms for registration, voting and the counting of ballots to be unnecessarily complex and time consuming".

The report said: "This creates a perceived risk of manipulation and potential abuse."

"The centralised registration and voting system creates possibilities for fraud. The plan for verifying voter identity and counting ballots is cumbersome, unnecessary, and jeopardizes ballot secrecy.

"The time involved in the counting process - a minimum of two weeks - will undoubtedly give rise to allegations of tampering and rigging," the report added.

INDEPENDENT ELECTION COMMISSION

"In Namibia," the report said, "we found a wide spectrum of the electorate does not believe that the present government can or will administer the process fairly."

"Simply put, these individuals believe that the government is aligned with the South African government and cannot be truly independent and impartial.

"The lack of confidence is a serious impediment to the government's ability to conduct the process efficiently and fairly, no matter what its intentions. It is also a serious impediment to assuring the peaceful acceptance of the results of the election, since it invites charges of fraud and manipulation of the results," it said.

The delegation recommended that the Administrator-General establish an independent Election Commission "to give all political parties and interested persons, without regard to their political views, a full and fair opportunity to organise and participate in the electoral process." (S/12636 para 6).

The NDI report suggested that members of the Commission should be appointed by the Administrator-General, subject to the approval of the Special Representative.

"The Commission would be responsible for the administration of all aspects of the election process. This recommendation is consistent with the approach taken by the AG in establishing the independent Commission of Inquiry into Intimidation," it said.

Pointed out that election commissions are common throughout the world, the delegation said "they exist primarily to ensure public trust in the system".

In conclusion, the delegation said that virtually everyone, "especially the younger generation in this country, have placed their hopes in 435".

"All they want is a stable society in which they can get on with their lives. What is needed is the combined efforts of all concerned, and the human will to succeed.

"If the United Nations does not succeed at this time, we may not have another Namibia to save in the future," the report said.

The NDI plans to send in July a delegation of US Democratic Party leaders to Namibia to "assess the political environment of the campaign period". A third delegation will visit Namibia at the time of the actual election.

The Institute, which has such prominent US politicians as Edmund Muskie, Cyrus Vance and Andrew Young serving on its Senior Advisory Committee, also intends to design a mass voter education programme to familiarise people with the process of voting.

Recent election observation missions by the NDI include the delegation to Panama, led by former President Jimmy Carter, and Poland, Paraguay, Chile, Pakistan and the Soviet Union.

Appendix J

JUN 2? 1989

FREDERIC J. COWAN
ATTORNEY GENERAL

COMMONWEALTH OF KENTUCKY
THE CAPITOL

MICHAEL B. RONEY
DEPUTY ATTORNEY GENERAL

June 12, 1989

Senator B. A. (Al) Graham
Canadian Senate
Room 263 - East Block
Parliament Building
Ottawa, Canada KIA 0A6

Dear Al:

I wanted to let you know how much I enjoyed
working with you in Namibia. The experience was
certainly one of the most rewarding ones in my
professional life. I felt that we did our work
thoroughly, expeditiously and fairly, and a large
part of our success is attributable to you. I don't
think I have ever worked with a group of people who
had as much genuine respect for each other and worked
as well as we all did. I count it as a real privilege to have been associated with you and NDI and I
look forward to maintaining our close association and
friendship in the future.

Sincerely,

FREDERIC J. COWAN
ATTORNEY GENERAL

FJC:as

Al, thanks for your great leadership.
I hope we can do it again sometime!
Let's keep in touch.

SERVICE • DEDICATION • EXCELLENCE
FRANKFORT 40601
502/564-7600

217

Appendix K

NATIONAL DEMOCRATIC INSTITUTE FOR INTERNATIONAL AFFAIRS

Suite 503, 1717 Massachusetts Avenue, N.W.   Washington, D.C. 20036   (202) 328-3136

■ FAX (202) 939-3166
■ Telex 5106015068 ND

September 24, 1992

The Honorable Al Graham, MP
Room 263 East Black
Parliament Building
Ottawa K1A 0A6
Canada

Dear Al:

On behalf of the National Democratic Institute for International Affairs (NDI), I would like to invite you to lead an international delegation to observe the October 11 elections in Cameroon.

This presidential election will be Cameroon's first multiparty presidential election in 20 years. The presence of this delegation of leading democratic political leaders and election experts will demonstrate important international support for free and fair elections and for the multiparty democratic transition in Cameroon.

The 20-member delegation of international observers will be sponsored by NDI in collaboration with GERDDES, a nonpartisan African democratic development organization, and will include political leaders and election experts from the United States, Europe, Latin America and Africa. The observers will be present in Cameroon from Wednesday, October 7 through Wednesday, October 14.

NDI will arrange travel, hotel accommodations and other logistics. We will cover basic expenses related to your participation, including airfare, hotels, meals and program-related in-country expenses.

Please let us know by Monday, September 24 whether you will be able to join us in what promises to be an exciting and rewarding experience. You can contact Senior Program Officer Ned McMahon or Program Assistant Anna Wang in the NDI Washington office at (202) 328-3136 or fax at (202) 939-3166.

Once you have confirmed your participation, NDI will send you a detailed agenda, additional logistics information, and briefing materials along with your plane ticket.   In the meantime, if you are able to participate, please send biographical information as well as copies of the first three pages of your passport.

I hope you will be able to participate in this historic event.

Sincerely yours,

J. Brian Atwood
President

Appendix L

MEMORANDUM

TO: Trainers and Observers

FROM: Ned McMahon

DATE: September 18, 1992

RE: Briefing Paper: Training Election Monitors and Observing Elections

I. BACKGROUND

a. Regional Focus

Building on a survey conducted in francophone Africa last year, NDI co-sponsored with GERDDES, a nonpartisan African democratic development organization, a seminar in Benin on nonpartisan and political party domestic election monitoring. Over 100 participants from 15 different countries participated. This project was aimed at disseminating information relating to international standards and norms for democratic elections. Cameroonian representatives from both the ruling party and the opposition attended the seminar. In March of 1992, NDI held election observation training seminars in Cote d'Ivoire, Niger and Congo. Emphasizing practical aspects of election monitoring, these three seminars focused on how to organize an observation mission, and how to observe the electoral process before, during and after the vote. The Cameroon training program would incorporate the essential elements covered by these seminars.

b. Country Focus

NDI 1991 Program in Cameroon

In response to an invitation from the Prime Minister of Cameroon, and with the concurrence of opposition parties, in September 1991 NDI sent a team of international experts to assess the democratic transition already underway. The Delegation focused on several legal and political questions central to the democratization process; drafting a new electoral code, access to media, and constitutional issues including decentralization and guarantees on political freedoms and the separation of powers. The mission's goal was to help break the political impasse that had developed between the government and the opposition over how to implement a multiparty system in Cameroon. In its final report, the delegation recommended adoption of a new electoral law that would stress the principles of accountability, transparency and neutrality in election administration. The delegation noted the vital role that civic organizations play in the transition process by participating in voter education and election monitoring programs.

The report received a positive response from across the political spectrum and has established NDI's reputation in Cameroon as an impartial, nonpartisan organization.

c. Cameroon's Path to Elections

Long-time President Ahmadou Ahidjo retired in 1982 and was succeeded by his Prime Minister, Paul Biya. Biya began a process of political opening, but a nearly -successful coup attempt in 1984 led to a period of retrenchment and caution regarding political development. In 1989, Yondo Black, a Cameroonian lawyer, attempted to create a political party, for which he was arrested. This resulted in wide-scale protests, led by the legal community. These protests reflected pent-up desires for greater political freedoms amongst a wide segment of the population, and in June of 1990, President Biya announced that a new era of political pluralism would be inaugurated.

A law permitting formation of political parties was enacted in December 1990; both new political parties and those which had existed before the advent of single-party rule were registered. Although having different goals and bases of support, a number of these parties subsequently joined together to form a coalition in opposition to perceived attempts by President Biya to control the democratization process, and to ensure a leading role for his party in a post-electoral period.

In June, 1991 the coalition declared "Operation Villes Morts", an attempt to force President Biya to call a sovereign national conference to guide the democratic transition. After months of limited effect, the strike failed. While a short-term result was to contribute to greater polarization within the country, its failure perhaps served to re-channel demands for political change to the electoral arena.

In November 1991, President Biya convened a tripartite meeting which included representatives of government and ruling party, civil society and part of the opposition. The meeting was designed to discuss the framework for parliamentary elections. Biya subsequently called for parliamentary elections in March, 1992. The election resulted in the ruling CPDM party losing its overall majority, but it formed a coalition with a small party to gain a working majority. The elections were boycotted b some important opposition parties, including the anglophone Social Democratic Front (SDF). The election results surprised many, who had anticipated widespread fraud, by resulting in such a large opposition representation.

In late August, President Biya announced that presidential elections, which must be held by mid-1993, would be scheduled for October 11. Most parties have previously indicated that they would participate in the elections, although it is not clear whether the elections would take place under the existing 1973 presidential electoral code, which includes a simple single-round plurality system, or whether a two-round system would be adopted.

The provision of trainers and election observers responds to a request made by the Government of Cameroon before the March legislative elections. At that time, the US embassy committed to explore the possibility of designing a program to train Cameroonian election observers for future elections with various NGOs, including NDI.

II. PROGRAM ACTIVITIES

a. Seminar on Election Monitoring

NDI, in collaboration with GERDDES Africa, is sponsoring a seminar to discuss detailed aspects of organizing domestic election observer missions and training trainers of election observers October 2-4. The intent of the seminar is to "train trainers", who will then disseminate the information to their constituencies prior to the election. The training faculty consists of eight international experts from Africa, Europe and North America who have election observation and training experience. GERDDES has named half of the international trainers from within its membership. As is standard operating practice, the international trainers have been drawn from a range of different fields, and include a former diplomat, a lawyer, academics and others with a regional or functional expertise.

The program consists of a 2 1/2 day seminar held in Yaounde for 200 participants from the range of political parties and interested civic groups. The American Embassy will assist in the delivery of invitations and facilitate some logistical arrangements, invitees will be asked to respond expeditiously to avoid a late surge of acceptances which could affect logistical arrangements.

The seminar will focus on interactive sessions designed to maximize the exchange of information and experiences. There will be plenary/workshop sessions on the organization of election observation missions, pre-election day activities and preparations, observation on voting day (including the vote counting process), and evaluating the transparency and legitimacy of the elections. Participants will rotate through the three workshops, which will be lead by one international and one GERDDES expert. A voter education slide show developed by NDI, and which uses examples from a number of countries which have recently held elections, will also be presented. Written materials will also be handed out to facilitate participant retention and dissemination of information provided.

Participants will be drawn from most political parties, although representation is weighted towards the five largest political parties. These include the ruling Cameroonian Popular Democratic Movement (CPDM), the Union of Cameroonian Peoples (UPC), the SDF, the National Union for Democracy and Progress (UNDP), and the Union of Cameroonian Democrats (UDC). Representatives from several civic organizations will also be invited.

As a condition of participation in the seminar, participants will commit to disseminate the information gained as a result of the seminar more widely, during the week prior to the October 11 election. Participants will thus disperse to their home regions and conduct meetings, seminars and other public gatherings to emphasize the importance of ensuring that the elections are conducted in a transparent and credible manner. Specific target audiences will include the constituencies of the participants, especially political parties, as they will be allowed to have representatives present in the polling places. Other targets will include civic organizations, local government figures and possibly traditional leaders. The international trainers will be divided into four groups of two and sent to different parts of the country to monitor, and as appropriate, participate in these activities.

After the training session, on October 6-7 the trainers will travel to the region that they will be observing during the election. During the period prior to the election their task will be to develop as comprehensive an understanding of the local dynamics and factors relating to the election as possible. In addition, they should also contact participants who had been at the Yaounde seminar to determine the extent to which the information provided in the seminar has been disseminated. They can attend and participate in any meeting where this may occur as long as their actions are not viewed in a partisan fashion. In other words, they should plan on attending more than one session if they are hosted by different political parties.

b. Election Observation

As the trainers will have been in Cameroon for 10 days prior to the election, they will have developed detailed information on pre-election day issues. in the Cameroonian context, questions of particular importance are:

What is the system for aggregating vote counts from individual polling places?

Are there any refinements to the system of election administration used for the March parliamentary elections i.e. the Ministry of Territorial Administration takes the lead role? Will the parties have any input into this process?

How will resolution of election-related complaints be handled?

How much controversy surrounds pre-electoral issues? Is the single-round voting system a matter of contention? The electoral code calls for a 30-day period between the issuance of a presidential elections decree and the actual election. Is the fact that this stipulation not being respected 30-day period controversial?

Are opposition parties criticizing voter rolls or voter ID card distribution? What about access to media questions?

Are electoral preparations moving ahead equally in areas where the opposition is strong as compared to CPDM regions?

Have there been any specific examples of repression or inhibiting opposition party activities related to the upcoming election?

have campaign finance issues come into play? Will there be a deposit requirement for candidates?

An additional twelve international observers will arrive in-country October 5-7 to supplement the election day observation team. After a day of briefings in Yaounde, they will be deployed into 4-5 different groups and sent to the regions of the country they will observe on election day. The election observation delegation will be co-led by a senior figure from the U.S. or Europe, and a respected African leader. A command and control center will be established in Yaounde in order to monitor the observers' activities and act as key communications link.

The observers will each visit 20-30 polling sites on election day and develop an assessment of the different stages of the voting process. Information on recommended election observation methodologies is contained elsewhere in this briefing book. The observers will also seek out information regarding voting in the region of the country they have been assigned. The entire team will reassemble in Yaounde on October 12 for de-briefing and to draft a statement on the elections prior to departure from Cameroon October 13. The content and nature of the statement will depend on the circumstances surrounding the election. NDI staff may remain in-country until the announcement of the final results by the Supreme Court on October 20, if needed.

A total of 5 NDI staff members will provide support services. The staff will include 1 logistics expert, 2 program assistants, a consultant/advisor and a senior program officer. The senior program officer will work closely with the delegation leaders and have primary responsibility for the day-to-day operation of the project.

CED
CENTRO DE
ESTUDIOS
DEMOCRATICOS

VERSION SIMPLIFICADA DEL ESTATUTO ELECTORAL (LEY 886)

MANUAL DEL
VEEDOR

ELECCIONES GENERALES, 1 DE MAYO 1989
ASUNCION, PARAGUAY

ES UN SERVICIO DE

EL DIARIO
noticias

II LA INSTALACION DE LA MESA

1. Tareas del veedor.

a. La llegada.

El acto electoral comienza a las 7:00 de la mañana, y el veedor debe llegar 30 minutos antes (a las 6:30 AM) y presentarse de inmediato ante el presidente de mesa con sus documentos y su credencial.

b. Comprobar que exista cuarto oscuro y boletines de voto.

El veedor debe comprobar, acompañado por el Presidente de la mesa, si existe una habitación o ambiente que funcione como "cuarto oscuro", si dicho cuarto está con todas las puertas y ventanas bien cerradas (excepto

la puerta cercana a la mesa) y si la mesa receptora de votos se halla próxima a dicho cuarto (Arts. 69 y 75).

El Presidente de la mesa debe colocar los boletines de voto de los distintos candidatos, y en cantidad suficiente, en un lugar visible dentro del cuarto oscuro (Art. 75).

Los boletines de voto contendrán las listas de candidatos de los distintos partidos. Serán de papel blanco e impresos en tinta negra (Art. 86)

Las listas de candidatos a Senadores, Diputados y Presidente de la República, presentadas por cada partido. deberán estar en boletas separadas.

c. Comprobar que exista urna.

La urna que se usará para depositar los sobres con los votos debe estar cerca de los miembros de la mesa. Debe estar VACIA, para que luego sea CERRADA y PRECINTADA con una faja de papel engomado que deberá ser firmado por los miembros de la mesa antes de comenzar el acto eleccionario. NADIE PODRA ABRIR LA URNA UNA VEZ QUE EMPIECE EL ACTO ELECTORAL (Art. 88)

JRNA

ES DE MADERA
Y TIENE
CERRADURA.

CONTENIDO

I.CUESTIONES GENERALES

1. El elector.

a. Quiénes son electores.
b. Protección del elector.
c. A quiénes se elige el próximo 1º de mayo.

2. Las mesas receptoras de votos.

a. Quiénes deben votar en la mesa.
b. Composición de la mesa.

3. El Veedor.

a. Qué es un veedor. Quién lo nombra.
b. Quién puede ser veedor.
c. Qué documentos necesita el veedor para acreditarse ante la mesa receptora de votos.
d. Protección del veedor.

4. El Apoderado.

a. Qué es un apoderado. Quién lo nombra.
b. Funciones del apoderado.

II. LA INSTALACION DE LA MESA

1. Tareas del veedor.

a. La llegada.
b. Comprobar que exista cuarto oscuro y boletines de voto.
c. Comprobar que exista urna.

CAMPAÑA POR LA EXPRESION CIUDADANA

2. El acta electoral.

III. LA VOTACION

1. Apertura de la votación.
2. Pasos de la votación.

   a. El elector se acerca a la mesa.
   b. En el cuarto oscuro.
   c. Depositando el sobre en la urna de la mesa receptora de votos.
   d. La tinta indeleble.
   e. Antes de retirarse el votante.

3. Qué ocurre si se impugna la identidad del elector.
4. Cierre de la votación.

IV. EL ESCRUTINIO

1. Apertura de la urna.
2. Revisión de las impugnaciones.
3. El recuento de los votos.

   a. Votos correctos.
   b. Votos nulos.
   c. Votos en blanco.

4. Resultado del escrutinio.
5. El veedor puede solicitar una constancia escrita de los resultados.

V. QUE DEBE HACER EL VEEDOR ANTE IRREGULARIDADES.
VI. APENDICE: GUIA PARA EL USO DE LA LEY ELECTORAL

VEEDORES

"Los partidos políticos participantes pueden designar un veedor en cada mesa receptora de votos, a quien en ningún caso se le impedirá el cumplimiento de sus funciones" (Art. 53).

* SOS EL REPRESENTANTE DE UN PARTIDO ANTE LA MESA RECEPTORA DE VOTOS.
* NADIE, POR NINGUN MOTIVO, PODRA HACERTE SALIR DEL RECINTO ELECTORAL.
* DE VOS DEPENDE QUE EL ACTO ELECTORAL EN TU MESA SE REALICE RESPETANDO LA TOTAL LIBERTAD DEL ELECTOR, EL SECRETO DEL VOTO Y EL CORRECTO RECUENTO DE LOS VOTOS EMITIDOS.
* LA LEY DEL ESTATUTO ELECTORAL (LEY 886) DETERMINA SEVERAS PENAS, DE 6 MESES A 3 AÑOS DE CARCEL, PARA AQUELLOS QUE INCURRAN EN IRREGULARIDADES.

* Cuando falsifiquen, alteren, destruyan o hagan desaparecer las actas y otros documentos electorales.
* Cuando obstruyan o impidan la formación o el funcionamiento de las mesas receptoras.
* Cuando sustraigan o abran indebidamente urnas electorales, se apoderen de boletines de votos, o lo permitan ilegalmente o de cualquier manera dificulten o impidan el escrutinio. (Art. 166)

I CUESTIONES GENERALES

1. El elector

a. Quiénes son electores.

Tienen derecho y deber de ser electores los ciudadanos paraguayos entre 18 y 60 años. Después de los 60 años se tiene el derecho, pero ya no la obligación (Art. 2).

Pero, para ejercer el derecho a voto, los ciudadanos deben estar inscriptos en el Registro Cívico Permanente (Art. 41).

En base a ese registro, se hacen listas de personas habilitadas para votar en cada mesa, local y sección electoral en una elección.

b. Protección del elector.

El votante está protegido por la ley. Nadie puede amenazarlo ni prohibirle que vote. En caso de que se presente algún problema, debe recurrir al Juez, quien deberá resolver el reclamo de inmediato.

> "Con el objeto de asegurar la libertad, seguridad e inmunidad individual o colectiva de los electores, el Juez de 1ra. Instancia en lo Criminal de Turno y en la Sección donde no la hubiere, el Juez de Paz en lo Criminal, o en su defecto, el Juez de Paz, mantendrá abierto su despacho desde media hora antes de comenzar la elección hasta que ella termine, para recibir y resolver, verbal e inmediatamente, las reclamaciones de los electores que se viesen amenazados o privados del ejercicio del voto, o coartado para desempeñar una función pública electoral (Art. 47).

c. A quiénes se elige el próximo 1 de mayo

Por voto directo los ciudadanos eligen al Presidente de la República, a 72 diputados titulares y 42 suplentes y a 36 Senadores titulares y 21 suplentes.

2. Las mesas receptoras de votos

a. Quiénes deben votar en la mesa.

A cada mesa receptora de votos le corresponde una serie de 200 ciudadanos inscriptos en el Registro Cívico Permanente. La lista de estos ciudadanos se encuentra copiada en el cuaderno del acta electoral.
A cada mesa le corresponde dos ejemplares de dicho cuaderno.

Sólo pueden votar en una mesa aquellos que figuran en el cuaderno, y también las autoridades de la mesa, los candidatos, los veedores y los apoderados.

b. Composición de la mesa.

Cada mesa se compondrá de un Presidente, un Secretario y un Vocal, nombrados por la Junta Electoral de cada sección. El Presidente y el Vocal corresponden al partido mayoritario de la respectiva Junta, mientras que el cargo de Secretario será ocupado por la minoría (Art. 53).

3. El veedor

a. Qué es un veedor. Quién lo nombra.

El veedor es la persona nombrada por un partido político para controlar los actos de una mesa receptora de votos. Es nombrado por el Presidente del respectivo partido político de la localidad (Art. 73). Los miembros de la mesa están obligados por ley a aceptarlos.

De él depende que el acto eleccionario se desarrolle limpiamente respetando la total libertad del votante, el secreto del voto y el correcto recuento de los votos.

Su función principal es controlar si el nombre y los datos personales del que vota son correctos, y presentar protesta por escrito sobre los hechos relacionados con las elecciones (Art. 73).

b. Quién puede ser veedor.

Para que un ciudadano pueda ser veedor, debe estar inscripto y hallarse en el momento de la elección en pleno goce de sus derechos políticos (Art. 74). No importa que sea de otra sección electoral. Tampoco necesita estar afiliado a ningún partido político.

NO PUEDEN SER VEEDORES LOS JEFES Y OFICIALES DE LAS FF.AA. DE LA NACION Y DE LA POLICIA EN SERVICIO ACTIVO, NI LOS EMPLEADOS MILITARES Y POLICIALES (ART. 74).

c. Qué documentos necesita el veedor para acreditarse ante la mesa receptora de votos.

El ciudadano nombrado como veedor debe presentarse ante la mesa con (a) su Libreta Cívica o Certificado de Inscripción, (b) su cédula de identidad y (c) su credencial firmada por el Presidente del partido político correspondiente de la localidad (Art. 75).

d. Protección del veedor.

"Los partidos políticos participantes puden designar un veedor en cada mesa receptora de votos, a quien en ningún caso se le impedirá el cumplimiento de sus funciones" (Art. 53)

4. El apoderado

a. Qué es un apoderado. Quién lo nombra.

El apoderado es un ciudadano que representa a un partido político en una localidad del interior del país, o en un local electoral en la capital. Cualquier ciudadano inscripto en el Registro electoral puede ser apoderado de un partido político (Art. 134 y 186)

Debe ser nombrado por escrito por la autoridad máxima del partido que representa. La lista de apoderados de cada partido, firmada por su Presidente y Secretario, debe ser enviada a la Junta Electoral Central para que ésta vise y selle la credencial de cada uno de ellos.

b. Funciones del apoderado.

El apoderado representa a un partido político. Puede nombrar veedores y es encargado de formular las protestas que se anotan en el Acta Electoral (Art. 65).

Las funciones del apoderado comienzan desde el momento en que es reconocido por la Junta Electoral Central, y terminan en el momento de aprobación de los resultados electorales por parte del Congreso (Art. 187).

SE DEBERA REVISAR PERIODICAMENTE EL CUARTO OSCURO PARA CONTROLAR SI HAN DESAPARECIDO LOS BOLETINES DE VOTO DEL PARTIDO QUE REPRESENTA.

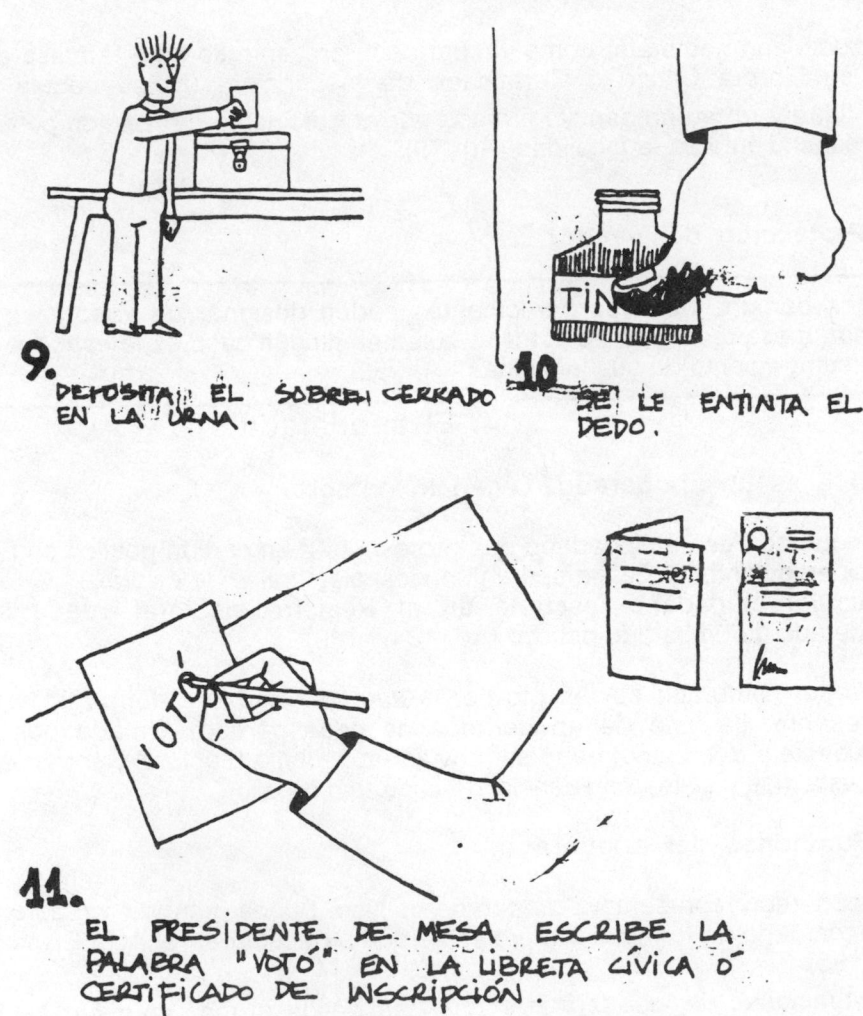

9. DEPOSITA EL SOBRE CERRADO EN LA URNA.

10. SE LE ENTINTA EL DEDO.

11. EL PRESIDENTE DE MESA ESCRIBE LA PALABRA "VOTÓ" EN LA LIBRETA CÍVICA Ó CERTIFICADO DE INSCRIPCIÓN.

CAMPAÑA POR LA EXPRESION CIUDADANA

234

c. Depositando el sobre en la urna de la mesa receptora de votos.

El elector saldrá del cuarto oscuro con el sobre cerrado. Volverá al lugar donde funciona la mesa y depositará el sobre en la urna. Se debe controlar que el sobre que trae el elector a la salida del cuarto oscuro es el mismo que se le entregó en la mesa firmado por el Presidente.

d. La tinta indeleble

Luego de esto, las autoridades de la mesa procederán a inpregnar el dedo pulgar del elector con tinta indeleble.

12. EL PRESIDENTE DE MESA FIRMA LA LIBRETA Ó CERTIFICADO Y LO DEVUELVE AL ELECTOR.

13. AL MISMO TIEMPO EL SECRETARIO Y EL VOCAL ESCRIBEN LA PALABRA "VOTÓ" AL LADO DEL NOMBRE DEL ELECTOR EN AMBAS COPIAS DEL ACTA.

¡¡ YA VOTAMOS!!

e. Antes de retirarse el votante

Después, el Presidente de mesa deberá escribir en la Libreta Cívica o Certificado de Inscripción la palabra "votó" y la fecha, firmando de puño y letra.
El Secretario y el Vocal de mesa escribirán lo mismo en la casilla con el nombre del votante en el ejemplar del acta electoral a su cargo (Art. 82).

2. El acta electoral

Por cada mesa receptora de votos se entregarán dos ejemplares del acta electoral. En el acta electoral deberá estar el nombre y la firma del Presidente, Secretario y Vocal de la mesa, y firmado por los veedores (Art. 65). EL VEEDOR NO SERA ADMITIDO SI NO FIRMA EL ACTA.

III. LA VOTACION

1. Apertura de la votación

La mesa dará comienzo al acto electoral llenando el acta de apertura (Art. 76). Se votará a partir de las 7:00 de la mañana.

Comenzarán votando los miembros de la mesa, los candidatos, los veedores y los apoderados de los partidos (Art. 65).

Acto seguido se dará comienzo a la recepción de los votos de los inscriptos en la serie electoral de la mesa, desde las 7 de la mañana hasta las 4 de la tarde. Pero, si a las 4 de la tarde aún quedan algunos presentes ante la mesa, se les permitirá votar (Art. 72).

Una vez abierta la mesa, las elecciones no podrán interrumpirse excepto por motivos graves. En caso de realizarse una interrupción, se anotará en el acta el tiempo que haya durado la interrupción (Art. 89)

SEGURIDAD

DEBERA HABER UN NUMERO SUFICIENTE DE AGENTES DE POLICIA A LAS ORDENES DEL PRESIDENTE DE MESA, PARA MANTENER LA SEGURIDAD Y LA LIBERTAD DEL ACTO ELECTORAL Y HACER CUMPLIR SIN DEMORA LAS RESOLUCIONES DE LA MESA.

236

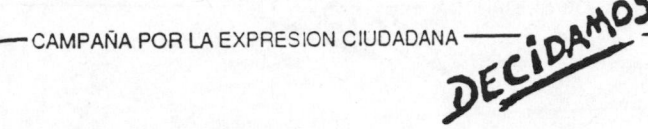

2. Pasos de la votación.

a. El elector se acerca a la mesa.

A medida que vaya llegando, el elector se presentará ante la mesa receptora dando su nombre y presentando su Libreta Cívica o Certificado de Inscripción, para comprobar si le toca o no votar en esa mesa. Acto seguido, el Presidente comprobará el nombre y los datos de la persona (Art. 79).

1. EL ELECTOR SE ACERCA A LA MESA.

2. ENTREGA SU LIBRETA CÍVICA O CERTIFICADO DE INSCRIPCIÓN.

SI EL VEEDOR CREE QUE DEBE IMPUGNAR LA IDENTIDAD DE UN VOTANTE, TIENE QUE HACERLO EN ESTE MOMENTO

CAMPAÑA POR LA EXPRESION CIUDADANA — DECIDAMOS

Si la identidad del elector no es cuestionada, el Presidente de la mesa le entregará un sobre abierto, vacío y no transparente, que firmará de inmediato por fuera, de su puño y letra.

Durante la votación NO PODRAN APROXIMARSE A LA MESA RECEPTORA DE VOTOS MAS DE DOS ELECTORES A LA VEZ (Art. 77).

SOBRE

3. EL PRESIDENTE DE MESA LE ENTREGA UN SOBRE VACÍO Y FIRMADO DE SU PUÑO Y LETRA

4. ENTRA AL CUARTO OSCURO, SOLO.

EL VOTO ES SECRETO

El secreto del voto es inviolable. ÑADIE PODRA INFORMARSE DEL CONTENIDO DEL SOBRE CERRADO. NINGUN ELECTOR PODRA PRESENTARSE A LA MESA RECEPTORA MOSTRANDO SU BOLETIN DE VOTO. NADIE PODRA ENTREGAR U OFRECER BOLETINES DE VOTO A LOS ELECTORES EN EL LOCAL DE LA MESA, NI EL UN RADIO DE 100 METROS ALREDEDOR DE ELLA (ART. 85).

b. En el cuarto oscuro.

Con el sobre vacío en la mano, el votante deberá pasar al cuarto oscuro, donde estarán puestos los boletines de voto de todos los partidos que participan (Art. 75). Dentro del cuarto oscuro no puede haber más que un elector.

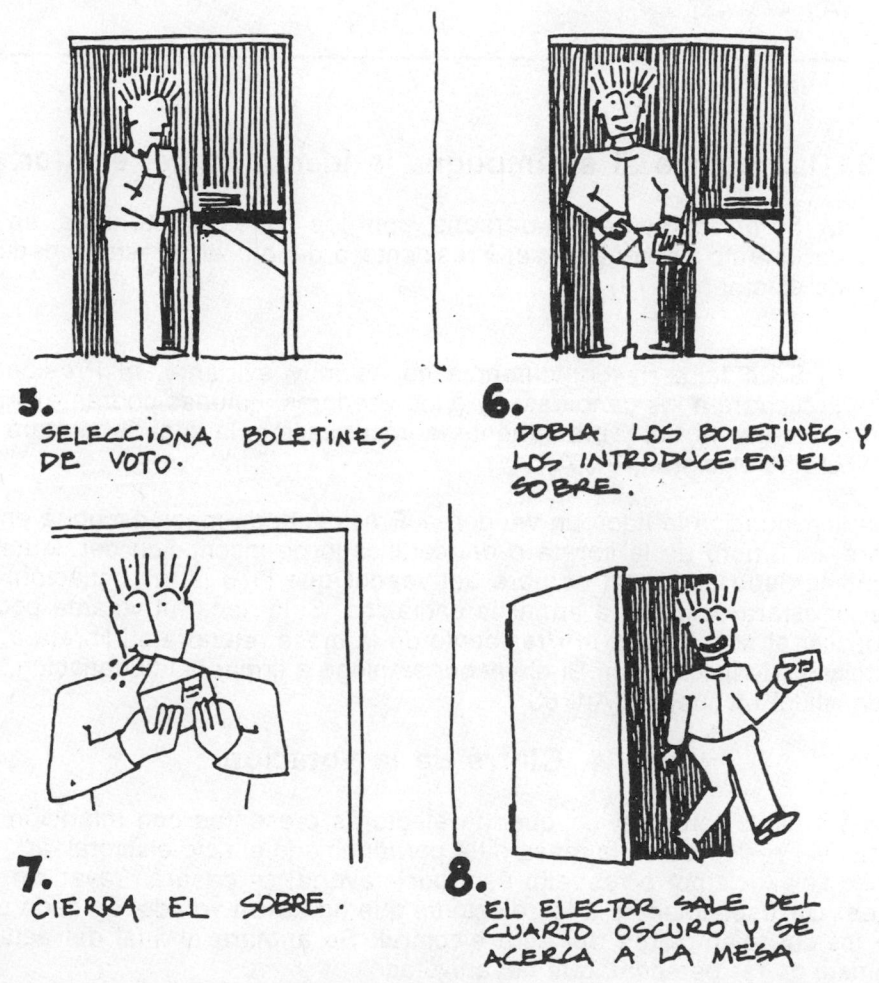

5. SELECCIONA BOLETINES DE VOTO.

6. DOBLA LOS BOLETINES Y LOS INTRODUCE EN EL SOBRE.

7. CIERRA EL SOBRE.

8. EL ELECTOR SALE DEL CUARTO OSCURO Y SE ACERCA A LA MESA

Luego, el elector introducirá los boletines correspondientes en el sobre. EL VOTANTE PUEDE ELEGIR BOLETINES DE VOTOS DE DISTINTOS PARTIDOS PARA LLENAR DISTINTOS CARGOS. Si prefiere votar en blanco, se limitará a cerrar el sobre sin introducir boletines de voto dentro de él.

Cualquier irregularidad que observe el ciudadano, deberá denunciarla ante la mesa, ante los veedores y apoderados de los partidos o ante el juzgado más cercano, que deberá estar abierto. (Art. 47 y 48)

3. Qué ocurre si se impugna la identidad del elector.

a) Si no coincide la persona con los datos contenidos en el documento presentado, el Presidente ordenará el arresto inmediato del elector (Art. 79).

b) Si la falta de coincidencia no es muy evidente, el Presidente escuchará a los candidatos y a los veedores, quienes podrán explicar en forma verbal y brevemente la impugnación, la cual se anotará en el acta electoral (Art. 79).

Si la impugnación la hace un veedor, el Presidente de mesa escribirá en el sobre el número de la libreta o del certificado de inscripción del votante. También debe anotar el nombre del veedor que hizo la impugnación. El veedor estará obligado a firmar la anotación. Si lo hace, el votante podrá depositar el sobre, pero el Presidente de la mesa retendrá su libreta o su certificado de inscripción. Si el veedor se niega a firmar la impugnación, no se la tendrá en cuenta. (Art. 83).

4. Cierre de la votación.

A las 4 de la tarde, si no quedan electores presentes con intención de votar, el Presidente de la mesa dará por terminado el acto electoral.
Si no hay reclamo, o resuelto éste por mayoría, se pasarán rayas en las líneas correspondientes a los electores que no hayan votado, en cada uno de los dos ejemplares del acta electoral. Se anotará al final del acta el número de las personas que hayan votado.
ESTA ANOTACION SERA FIRMADA POR LOS 3 MIEMBROS DE LA MESA Y POR LOS VEEDORES Y CIUDADANOS PRESENTES QUE DESEEN HACERLO (Art. 92).

IV. EL ESCRUTINIO

1. Apertura de la urna.

El Presidente de la mesa abrirá la urna que contiene los votos para comenzar el recuento EN EL MISMO LUGAR EN EL CUAL SE LLEVO A CABO LA VOTACION. NO SE PUEDE SACAR LA URNA Y LLEVARLA A OTRO LUGAR. Comparará el número de sobres que están dentro de la urna con el número de personas que hayan votado.

Separará los sobres que tengan la anotación de "impugnados" y VOLVERA A DEPOSITAR LOS OTROS SOBRES EN LA URNA (Art. 93).

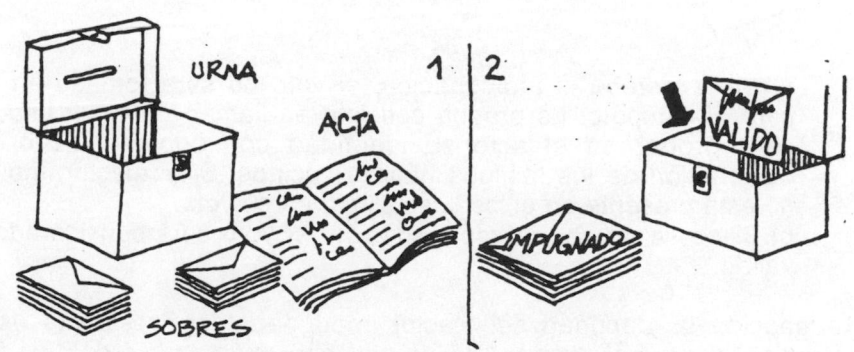

1.
SE ABRE LA URNA. DEBE COINCIDIR EL Nº DE SOBRES CON EL Nº DE VOTANTES QUE FIGURAN EN EL ACTA ELECTORAL.

2.
SE SEPARAN LOS SOBRES QUE DIGAN "IMPUGNADO". SI NO SE PRUEBA LA IMPUGNACIÓN, EL PDTE. DE MESA ESCRIBIRÁ DETRÁS DEL SOBRE "VALIDO POR RESOLUCIÓN DE LA MESA", LO FIRMARÁ Y LO DEPOSITARÁ EN LA URNA.

2. Revisión de las impugnaciones

Inmediatamente después de esto, se examinarán uno a uno los sobres que contengan la nota de "impugnados" (Art. 94):

3. LUEGO, EL PDTE.
SACARÁ UNO A UNO
LOS SOBRES, EXTRAERÁ
DE ELLOS LOS BOLETINES
Y LOS LEERÁ EN VOZ
ALTA.

a) Si se prueba la impugnación, el voto no será tomado en cuenta para el cómputo. La prueba consiste en llamar al elector impugnado para probar en el acto su identidad con documentos o con la declaración de los testigos hábiles vecinos. Si el elector impugnado no está presente en el local, se eliminará su voto.
b) Si no se prueba la impuganación, el voto será considerado como válido.

Reconocida la identidad del elector impugnado, el Presidente escribirá detrás del sobre impugnado "Válido por resolución de la mesa", lo firmará y lo depositará en la urna. Se devolverá la Libreta Cívica o Certificado de Inscripción a su dueño, anotándose encima de la impugnación la palabra "anulada" bajo la firma y sello del Presidente.

3. El recuento de los votos.

Terminado este procedimiento, el Presidente sacará uno a uno los sobres de la urna, extraerá de ellos los boletines y los leerá o hará leer en voz alta. En caso de que un miembro de la mesa tenga duda sobre el contenido de la boleta leída, podrá pedir en el acto su exámen y le será concedida.

DURANTE EL ESCRUTINIO O RECUENTO DE VOTOS SE PROHIBE
A LOS ELECTORES ENTRAR EN EL LOCAL O ACERCARSE A LA
MESA. SOLO PODRAN ESTAR LOS VEEDORES PARA
CONTROLAR EL RECUENTO. Bajo ningún concepto el recuento
podrá suspenderse, interrumpirse o postergarse. (Art. 93)

---

a. Votos correctos.

Se consideran votos correctos los sobres que contengan papeletas para
Presidente, lista de senadores y de diputados de un mismo partido.

TAMBIEN SON VOTOS CORRECTOS LOS SOBRES CON
PAPELETAS PARA PRESIDENTE, SENADORES Y PARA DIPUTA-
DOS DE DISTINTOS PARTIDOS PARA DIFERENTES CARGOS.

---

b. Votos nulos.

Son votos nulos los sobres con 2 o más boletines con listas de candidatos
de diferentes partidos para llenar una misma clase de cargo. También
serán nulos los boletines de voto imposibles de leer o que no contengan
nombres propios (Art. 96), al igual que LOS SOBRES HALLADOS EN LA
URNA SIN LA FIRMA DEL PRESIDENTE (Atr. 81)

c. Votos en blanco.

Se considerán votos en blanco a los sobres que no contienen boletines en
su interior.

4. Resultado del escrutinio.

Terminado el escrutinio, el Presidente de la mesa preguntará si hay algún
reclamo escrito y firmado. De no haberlo, o después de resolver por
mayoría el que se presentase, anunciará el número de votos obtenido por
cada canditato (Art. 97).

Se dejará constancia escrita de los resultados del escrutinio al final del
acta electoral (Art. 99).

En un sobre o paquete certificado, cerrado, lacrado y sellado, se colocará
un ejemplar del acta electoral, los sobres y las protestas de los veedores y
apoderados para ser enviado al Congreso (Art. 98 y 99).

VOTOS

CORRECTOS NULOS BLANCOS

4. HABRÁN VOTOS CORRECTOS, NULOS Y EN BLANCO.

5. LUEGO DE RESOLVER LOS RECLAMOS, EL PDTE. DE MESA ANUNCIARÁ LOS RESULTADOS.

VOTOS REVISADOS

6. SE ESCRIBIRÁ EN EL ACTA LOS RESULTADOS DEL ESCRUTINIO

7. SE ENTREGARÁ UNA COPIA DE LOS RESULTADOS A LOS VEEDORES.

8. LAS AUTORIDADES DE MESA FIRMARÁN EL ACTA ELECTORAL.

CAMPAÑA POR LA EXPRESION CIUDADANA – DECIDAMOS

5. El veedor puede solicitar una constancia escrita de los resultados.

> LAS MESAS RECEPTORAS DE VOTOS ENTREGARAN A LOS VEEDORES QUE LO SOLICITEN, UN CERTIFICADO DEL RESULTADO DE LA ELECCION, ESPECIFICANDO EL NUMERO DE VOTOS OBTENIDO POR CADA LISTA, EL DE VOTOS EN BLANCO Y EL DE VOTOS NULOS O IMPUGNADOS (Art. 100).

V. QUE DEBE HACER EL VEEDOR ANTE IRREGULARIDADES.

El veedor deberá hacer constar en el acta por escrito cualquier irregularidad observada. También, sin abandonar la mesa, deberá hacer llegar al juez competente los reclamos por irregularidades cometidas durante el acto electoral, sea en la instalación de la mesa, la votación o el escrutinio.

Appendix N

Voting Times

Issued by Project Vote, in association with Matla Trust
YOUR VOTE COUNTS!

Issue No. 1
January 1993

COUNTDOWN TO DEMOCRACY

D emocracy is everything apartheid is not.
Vote for democracy.

Because by voting you can make sure that your children get a better education. You can make sure that they have better books, better teachers and ultimately better paying jobs.
By voting you can also make sure that you get better housing, jobs, water, electricity and sanitation.
Democracy means freedom, equality, unity, respect, peace, opportunity and majority rule.

All it takes for all of this to come about is enough votes.
You have the right and the power to vote and your vote counts.
So if you want to do something to improve the quality of your life make sure you cast your vote.
If not for yourself, for your children.

What your vote means

Y our vote means that you can choose a government that you believe will work for you.
A government that will strive to give everyone water, electricity and better schooling and jobs.
Voting means that you can restore your dignity and end the humiliation you and your children have felt.
Voting means that your children will grow up to have a sense of self-worth and individual dignity.
Your vote is a beginning of a better life for everyone.

Democracy must bring a better future for our children

Vote for a political party or organisation that will help create a better future for everyone

PROJECT VOTE IS AN ELECTION EDUCATION PROGRAMME OF THE CENTRE FOR DEVELOPMENT STUDIES (CDS) AND THE NATIONAL DEMOCRATIC INSTITUTE (NDI)
P.O. BOX X17
BELVILLE 7535

Voting Qualifications

All South Africans, (doctors, farm workers, teachers, domestic workers, students etc.) regardless of sex, colour or creed, as long as they are over the age of eighteen on or before the day of voting will be allowed to vote in South Africa.

HOW DO YOU VOTE?

Take your ID book, or some other form of identification and go along to your nearest polling station. There will be a person at the door who will check your identification to see if you are who you say you are and if you are the correct age to vote.

Your vote is secret

To cast your vote you will be taken into a small cubicle or room. This is called a voting booth.

You go into the voting booth alone. No-one else can see who you vote for.

You will then be given a ballot paper which has a list of all the political parties or organisations who will contest the elections. Next to each political party or organisation's name there is a little block.

You have to make a mark in the block next to the political party or organisation that you want to vote for.

Once you have made a mark next to the political party or organisation that you want to vote for all you have to do is fold your ballot paper and place it into a ballot box.

And that's all you have to do to cast your vote.

It's that simple.

BALLOT PAPER

(Make a cross next to the party or organisation of your choice)

AFRICAN NATIONAL CONGRESS	ANC	
AFRICAN DEMOCRATIC PARTY	ADP	
AFRIKANER-VOLKSUNIE	AVU	
BOPHUTHATSWANA NATIONAL PARTY	BNP	
AZANIAN PEOPLE'S ORGANISATION	AZAPO	
CONSERVATIVE PARTY	CP	KP
DEMOCRATIC PARTY	DP	DP
DIKWANKWETLA PARTY	QWAQWA	
INKATHA FREEDOM PARTY	IFP	
INTANDO YESIZWE PARTY	IYP	
INYANDZA NATIONAL MOVEMENT	INM	
LABOUR PARTY OF SOUTH AFRICA	LP	
NATIONAL PARTY	NP	NP
NATIONAL PEOPLE'S PARTY	NPP	
PAN AFRICANIST CONGRESS	PAC	
SOLIDARITY PARTY	SP	
UNITED PEOPLE'S FRONT	UPF	

This is a sample and not an official ballot paper. Some of the above political parties / organisations may choose not to enter the elections

WHAT IS A BALLOT?

A ballot is the official form on which all the names and symbols of all the political parties or organisations contesting the elections appear.

Next to each political party or organisation's name and symbol is a block or circle.

On this ballot form you will be required to make a clear mark inside the block or circle next to the political party or organisation that you want to vote for.

ONLY YOU KNOW WHO YOU VOTE FOR

Your vote is secret. Don't be afraid to vote for the political party or organisation of your choice. Only you are allowed into the voting booth.

You mark your ballot paper. Therefore no-one else can see who you voted for.

You are not allowed to write your name on the ballot.

All of these things make sure that your vote is secret.

You are the only person who will know who you vote for.

What is a voting station?

The electoral commission will identify the place where voters will cast votes on election day.

As it is only temporary and for the duration of the elections, voting stations, also called polling stations, are usually set up in school halls, churches, community centres and other places.

3

HOW T

1 On the day of the election you go to your nearest
polling station and cast your vote.
(You must have some form of identification with you.)

5 Once inside the booth you put a
mark in the block or circle next to
the political party or organisation that you want to vote
for.

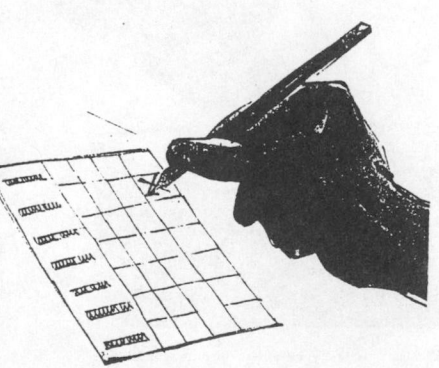

4 You then proceed to the voting booth to cast your
vote in private.
(This booth is designed so that only you know who you
are voting for.)

EVERY V

MAKE SURE YOU VOTE FOR A POLITICAL PARTY OR ORGANISATION TH.

⊃ VOTE

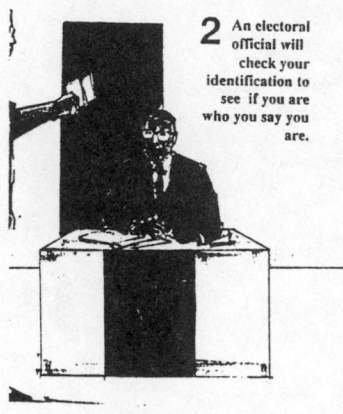

2 An electoral official will check your identification to see if you are who you say you are.

3 You will be given a ballot paper listing all the political parties or organisations contesting the elections.

BALLOT PAPER
(Make a cross next to the party or organisation of your choice)

Party	Abbrev.	
AFRICAN NATIONAL CONGRESS	ANC	
AFRICAN DEMOCRATIC PARTY	ADP	
AFRIKANER-VOLKSUNIE	AVU	
BOPHUTHATSWANA NATIONAL PARTY	BNP	
AZANIAN PEOPLE'S ORGANISATION	AZAPO	
CONSERVATIVE PARTY	CP	
DEMOCRATIC PARTY	DP	
DIKWANKWETLA PARTY	QWAQWA	
INKATHA FREEDOM PARTY	IFP	
INTANDO YESIZWE PARTY	IYP	
INYANDZA NATIONAL MOVEMENT	INM	
LABOUR PARTY OF SOUTH AFRICA	LP	
NATIONAL PARTY	NP	
NATIONAL PEOPLE'S PARTY	NPP	
PAN AFRICANIST CONGRESS	PAC	
SOLIDARITY PARTY	SP	
UNITED PEOPLE'S FRONT	UPF	

*This is a sample and not an official ballot paper. Some of the above political parties / organisations may choose not to enter the elections.

6 Then you fold your ballot paper and put it into a ballot box.

7 The counting of votes takes place at the end of the last day of the election.

We've voted for a just and peaceful South Africa

8 Voting means that you can choose a government that you believe will work for you. And with a government that works for you things can only get better.

E COUNTS!
'ROMISES TO DELIVER A BETTER FUTURE FOR YOU AND YOUR CHILDREN.

Page 5

Al Graham

The Electoral Commission

This is the group of people who handle all the administration in an election. They draft electoral laws and procedures to ensure that people are familiar with the rules and regulations of voting. They also arrange venues for voting stations and make sure that the whole election throughout the country runs smoothly. The Election Commission may be composed of a multi-party committee. They are the supreme voting authority to whom all electoral officials are accountable.

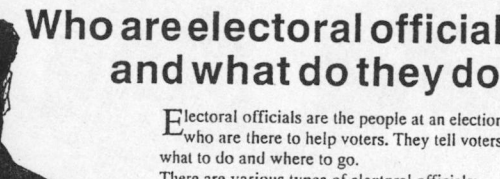

ELECTION TIME

The Electoral Commission will announce a day or days and times when voting will take place.

Who are electoral officials and what do they do?

Electoral officials are the people at an election who are there to help voters. They tell voters what to do and where to go.

There are various types of electoral officials;
Poll Watchers, also called monitors, are party officials or even independent local and international monitors who watch over the voting process on election day.

They also watch over the counting of ballots when the polls have closed.

The **Presiding Officer** is the electoral official who supervises balloting in each polling station. He or she is responsible for the general operation of the polls on election day.

Another electoral official is the returning officer. The **Returning Officer** accepts nominations, arranges polling places, election machinery and personnel, presides over the poll and conducts the count.

What are political parties or organisations

A political party or organisation can be made up of a small group of concerned individuals or millions of citizens.

A party or organisation's ideology and policy objectives shows how its members generally share the same concerns and values.

Most parties or organisations use symbols as their trademark.

Symbols are easy to recognise so they make voting a lot easier for people who can't read.

The official statement of a political party or organisation's approach to government, vision of society, values and ideals are presented in a manifesto. This often lengthy document is the product of a broad-based process of consultation and decision-making within a political party or organisation.

A political party or organisation will present its manifesto to voters in many forms.

Newspaper adverts, books, pamphlets, speeches, songs and slogans are all popular methods.

Canvassing

This takes place when political parties or organisations put up posters and hold rallies to get people to vote for them. It will involve door to door campaigning. You can expect representatives from many different parties to visit your home to canvass for your vote.

Canvassing can also take the form of public meetings where two or more political party representatives debate.

This can also take place on radio or television where their positions on issues are discussed.

One person, One vote

Any person who qualifies to vote can do so on voting day and is allowed only one vote. Your vote will carry the same value as any other person's.

IT'S YOUR RIGHT TO VOTE

If you are over the age of eighteen on or before the day of an election it is your right to vote in South Africa.

It is also your duty.

Voting is safe.

On voting day the Presiding Officer will count the total number of unused ballots.

He or she will then open the ballot box to show everyone that it is empty. Having done this the Presiding Officer will close the ballot box again and fasten it with string.

This is done to make sure that there is no cheating going on and that the election is free and fair.

Only you are allowed into the voting booth to make your mark on your ballot. So only you know who you voted for. If anyone tries to intimidate you; to get you to vote for them or to find out who you voted for, remember this: It's your vote and you don't have to tell anyone anything no matter what they do. There will be plenty of electoral officials around for you to report intimidators to.

So don't be intimidated!

You've got the protection. You've got the right.

And you've got the vote.

All you have to do now is go out there and use it as responsibly as you can.

Your vote counts!

By voting you can shape your own life.

You can shape your children's lives. You can shape the future of your country. Don't think that your vote doesn't count. It does and it counts a lot. Because just as one cent can make the difference between 99 cents and one rand, one vote can make the difference between a government that you want and one that you don't.

DON'T BE INTIMIDATED!

Some individuals may try to force people to cheat or vote in a particular way. They may do this by telling them things like:

You may lose your job if you don't vote for a particular party. They may also be violent in their intimidation. Don't be intimidated! There is no way that anyone can know who you actually vote for. And you can report intimidators to either the authorities or an electoral official.

Printed by Caxton Ltd

SECTION 1: INFORM AND MOTIVATE

A. Some commonly asked questions and how to answer them

1. What is a democratic government?

A popular definition of democratic government is: government of the people, by the people, and for the people. This means:

> The word **democracy** comes from two ancient Greek words – *demos*- means the people; and -*kratos* means to rule.

+ People **participate** in decisions which affect their lives; and
+ People **elect** their own government which represents their views, beliefs, values, and wishes.

How can we make sure that there is government by the people?
In a large country like ours, not everyone can be part of the government. So we choose a small number of people to represent us in government. And to make sure that the members of the government **remain** responsible and accountable to the people, countries usually have elections every four or five years.

"I need to know everything, because I've never voted."

"I can't vote because I don't know how to vote."

"Voting. What's voting?"

A democratic government represents most of the people, rather than all of the people. In other words, there is **majority rule**. It is not possible or practical for all the representatives and all the parties to be in power. That's why compromise is an important part of democratic rule – everyone must accept what the majority wants. However, democratic rule must also aim to accomodate the minority.

2. What is an election?

In democratic countries people exercise their right to vote in **free and fair elections**. Voters are **free** to vote for the person or party of their choice without intimidation, bribery, violence or force. And the way the elections are carried out must be **fair** – everyone must be able to vote, even those who cannot read or write. The election process must guarantee a secret vote, accurate counting of the votes, and the announcement of the results as quickly as possible.

"Elections are when people vote for the best party that they hope will truly represent their own needs."

Al Graham

There are various ways that a country can make sure that elections are free and fair:
- through the electoral system that is used;
- through election laws;
- through protecting voters' rights;
- through a monitoring system.

3. What is an electoral system?

Elections can happen in many different ways. Each way determines how many seats each party will win in the government.

"First-past-the-post"
In South Africa in the past there was an electoral system called "first-past-the-post".

> The system called "first-past-the-post" comes from the British Westminster system.

The country was divided into geographical **constituencies**. In each constituency people voted for a candidate from a particular political party. The **candidates** who won the most votes in their constituency went to parliament. The political party that got the most seats in parliament became the government. The governing party since 1948 has been the National Party. All the other parties formed the opposition.

> For the purposes of the election the country is divided into several geographical areas or constituencies. In the past people criticised the way the constituencies were chosen, as they seemed to favour the ruling party.

Over the last two-and-a-half years there have been multiparty negotiations. The parties have agreed that "first-past-the-post" is not the best electoral system for South Africa. The main reason is that there is no relationship between the number of votes and the number of seats in parliament. Rather, these parties have agreed to an electoral system called proportional representation.

> A **candidate** is a person from a political party who stands for elections.

What is proportional representation?
In proportional representation people vote for a **political party**. The number of votes that the political party wins in an election determines how many seats each party gets in the government. However, parties need to get a certain minimum percentage of the vote (3–5%) in order to gain representation in parliament. So, this system makes sure that all groups have a say, and this is related to how much support they have. The party that gets the most votes will get the most seats and become the governing group. For example, if a party wins half the votes, then it is entitled to half the seats in government.

255

Before the elections, each political party draws up a **list** of their candidates which it presents to voters. This list will accomodate both national and regional candidates. When the voting is over, the party candidates are given seats in parliament in the order they appear on the party's list. For example, parliament will consist of 400 seats which will cater for national and regional candidates. So a party will draw up a list of 400 candidates in rank order, from 1 to 400. If the party wins 60% of the votes, then the first 240 candidates on the list are given seats in parliament.

There are many different kinds of proportional representation. South Africa has not yet agreed on the kind of proportional representation it wants.

Since 1948 the National Party has won every election without getting a majority of votes. In the 1981 white elections, for example, with 59% of the votes, it won 79,5% of the seats in parliament. In the same election the HNP won 14,8% of the votes, but it won no seats at all. This is because there was no proportional representation.

4. What are electoral laws?

No election system can work without laws and regulations which assure free and fair elections. In South Africa electoral laws will soon be passed to cover:

◆ How voters register.
◆ How political parties are formed and their role in the election process.
◆ Election campaigns.
◆ How elections are administered and by whom.
◆ Election day – from the time voters enter the polling stations to the announcement of the results.

These laws and regulations allow elections to happen again and again in an orderly way.

5. Who can vote?

All South African citizens of 18 years or older will have the right to vote. This includes men and women, people who can read and write, those who are illiterate, and people living in rural and urban South Africa.

Each voter needs to identify herself as a South African citizen to vote. She must show who she is and her age, as well as proof that she is a South African citizen. The voter can use any of the following documents:

- pension card;
- driver's licence;
- employment card;
- birth certificate;
- baptismal certificate;
- passport;
- Book of Life;
- voter registration card;
- pass book;
- any other identity card.

We urge people to get their identity documents (I.D.) immediately.

People can still vote even if they do not have any identity document. In this case, they need at least two South African citizens to confirm their identity and citizenship.

You have to be a South African citizen to vote.

People who are South African citizens by **naturalisation** can also vote. For example, migrant workers from Southern African countries who have worked in South Africa for at least 5 years can become naturalised South African citizens and can vote. Or citizens of another country who have married a South African can become naturalised South African citizens and can vote.

Voter Registration

Potential voters will have to **register** in order to vote. The purpose of registration is to record the names of everyone who qualifies to vote. It stops people from voting more than once. It also stops people who are not South African citizens from voting.

When people go to register they must produce some proof of their identity (any of the documents mentioned above can be used). Then people will be issued with a **voter's card**. Every voter must present this card or any other identity card at the polling station on election day.

Showing identification.

By mid-1994 the body who oversees the election (Election Commission) will start issuing people with voter's cards as part of the voter registration process.

In some countries a **voter's roll** is used. This is a list of all potential voters in the country. It is used to make sure that people can only vote once. Before election day people need to register their names on the voter's roll. We are not sure yet if we will have a voter's roll in South Africa. But even with a voter's roll, people who do not register can still vote.

6. What is a ballot?

A ballot is the form voters are given on election day. This is where they can mark their vote. Ballots are printed on special paper and have secret markings to make sure that no-one can make copies of the ballot and vote more than once.

People can only vote once – in other words, there is one person, one vote.

How do you mark a ballot?
We are not yet sure what system will be used in South Africa for marking the ballot. Usually a pencil is used, and people either make a cross (×), or a tick (✓) or circle (AFG party) the party of their choice. Sometimes a rubber stamp is used, or people make a thumb-print in the correct place.

See Ballot on the poster in the pocket.

Tell people not to write their names on the ballot, or the name of the party they are voting for.

If you mark your ballot incorrectly then it won't be counted as a vote for the party of your choice.

The ballot is secret – no-one knows who you have voted for.

What is a spoiled ballot?
Sometimes people do not agree with the policies of any party and do not wish to vote for any of them. People may spoil their vote by putting any mark on the ballot which should not be there. The number of spoiled votes is also published after the elections.

See spoiled Ballot on the poster in the pocket.

Often ballots are spoiled because people do not know how to fill them in properly. In Section 2 of this manual there is a role-play of an election for your workshops. This gives people practice in filling in a ballot correctly.

"How can I fill in a ballot paper if I cannot read or write?"

Six in every ten adults in this country are illiterate. Illiterate people have the right to vote. In the short term we will need to teach illiterate people how to "read" the ballot and how to mark their choices. More importantly, we need to give illiterate people as much information as possible about elections so that they do not feel too intimidated to vote. There are some suggestions for how to work with illiterate people in Section 2.

8. Why is the ballot secret?

Many people say, "Democracy is about honesty and openness, so why should we have a secret ballot?" or "The very word secret shows that something is happening which we cannot control." A secret ballot means that no-one, except you, knows or sees who you have voted for. The right to a secret ballot exists to ensure that you are free to vote for the party of your choice, without fear of intimidation or force.

Your right to secrecy is guaranteed and protected by the election laws and procedures. You must not write your names on the ballot. So no-one can ever find out who you have voted for, unless you tell them. No-one may enter the voting booth with you. You vote alone, with no witnesses. You fold your own ballot before placing it in the box – no-one sees where you have placed your mark. A secret ballot ensures your right to free and fair elections.

9. What is a ballot box?

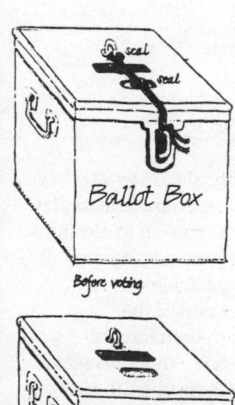

Ballot Box

Before voting

During voting

The ballot box is the box in which voters put their ballots, after they have voted. In your election kit there is a model ballot box to use in your workshops.

The ballot box is **locked** before voting begins and **sealed** when voting ends. This security measure makes sure that once voters have put their ballots into the box they cannot be taken out until the seal is broken. Sometimes ballot boxes must be transported to other places before votes can be counted. These boxes must also be sealed. Officials from political parties must see that this is done and they must place their own seal on the box as an extra security measure. Officials from political parties must be present when ballot boxes are transported.

Only an election official called a returning officer can break the seals to count the votes. This is done in the presence of party officials and monitors. On election day the ballot box is guarded by an election official to make sure that no-one tampers with it.

The roles of the various election officials are explained in the role-play on page 39.

10. What are the rights of voters?

◆ Voters have the right to vote in secret.

◆ Voters have the right to vote for the party of their choice, without fear of intimidation or violence.

◆ Voters have the right to free and fair elections.

◆ Voters have the right to vote once.

◆ Voters must have access to all the parties' views and positions, so that they can make informed choices. The mass media – radio, newspapers, television, and magazines – should allow each party equal space and time to present their positions.

11. What is the role of monitors during elections?

Monitors work to protect the election process – their job is to ensure that elections are free and fair. There may be different types of monitors:

◆ **Poll watchers** are representatives from political parties who monitor the voting process on election day.

◆ There may also be **monitors who are neutral** and do not belong to any one political party. For example, church officials or ordinary citizens may volunteer to be trained as monitors. These people observe the activities leading up to election day – for example, the media, the political parties, the election laws, the campaigns, the atmosphere in the country. They also observe the actual voting process and the counting of the votes. They report irregular practices to the election officials.

Political parties also have an important role to play in the run-up to elections. They must bring any irregularities to the attention of the international monitors or the body that oversees elections (the Election Commission).

♦ During a transition period there may also be an **international election monitoring team**. This team observes the process leading up to the election, election day procedures, the counting of the votes and, where necessary, the transfer of power to the new government. It is likely that the United Nations (UN), the Organisation for African Unity (OAU), the Commonwealth of Nations, and the international churches will monitor our elections.

Election laws will state the rights and duties of domestic and international monitors.

12. What is the role of the media during elections?

The media consists of the public media which includes radio, television and newspapers, and the mass communications of political parties during their political campaigns. The media's role is important during elections. The media should:

♦ Inform the public about election issues, e.g. the dates of elections.
♦ Make important announcements, such as where and when to vote.
♦ Be open to all points of view and not favour one candidate or party.
♦ Report election information fairly and in a balanced manner.
♦ Allow all parties equal space to present their positions.
♦ Cater for illiterate people. At present the media favours literate people.

13. How do people vote?

On election day people cast their vote – they choose the party who they wish to govern them.

In and around the polling station:
In every area, polling stations are set up for people to cast their votes. There are many polling stations so that people can vote without having to travel. They may be set up in

church halls, community centres, schools, public buildings, or they could be mobile polling stations. Normally people will vote at the polling station closest to their homes.

Polling stations are usually open from early in the morning until the evening, and voting may happen over several days or on only one day.

In each polling station there are:
♦ paid election officials;
♦ a presiding officer – in charge of that polling station;
♦ one official representative from each political party to monitor the voting;
♦ one agent from each party who tells her political party how many votes are cast;
♦ security forces who must help with the smooth running of the voting;
♦ neutral monitors to watch the process.

All of these people take an oath of secrecy.

How to cast your vote:
♦ Voters must usually queue to go into the polling station.

♦ The election officials sit at tables inside the polling station. Voters need to show these officials some proof of their identity, age and citizenship.

♦ Sometimes an official marks the voter's hand with a harmless invisible ink. The mark lasts a few days and then wears off. Each polling station has special equipment to make sure that the voter's hand has not already been marked. This allows officials to check whether someone has already voted. Each person can only vote once.

♦ The ballot clerk gives the voter a ballot to take into the voting booth. This is a private area where voters go to mark their ballot papers. Voters must do this on their own – their votes are secret. However, disabled people may be helped into the **voting booth**.

♦ After voting, each voter on her own folds her ballot and puts it in the ballot box.

There are about 20,5 million South Africans who will have the right to vote. This means there will be about 20 000 polling stations around the country.

Voting

Placing the Ballot into the Ballot box.

Remember, no-one knows who you have voted for. You vote in secret.

14. What happens after everyone has voted?

♦ Before the counting of the votes begins, the returning officer must show officials that the seals on the ballot boxes have not been broken. The returning officer is the only person who can break the seals so that ballots can be counted under her supervision.

♦ The ballot box is opened and the votes are counted. Party officials and monitors must be present when votes are being counted. The ballots may be counted twice to check that the final totals are correct.

♦ When the counting is finished, the presiding officer tells the public the results. These are also broadcast on the radio, television and in newspapers.

B. Why vote?

Reasons for voting

Workshop participants gave two main reasons for voting:
♦ The first reason has to do with **democracy.**
♦ The second reason is about **improving the quality of life** for present and future generations of black South Africans.

The reasons are presented here in the order that people prioritised them.

VOTE: FOR EDUCATION, JOBS, HOUSING, PEACE

People say that by voting for a new government we can make sure that our children get better education. They say that education is the main hope for the next generation. Over and over again, they discuss their desire for better teachers, better books, better school buildings, and a quality of education that is as good as "white" education. People want their children to have more jobs, better jobs, and better paying jobs. They believe the way to achieve these goals is through education.

After education, people said that better housing, jobs, water, electricity and sanitation were important reasons for voting.

VOTE: FOR DEMOCRACY IN SOUTH AFRICA

Democracy represents everything that apartheid is not. Here is a list that workshop participants drew up to show what apartheid and democracy mean to them.

Apartheid	Democracy
Oppression	Freedom
Discrimination	Equality
Segregation	Unity
Humiliation	Respect
Violence	Peace
Poverty	Opportunity
White minority rule	Majority rule

VOTE: FOR A BETTER FUTURE FOR OUR CHILDREN

"I am married and I have children. Those children haven't got the right to go and vote. So what I'm doing I'm doing for my children, for the future of my children."

People express their hopes that their children will grow up to have a sense of self-worth and individual dignity. They worry that their children will experience the kinds of humiliations that the older generation experienced under apartheid.

Some other messages that motivate people to vote are:

VOTE: TO END APARTHEID FOREVER

VOTE: TO SUPPORT YOUR PARTY

VOTE: FOR A NEW SOUTH AFRICA

VOTE: SO WE CAN STOP THE VIOLENCE.

We must encourage people to **want** to vote. They must see the opportunity to vote for the first time as the kind of experience that gets told and retold to their children and their children's children. At the same time, we must explain that a new government will not be able to change everything overnight – apartheid was established over a long period of time and it will take a long time to break it down. But a new government should be accountable to the people who voted for it and put it in power.

Voting is the first step towards changing our lives for the better. But there are also other steps that will maintain the changes in the quality of people's lives. For example, community initiatives and structures will ensure that the government rules in people's interests. We must encourage people to participate in these structures.

Why would some people not vote?

In our workshops some people said they will not vote for some of the following reasons:

♦ Often people do not connect voting with realising their hopes for the future, and solving the problems they face every day.

> "People believe the elections won't change anything. They say that after voting there will be no changes in the procedure and in the oppression in their villages."

♦ Some people have voted before in elections. These people talk about lies, unfulfilled campaign promises, and elections that make no difference to the quality of their lives.

> "Nothing will come of it."

♦ Many people doubt that the present government will hold a fair and honest election.

> "People believe elections will not be conducted in an honest way. They believe that some partisan movements will try to steal votes and manipulate results."

♦ People take it for granted that any national elections will be accompanied by intimidation and violence.

> "People are fearing . . . and they will be fearing to vote."

♦ People are naturally anxious and fearful about doing something they have never done before.

> "I wouldn't take part because I have never taken part in an election before."

How do we change these people's minds? How do we convince them that by voting they can shape their own lives, their children's lives, and the future of the country? One way is to give people as much information about elections and voting as possible. In your workshops listen to people's fears and try to respond honestly and truthfully. Focus on the positive reasons for voting, on the democratic process, on the benefits to people's own lives.

The message which runs through this manual and
through the workshops is this:

By voting you can bring real democracy to South
Africa. Democracy can bring dignity and an end to the
humiliation you and your children have felt.
Democracy can result in a better life – education, jobs,
decent housing. Voting is not just your right . . . it's
your responsibility. Because, for the first time, you can
shape the future for you and your children.

Index of Names

K
Karadzic, Radovan 56
Kaunda, Kenneth 49
Keefer, Patricia 131
Kennedy, Bobby 3
Kennedy, Edward 88
Kent, Tom 14
Khan, Mohammad Humayun 131, 169
Kidd, Bruce 10
Koestler, Arthur 138
Kozyrev, Andrei 30

L
Laino, Domingo 99, 123
Lambsdorff, Count Otto 19, 45
Lamontagne, Maurice 14
Lavoie, Louis 84
Laxalt, Paul 91
Locke, John 79
Lugar, Richard 90
Lujambio, Alonso 53

M
Macdonald, John 125
MacDonald, Father Charles 3
MacDonald, Finlay 13
MacEachen, Allan J. 7, 12, 13, 14, 15, 16, 29
MacGregor, Roy 11
MacLaren, Roy 29
MacLellan, Ronalda 90
MacLeod, Father Greg 7
Mahathir, Prime Minister 41
Malagodi, Senator Giovanni 18
Mandela, Nelson 27, 36, 46, 47, 48, 97, 106, 160
Marcos, Ferdinand 34, 60, 85, 86, 87, 88, 89, 90, 94, 108,110, 111, 112, 113, 114, 115, 116, 117, 161
McCurdy, Howard 47
McGrory, Mary 27
McMahon, Ned 158
McMurtry, Roy 47
Menchu, Rigoberta 85
Mokobi, Charles 128
Molgat, Senator Gildas 17, 152
Mondale, Walter 61
Montt, Rios 86
Morodo, Raul 124
Morrison, Bruce 125
Mulroney, Brian 13, 28

N
Namphy, Henry 151, 152
Noriega, Manuel 29, 93

O
Ortega, Daniel 72, 73,74, 75, 97
Ouellet, André, Hon 28

P
Paine, Tom 62
Pastor, Robert 73
Pearson, Lester B. 17, 18
Pienaar, Louis 92, 127, 129, 132, 133, 138
Pinochet, Augusto 81, 166, 169
Preval, President Rene 149
Price, George, Prime Minister 68

R
Ramphal, Sir Shridath 94
Richardson, Elliot 73
Rodriguez, General 46, 65, 103, 104, 119, 120, 121, 122, 123, 124
Rosenau, James N. 33, 169

S
Salamon, Lester M. 34
SaroWiwa, Ken 163
Scattalon, Geno 9, 10
Schlesinger, Joe 73
Scott, Archbishop Ted 47
Simmons, Robert 107
Sinclair, Huntley 18
Sithole, Masipula 131
Smith, Dennis 128
Smith, Hugh 45
Somoza, Anastasio 30, 74, 75
St. Laurent, Louis 12
Stanbury, Senator Richard 17
Steel, Sir David 19, 94
Stewart, Dr. John B. 15
Stroessner, Alfredo 46, 122, 123, 175, 126
Suarez, Adolpho 18, 46

T
Thornberry, Cedric 92
Tierney, Jim 158
Tobin, Brian 20
Tompkins, Father Jimmy 3, 6, 7, 8
Trudeau, Pierre 17

V
Victores, Megia 84

W
Wollack, Ken 96

Y
Yeltsin, Boris 41
Yew, Lee Kuan 41

Z
Zedillo, President 53, 54
Zhelev, Zhelyu 142, 143, 144
Zhivkov, Todor 139